# ESSENTIAL
# BICYCLE

# ESSENTIAL BICYCLE

## RACING ◎ SAFETY ◎ REPAIRS

**RONI SARIG**

**BARNES & NOBLE**

NEW YORK

Originally published as *The Everything Bicycle Book*

© 1997 by F+W Publications, Inc.

This 2008 edition published by Barnes & Noble, Inc.,
by arrangement with Adams Media, an F+W Publications Company.

ISBN-13: 978-0-7607-9378-7
ISBN-10: 0-7607-9378-6

Printed and bound in China

10 9 8 7 6 5 4 3 2 1

For my mom, who taught me how to ride;

and for my wife, who showed me how to tandem.

# Table of Contents

## Chapter 10
### Bicycling for Transportation

## Chapter 11
### Bicycling for Sport

## Chapter 12
### Bicycle Touring

## Appendix

# Acknowledgments

I would like to thank my assistant, Amy Eldridge, for her help with research and fact-checking. In addition, thanks to all the bike experts for their advice and opinions, especially in the technical chapters: Mike Keck of Mike's Bikes in Charleston, South Carolina; Brad Eller of The Bicycle Shoppe, also in Charleston; Jeff Hutchinson of All-Star Bike Shops in Raleigh, North Carolina; James Grigg; and Bruce MacLean. Thanks as well to the fine folks at the League of American Bicyclists and the International Mountain Bicycling Association for their help with resource material. And most of all, thanks to my wife, Danielle, who ably took on the extra duties of proofreader and cheerleader during the writing of this book.

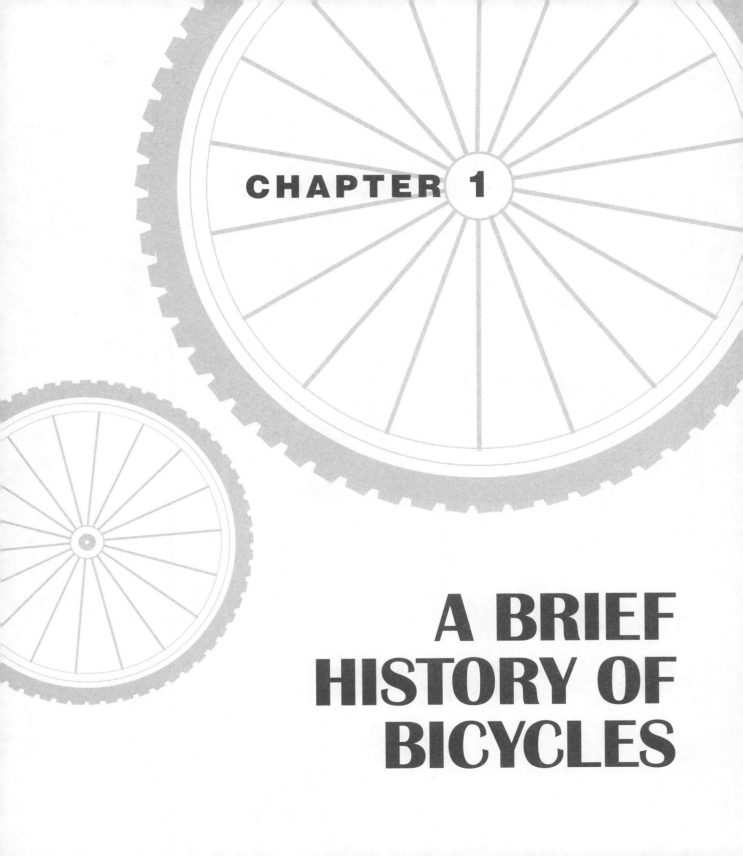

CHAPTER 1

# A BRIEF HISTORY OF BICYCLES

# Prehistory

Hard to believe, but that wonderfully simple two-wheeled marvel we call the *bicycle* probably did not exist before the latter part of the nineteenth century. Before then, few people understood what strange forces would allow human beings to balance on two thin wheels in line (even today, few of us could explain it!). For thousands of years our ancestors labored along the path of technology, from that first great invention—the wheel—to what has proven to be the most efficient human-powered vehicle ever created: the bicycle.

It's impossible to overestimate the importance of the wheel; indeed, it could be said that the history of technology is the story of the wheel's development. Historians agree the wheel was first used around 3500 B.C. in Sumeria (an area that is now part of Iraq). Sumerians used wheels to make plows for farming, and they constructed chariots for use in war.

There's a lot less agreement when it comes to tracing the ancestors of bicycles. Ruins from at least three ancient civilizations suggest two-wheeled vehicles have been around for thousands of years. Babylonian bas-relief, Pompeiian frescoes, and Egyptian hieroglyphics all depict what looks something like a crude bicycle. Some say the Chinese invented a bicycle in the first millennium A.D. If these cultures really had developed bicycles, no doubt it was little more than two wheels connected by a board. But no ancient relics have ever been found to further support the existence of these bikes; and if they ever existed, they sure disappeared in a hurry.

## Da Vinci Does It?

A popular belief in recent decades has been that Leonardo da Vinci invented the bicycle. Why not? After all, the most accomplished of Renaissance men conceived of flying machines and automobile engines hundreds of years before they were invented, plus he managed to find time to be one of the greatest painters, sculptors, and architects of his day. In 1966, during the restoration of a da Vinci notebook from 1493, a previously hidden drawing was uncovered. Though small, the sketch unmistakably depicts a modern bicycle, complete with handlebars, two wheels, pedals, and a chain drive similar to the kind first used almost 400 years later, in the 1880s.

Given that da Vinci conceived of the chain and cog mechanism and also of ball bearings, it is certainly possible that the drawing is authentic. However, most experts don't think so. Because the drawing is not in da Vinci's handwriting, scholars believe the bicycle sketch is, at best, the work of one of da Vinci's assistants—who perhaps applied his master's discoveries to practical use—or at worst, a fake drawn long afterward, between the 1880s and the 1960s.

Other historians think da Vinci's contemporary, the German artist Albrecht Dürer, worked on bicycles, though there's no evidence to support that. By the end of the eighteenth century, it seems the two-wheeler had yet to see the light of day.

# Dawn of the Hobby Horse

If it seems like the prehistory of bicycles is filled with contradictory and unsubstantiated claims, the intrigue pales in comparison to the modern story of bicycle development. Just like the old, long-discredited story about Abner Doubleday inventing baseball in Cooperstown, New York, the tale of who actually invented the bicycle is full of legend, inconsistencies, and flat-out lies. One thing that seems indisputable, though, is that the bicycle is a direct descendant of the late-eighteenth century piece of recreational equipment called the *hobby horse*.

The hobby horse was a popular fad for the French upper class and nobility of the late 1700s, including the soon-to-be-beheaded Marie Antoinette. Hobby horses were little more than a wooden rocking horse or simply a pole with a wooden horse head at the end. Legend has it that in 1790 a French courtier named Comte Médé de Sivrac got the idea to add two wheels to the hobby horse. That enabled gentlemen and ladies of the court to zip around the yards of the palace straddling the horse and walking, running, or pushing off with their legs. It was a hit. Sivrac's invention was essentially a wooden scooter, either called a *célérifère* or a *vélocifère*. Though Sivrac's hobby horse had neither steering nor brakes, it was the first documented case of a vehicle with two wheels in tandem—therefore, an important step in the birth of the bicycle.

But while the wheeled hobby horse definitely existed at the end of the 1700s, there's some doubt about Sivrac. Records are sketchy at best. Perhaps due to Sivrac's questionable existence, he never earned the title Father of the Bicycle. That distinction belongs to the man responsible for the bicycle's next evolutionary step: Karl von Drais.

## Von Drais and His Swift-Walker

Baron Karl Drais de Sauerbrun, or Karl von Drais for short, was a nobleman from the German province of Baden, where he was appointed Master of the Woods and Forests. This job required that von Drais travel long distances on foot in order to inspect the forests. Out of practical need, he developed a vehicle that could increase his walking speed while at the same time alleviate some of the strain walking put on his feet. Sometime around 1817, von Drais invented what came to be known as the *draisine*. The draisine was little more than a well-constructed hobby horse: it had two wheels in line and a simple frame made of wood. But von Drais's machine had steering, which made all the difference. Where hobby horses had been toys, the draisine was actually useful as a walking aid.

Upon patenting his creation, von Drais took his draisine to Paris, where he demonstrated it to curious crowds in the city's parks. Onlookers were impressed to find that the machine could more than double walking speed on level ground and reach even higher speeds downhill. Parisians were shocked to see von Drais riding at up to ten miles an hour, faster than they'd ever seen a human move before.

Around the time von Drais unveiled his two-wheeler, a number of other inventors, either independently or with full knowledge of the draisine, made similar walking machines. In England, the swift-walker caused quite a stir. In the United States, our first brush with two-wheeled vehicles came when W. K. Clarkson patented his own swift-walker in 1820. Though swift-walkers became a popular site in the New York City parks of the early 1820s and even led to the creation of several new laws in the city, by the end of the decade they had largely disappeared. While they successfully increased walking speed, swift-walkers were still too heavy and inefficient, especially on hills and bumpy ground, to take hold in any permanent way.

## Michaux's Pedals

By the late 1850s in Paris, the old swift-walkers (or *vélocipèdes*, as they were called in France) were a familiar, if uncommon, sight. At the time, Parisian Pierre Michaux and his sons were in business building coaches and were interested in new ways to improve the efficiency of self-propelled four-wheeled vehicles. But sometime around 1860 a man happened to bring into the Michaux shop an old *vélocipède* in need of repair. Though Michaux was in no way involved with the *vélocipède* business, he agreed to give the machine a look.

After watching the *vélocipède* lay around his shop for a while, Pierre and his fourteen-year-old son Ernest came up with an idea to help the walking machine work a little better. The Michaux attached the crank handles of an old grindstone to the *vélocipède*'s front wheel, thereby enabling a rider to turn the wheel by cranking with his feet. What they created was the world's first pedal-driven two-wheeler, or in other words, the first bicycle.

As usual, though, the story is not without contention. Pierre Lallement, a Frenchman who at one time worked for Pierre Michaux, claimed to have conceived of the pedaled *vélocipède* first. Lallement eventually took the new invention to the United States, where in 1866 he patented the *vélocipède* and introduced it to the American public. With the vehicle's small, iron-rimmed wooden wheels creating a very rough ride, the *vélocipède* came to be known in the United States as the *boneshaker*.

Back in France, Michaux improved on his original pedal *vélocipède* design, and the two-wheeler exploded in popularity. Cycling was fast becoming a favorite pastime:

On May 30, 1868, the first recorded bike race was held on the outskirts of Paris. Englishman James Moore won the race, and many more contests soon followed.

## The High-Wheeler and the Bicycle Explosion of the 1870s

Keep in mind that bicycles did not develop in a vacuum. Alongside the *vélocipèdes* the 1860s and 1870s saw the rise of a number of vehicles that utilized the pedal crank mechanism, including various models (some downright strange) of tricycles, unicycles, and something called a monocycle that had riders actually sitting in the center of a huge wheel! These other new human-powered vehicles shared innovations with the bicycle and developed simultaneously. The early 1870s saw a wide range of *vélocipède* innovations that improved comfort and efficiency: solid rubber tires, lighter steel frames, tension-spoked wheels, ball-bearings in the hub, brakes, and lights. With all the changes the *vélocipède* went through during the period, it became virtually a different machine. At the very least, it deserved a new name. The 1870s was the first time the two-wheeler became known as a *bicycle*.

Still, the bicycle had not yet become the practical, comfortable vehicle it would one day be. With the pedals attached directly to the front wheel, two-wheelers were difficult to ride anywhere but on the smoothest, flattest roads. Uphill riding required great effort to crank the wheel, while downhill riding turned the wheels so fast it sent the pedals spinning out of control, too fast for the rider's legs to handle. To address some of these problems, English designer James Starley decided in 1870 to increase the size of the front wheel. This made the vehicle move much faster—sometimes up to forty miles per hour—because one turn of the pedal (and therefore one turn of the wheel) would move the rider farther. The larger wheel also made the bicycle easier to pedal. Plus, it made the bicycle more comfortable because the larger wheel increased the shock absorption. Soon, front wheels were being made as large as could be—up to five feet in diameter—while still enabling a rider's leg to reach the pedals.

The new high-wheel bicycles were a smash; soon they were so common they became known as *ordinary* bicycles to distinguish them from earlier *vélocipèdes* (later the high-wheel was called the *penny-farthing*). The elevated seat position of the ordinary ensured that proper Victorian ladies, who wore long skirts and did not wish to expose their undergarments, could not ride the bicycle. Though it was a step backward for women, the high wheel otherwise brought the bicycle a newfound popularity.

In 1874, Colonel Albert A. Pope, along with Pierre Lallement, started the first U.S. bike company, the Columbia Bicycle Manufacturing Company. The League of American Wheelmen, the country's first cycling club,

formed in 1880 as bicycling became a popular mode of transportation. New roads and traffic laws were created to facilitate safe riding. The bicycle had finally taken hold.

By 1885, hundreds of thousands—if not millions—of bicycles existed in the United States and Europe. Still, the high-wheeler was far from perfect. For one, large wheels had made uphill riding difficult. Also, the huge wheel size and seat location (near the top of the large wheel) made mounting treacherous and maneuvering difficult. Finally, many riders found themselves falling face first over the top of the wheel when they tried to stop. Clearly, there was room for improvement.

## The Safety Bicycle

Though the modern chain-drive transmission had been developed in the late 1860s or early 1870s, it did not come into wide use for decades. In 1884, John Kemp Starley became the first inventor to apply the chain-drive mechanism to the two-wheeler, thus creating the first truly modern bicycle. He called his new model the *rover safety bicycle* because the chain drive made dangerously large front wheels unnecessary. Riders could safely touch the ground while on the bicycle, and women could ride without causing a spectacle. Within a few years the safety bicycle boasted two wheels of equal size and a diamond-shaped frame that made it look very much like the bicycles we ride today.

But there was still one catch. One of the high-wheelers' advantages was shock absorption. A return to smaller wheels meant a revival of the boneshaker. To make bicycles comfortable, significant improvements still needed to be made. The answer came in 1888, when a Scottish veterinarian named John Boyd Dunlop created a tire with an inflatable tube for his young son's tricycle. It worked well, and soon Dunlop's invention, the pneumatic tire, found its way onto many bicycles.

Diehard racers considered pneumatic tires wimpy and resisted them at first, but their advantages in comfort, speed, and stability were impossible to resist. By the early 1890s, Dunlop's tires were standard on all bikes, and the safety bike quickly overtook high-wheelers as the model of choice for bicyclists.

## The Golden Age of Bicycles

One of the most fascinating aspects of bicycle history is that, for the most part, bicycle design and mechanics were perfected more than a hundred years ago and little has needed improving since (consider how much cars have changed since then!). By the 1890s, all the major flaws in previous designs had been addressed to make bicycles the most sophisticated means of individual transportation of the time. A decade before the automobile changed the face of America, bicycles had a similarly mobilizing effect on the nation. The 1890s, a decade of incredible growth and popularity of the bicycle, became commonly known as the Golden Age of the Bicycle.

Three major innovations in the 1890s brought the bike fully up to speed with twentieth-century cycles: the freewheel did away with the fixed gear system and enabled coasting; caliper rim brakes made braking more effective; and multigear derailleur systems allowed bikes to have a variety of easily adjustable gears (these didn't catch on, though, for a few decades).

The Golden Age also brought the rise of great bicycle manufacturers whose names are still synonymous with the industry today. Frank Bowden of Nottingham, England, started the Raleigh Cycle Company in the early 1890s and by 1896 was making 30,000 cycles a year in the largest factory in the world. German bicycle manufacturer Ignaz Schwinn immigrated to the United States and cofounded the Arnold Schwinn Company in Chicago in 1895. By the turn of the century, over ten million Americans (out of a total population of 75 million) owned bikes. More bicycles were sold per capita than are sold today—bicycles had become a major industry with sales nearing a billion dollars a year. As hundreds of young bicycle manufacturers competed for sales, prices dropped from over $100 to as low as $20 for a new bike, making them affordable to just about anyone.

Hand in hand with the booming bicycle business, bikes had a tremendous impact on society in the final decade of the nineteenth century. Bike racing became a major international sport, second only to baseball in the United States. Top stars of the time included Arthur August Zimmerman, who set many early cycling records, and Major Taylor, the first black professional cyclist who went on to become world champion and remains a key figure in the sport's history. Bicycle clubs also boomed as cycling became, in addition to a key mode of transportation, a favorite recreational activity for Americans. Bicycles proved especially liberating for women, who became more mobile than ever before. Bicycling also created a need for comfortable new fashions, such as bloomers, that changed women's dress forever.

## The Industry Crash and the Auto Boom

Inevitably, the Golden Age had to end; indeed, by 1899, the industry had become over-stocked. Over a four-year period, four-fifths of American bicycle manufacturers either went out of business or merged with other companies. Major capitalists of the day such as John D. Rockefeller and A. G. Spaulding tried to take hold of the situation by forming a monopoly on the bicycle industry. But they failed, and by 1903, the bicycle industry was severely diminished from the glory days less than a decade earlier.

The biggest contributor to the bicycle's decline was the automobile. The car was faster, more comfortable, and required less human energy to operate—bikes couldn't compete. Engineers focused their attention on the auto, and companies that had produced bicycles switched to making cars and motorcycles. Men like the Wright Brothers and Henry Ford, who had applied bicycle technology in the development of the airplane and car, helped turn the bicycle into yesterday's news. Almost overnight bicycles ceased being the most advanced form of individual transportation.

Just as the horse's role in transportation had been greatly diminished by the bicycle, the birth of the automobile left the bicycle little more than a recreational toy. Though bikes remained popular in Europe, their use as everyday transportation in the United States became negligible. The Golden Age of the Bicycle, it seems, ended before it really began.

## Bicycles in the Twentieth Century

The story of bicycles in this century is a rollercoaster ride of highs and lows. While little has changed in the basic design of the bicycle, slight advancements have steadily improved bike efficiency. Increasingly, bicycles have become sturdier, as well as more lightweight and aerodynamic.

In the 1930s and 1940s, while the Great Depression and World War II's gas rationing kept car ownership expensive, bicycles experienced a new boom. Sales reached levels comparable to those in the 1890s. With their silver fenders, chain guards, headlights, horns, and balloon tires, designers clearly attempted to make

### THE WORLD'S FASTEST BICYCLES

Ever since 1899, when Charles "Mile-a-Minute" Murphy proved he could ride a bike over sixty miles an hour, cyclists have battled to out-speed each other and earn the title of "fastest human." With the help of motor-pacing, where bikes draft behind high-speed motor vehicles, cyclists have continually pushed the record to new heights.

It was back in 1941 when Frenchman Alf Letourner became the first person to travel over 100 miles per hour on a human-powered vehicle, clocking in at almost 109 m.p.h. By the 1960s, his fellow countryman Jose Meiffret had upped the record to 127 m.p.h. In 1973, American Allan Abbot rode his bicycle 138 m.p.h. across the salt flats of Bonneville Speedway in Utah.

The current record is held by John Howard, another American. In 1985, he rode the Bonneville flats at a staggering 152 m.p.h. I guess that makes him John "Two-and-a-Half Miles-a-Minute" Howard.

bicycles look as much like motorcycles as possible. The popular roadsters of the day were dubbed *moto-bikes*.

The prosperity of the late 1940s and 1950s meant another low for bike sales, although they remained popular with kids. But a second twentieth-century bicycle boom came in the late 1960s and lasted through the 1970s, when the back-to-nature movement collided with an energy crisis to revive interest in environmentally friendly human-powered vehicles. Along with traditional bicycles, recumbent bikes (on which the rider reclines) and human-powered cars received lots of attention, if not wide-spread use. As these developments combined with the fitness craze of the 1970s, bicycle sales reached record levels.

Recent decades have brought the rise of two new bicycle models. The thin-framed ten-speed bike, which had been introduced in the late 1950s, became the most common road bike of the day. As the 1980s approached, groups of designers in California and Colorado created a bicycle to better handle rugged off-road riding. By combining the durability of the balloon-tire roadster with lightweight racing components and design, the makers invented a new kind of bike. By the end of the 1980s, the bike's strength and versatility would make it the most popular choice for riders both on the road and off. The age of the mountain bike had arrived.

With the continuing dominance of the mountain bike, the 1990s also saw the rise of hybrid bikes that combine the sturdiness of the mountain bike with the practicality of the road bike. Even more recently, bicycle engineers have again taken a cue from auto makers and designed the world's first automatic transmission bike. But these bikes, which forfeit the ease and control offered by manual gears, are unlikely to cause major waves in the biking industry. More likely, bicycles will continue to make slight improvements in design and materials, but will probably remain similar to the brilliantly simple creation perfected over one hundred years ago. With bicycles still the most efficient human-powered vehicle in existence, why mess with a good thing?

# The Wide World of Cycling

While this brief bicycle history focuses on Western nations such as France, Germany, England, and the United States, the story of bicycling is very different when told from a non-Western perspective. While bicycles developed more slowly in other parts of the world, they currently rank as the dominant form of individual transportation for the billions of people on the continents of Asia and Africa.

Like many Western inventions, the bicycle made its way around the world during the era of colonialism. As England, France, Holland, Spain, Germany, and later, the United States, carved up the world into their own empires, each conquering power brought with them customs and tools from home. As early as the 1860s, bikes had been introduced on all continents. For the most part, though, they stayed in the hands of foreign colonialists, away from native people. With the exception of royalty, bicycles were either too scarce or too expensive to have much impact on the lives of people in colonized lands.

As automobiles became the vehicle of choice for Europeans and Americans, though, bicycles became more affordable and more common around the world. By the middle of the twentieth century, as countries began to assert their independence from colonial powers, bicycles became firmly rooted as the major mode of transportation.

Today, the relative poverty in many of these countries, particularly in eastern Asia, makes bicycles more common than cars. While few people in the world can afford to buy a car, most have the money for a bicycle. Not surprisingly, there are more than sixty bicycles for every car in China (cars outnumber bicycles three-to-two in the United States). Even in well-developed Eastern countries like Japan, the tremendous traffic jams caused by overcrowding make riding a bicycle more practical than driving a car.

Most of the one billion bicycles in the world today are found in countries such as China and India, where they're used for individual transportation, commercial transit (as pedi-cabs or rickshaws), and even to transport cargo. In small villages around the world, bicycles are often the only vehicle available. While the automotive age long ago swept the United States and other Western countries, as far as most of the world is concerned, the age of the bicycle continues.

## References

Ballantine, Richard, and Richard Grant. *Richard's Ultimate Bicycle Book.* New York: Dorling Kindersley, 1992.

Chauner, David, and Michael Halstead. *Tour de France Complete Book of Cycling.* New York: Villard Books, 1990.

LeMond, Greg, and Kent Gordis. *Greg LeMond's Complete Book of Bicycling.* New York: G. P. Putnam's Sons, 1990.

Nye, Peter. *The Cyclist's Sourcebook.* New York: Perigee Books, 1991.

Perry, David B. *Bike Cult.* New York: Four Walls Eight Windows, 1995.

Van der Plas, Rob. *Bicycle Technology.* San Francisco: Bicycle Books, 1991.

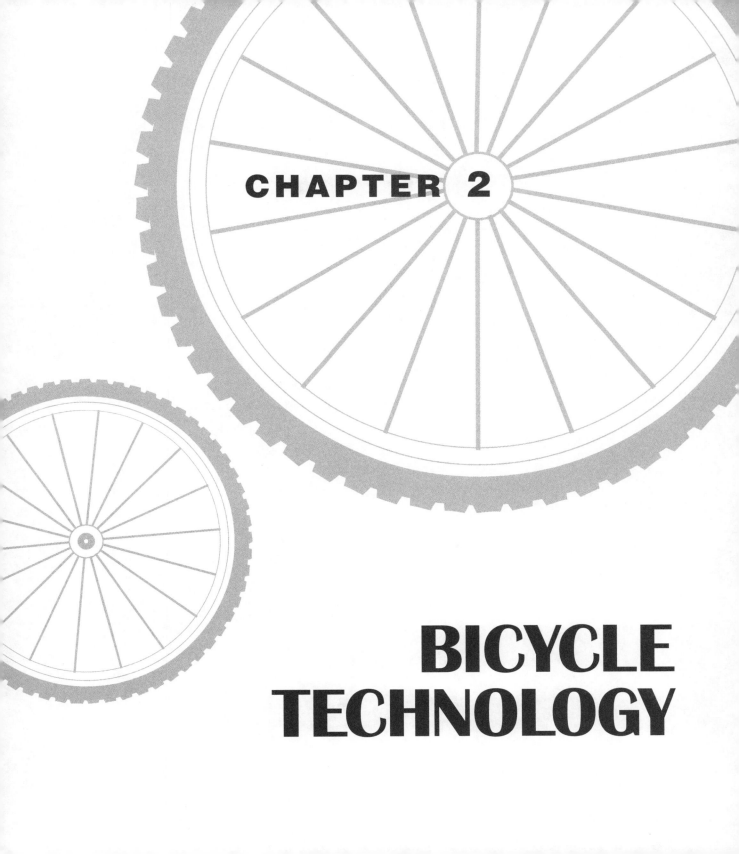

# CHAPTER 2

# BICYCLE TECHNOLOGY

# Parts of a Bicycle

Behold, the bicycle! It is the most efficient form of transportation ever created.

Though there are many styles of bikes—including racing bikes, touring bikes, and mountain bikes—all share certain design characteristics and parts. The bicycle in **Figure 2–1** is actually a racing bike, but most of its parts (with the exception of the drop handlebars) are common to all bikes. To get acquainted with the parts that make up all bicycles, refer to the figure while you read the explanations that follow.

## The Frame

The *frame* is the body of the bike. It holds the bike's parts together and gives the bike structure and definition. The frame is made of four main cylindrical tubes: the top tube, the head tube, the down tube, and the seat tube. Each is designed to be strong and sturdy, and all are held together through welding and/or lug attachments.

The *top tube*, across the top of the bike, connects the seat area to the steering area. Usually, the top tube runs roughly parallel to the ground, though on traditional women's bicycles the top tube slopes up (so skirts stayed in place).

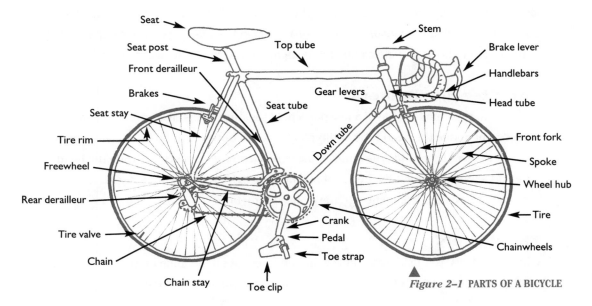

*Figure 2–1* PARTS OF A BICYCLE

The *head tube* is located just above the front wheel and below the handlebars. It connects the steering system to the front fork, which holds the front wheel.

The *down tube* extends diagonally down from the bottom of the head tube to the bottom bracket (the intersection of the seat tube and the down tube), which is where the crankset (chainwheel, crank, and pedals) is based.

The *seat tube* connects the bottom bracket to the top tube.

In addition to the four main tubes, which give the bike its diamond-shaped bone structure, the frame consists of two pairs of thinner tubes. Two *seat stays* connect the point just below the seat, where the seat tube and the top tube meet, to the two sides of the rear axle. Two *chain stays* connect the same points on the rear axle to the bottom bracket. The area where the seat and chain stays meet at the rear wheel axle is called the *dropout*. The seat stay, chain stay, and seat tube form a section of the frame known as the *rear triangle*.

## The Seat

The bike *seat* or saddle is attached to the *seat post*, which extends out of the seat tube above the top tube. The seat post and seat itself can be adjusted vertically by loosening and tightening the seat lug on the seat tube. The seat can also be adjusted horizontally (called the *fore-and-aft position*). Though the seat is generally setparallel to the ground, the seat angle can be tilted slightly forward or backward as well.

## The Steering System

The steering system is made of a few parts held together in the head tube. The *stem* extends out above the head tube and typically bends outward to hold the handlebars. The rider steers by turning the *handlebars*, which turn the stem. Held inside the head tube and allowed to pivot by means of ball bearings, the stem is connected to the *front fork*, which turns the front wheel in the desired direction.

## The Wheels

While wheels vary considerably in weight and thickness depending on the type of bike, all bicycle wheels have a *hub* at the center where the wheel axle is located. The axle connects to the bike frame in the front by means of the fork (at the fork ends) and in the back by the seat stay and chain stay. Ball bearings in the hub allow the wheel to rotate while the axle is held in place on the bike.

The circumference (or outer edge) of each wheel consists of a *rim*, onto which the inner tube and *tire* are mounted. On most bikes, the rim connects to the hub through a network of *spokes*.

## The Drivetrain

This is the engine of the bicycle (your feet serve as the gasoline). The drivetrain starts with the *pedals*, which is where the power source (the rider) meets the locomotive mechanism. The pedals are held in place by the *cranks*, which are strong bars that jut out of the chainwheel. The *chainwheel* is the set of circular gears or sprockets (on the right side of the frame) that the pedals turn. At its center, called the *crank spindle*, the chainwheel connects to the bottom bracket of the bike and turns by means of ball bearings.

The *chain* runs around the sprockets of the chainwheel and connects around the back wheel's axle at the *freewheel*, which has sprockets of its own, called *cogs*. The freewheel attaches to the back wheel's hub, turning the back wheel whenever the chain moves—which in turn makes the bike move.

Put simply, locomotion works like this: the pedals turn the cranks, which turn the chainwheel, which set the chain in motion, which turns the back freewheel, which turns the rear wheel, which moves the bike.

## The Gears

Most bikes have a gear system that allows riders to adjust pedaling difficulty by moving the bike chain onto larger or smaller sprockets. Gears on nearly all bicycles are operated by mechanisms called *derailleurs*. Derailleurs move the chain sideways onto the desired sprocket wheel. They are activated by *gear levers*, which are shifted by hand, located either on the handlebars, stem, or on the upper part of the down tube. Gear levers are connected to the derailleurs by cables.

The front derailleur, which is located just above the crankset (attached to the seat tube), moves the chain between the large *chainwheels* or sprockets on the crankset.

The *rear derailleur*, which is located below the rear wheel axle, moves the chain between cogs on the *freewheel* and adjusts to hold the chain taut no matter what gear it is in.

### The Brakes

Brakes are operated by *brake levers* located on the handlebars. The brake levers connect to brake cables that extend to the *brakes* near the top of the front and rear wheels. As the brake levers are pulled, the cables pull the brake arms that tighten the brake pads against the rims of the wheels and stop the wheels from turning.

There are a few different brake designs, including caliper (side-pull or center-pull) and cantilever. Some bicycles use drum brakes, in which brake pads are built into the hubs of the wheels, while other bicycles use the old-fashioned coaster brake that enables the rider to stop the bike by pressing backward on the pedals.

# Frame Design

The bike frame is generally what we talk about when we talk about the bike. Bike manufacturers are generally in the business of making frames; component manufacturers make the rest of the parts and sell them to bike manufacturers. While the frame is not necessarily the most expensive part of the bike, it is the biggest and, arguably, the most important. A good bike design begins with (and practically ends with) the frame. Refer to **Figure 2–2** while you read the explanations that follow.

### Frame Geometry

The tubing on most conventional bike frames is designed to form a diamond shape. This arrangement goes back at least a hundred years to the earliest safety bicycles and hasn't changed much since. The diamond frame's nearly triangular shape (made by the seat, top, and down tubes) provides strength—because the triangle is the sturdiest shape for construction—while the short head tube holds the steering mechanism comfortably in place.

The subtle but important variations in frame design come in the area known as *frame geometry*, how the angles and lengths of the tubes relate to each other. Though all bikes may appear similar in shape, very slight differences in the angles of the tubes can make huge differences in the comfort and performance of the bike. The two main angles discussed in frame geometry are the *head tube angle* and the *seat tube angle.*

The head tube angle is the angle measured between the top side of the top tube and the head tube's extension above the top tube. The seat tube angle is the angle measured between the bottom side of the top tube and seat tube below. While head and seat tube angles are usually not equal on a bike, they do roughly correspond to each other. That is, a bike with a relatively sharp head angle will also have a sharp seat angle.

Bikes with smaller, more acute angles (head tube angles between 70 and 72 degrees and seat tube angles between 72 and 74 degrees) are said to have a shallow or slack geometry. Because the angles are smaller, the frame's height is shorter and longer. A

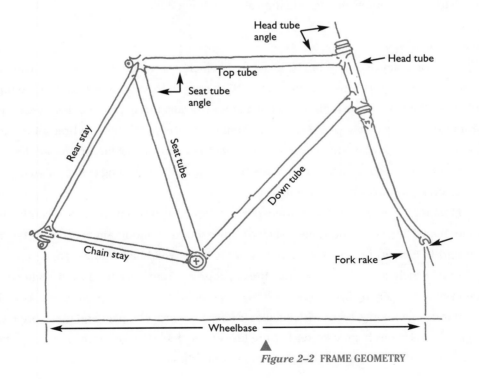

*Figure 2–2* FRAME GEOMETRY

longer frame means the bike will have a longer *wheelbase*, which is the distance between the two wheel axles. To allow room for the wheels to fit in this shallow geometry, chain stays must be longer in back and *fork rake* (the amount the fork slopes outward before reaching the wheel) must be greater in front.

Bikes with slack geometry will be slightly slower through turns (because of the longer wheelbase) and less responsive in handling (because they are more spread out). However, a less compact, longer wheelbase means the bike will be more stable and have better suspension built into the frame, making it more comfortable to ride.

On the other hand, bikes with larger, less acute head tube angles (73 to 75 degrees) and seat tube angles (73 to 76 degrees) are said to have a tight or aggressive frame geometry. Larger angles make the frame taller and the bike more compact, with a shorter wheelbase and therefore shorter chain stays and smaller fork rake. Bikes with tight geometry handle better and are quicker through turns. They are also stiffer and therefore less comfortable to ride than shallow framed bikes.

## Frame Size

The size of a bicycle frame can be measured in inches or centimeters. The measure is typically the length of the seat tube, from the center of the bottom bracket to the top of the seat lug. However, some bike companies (usually foreign companies) measure frame size as the length of the seat tube from the center of the bottom bracket to the center of the top tube. The difference between the two styles of measuring will be about one-half inch, which is a lot in the precision world of cycling design, so make sure you know how size is being measured.

Most bike frames come in a variety of sizes, typically in two-inch (or two-centimeter) increments. Smaller adult frames, such as those found on mountain bikes, will start at around 16 inches and go up to 24 inches, while larger road bike frames range from around 18 inches to 26 inches. While the appropriate frame size for a cyclist will be determined largely by body size, there is some room for personal preference. As with tight frame geometry, bikes with smaller frames are more compact and therefore more rigid. Small frames handle better but are less comfortable. Larger frames, on the other hand, are more flexible and therefore more comfortable.

# Materials

The most desirable characteristics in bike parts are light weight and strength. Materials should also be sufficiently rigid, meaning they'll keep their shape and won't give way under stress, and noncorrosive. While a flexible bike is valued by most riders, suspension should be provided through design (or through the use of shock absorbers and tires), not through the frame material.

While frames and components can be made of this material or that, it's important to remember that within the few categories there is an infinite variety. While the vast majority of bike parts and frames are made of either steel or aluminum *alloys* (mixes of metals), different combinations of alloys yield slightly different materials. Various levels of processing and refining also create a range of qualities and properties. So when we speak of one material being better than another, keep in mind that we're just making a generality. Each material can be used to make a good bicycle, otherwise the material would not be used at all.

## Steel and Steel Alloys

For decades steel was the standard material in the manufacture of bike frames. Today, steel remains the most popular material, particularly with lower priced bikes, while significantly lighter materials have become popular with more expensive models. The major drawback of steel frames is their greater weight, though steel has a number of qualities other materials can't beat. For one, it can be repaired easily. Other materials may break under stress, but steel is more likely to bend slightly. Good bike mechanics will be able to bend most steel frames back into shape, while other frames would be irreparable.

Steel tubing is often held together with lugs that are welded onto the frame, or the frame may be lugless. Tubes made of steel, as well as tubes made of other materials, are commonly butted, which means the inner walls of the tubes are reinforced with thicker metal near the joints to provide more strength where it is needed most.

Steel frames are actually made of steel alloys, mixtures of steel and small amounts of other metals. High tensile steel, for instance, contains more carbon (steel already has some carbon) to make it a stronger material. A common bike material known as chromoly is actually a steel alloy that mixes chromium and molybdenum with steel to make it even stronger, as well as more expensive.

## Aluminum Alloys

Aluminum is a good deal lighter than steel but is not very strong. However, by mixing aluminum with other metals to make aluminum alloys, the resulting material is stronger and lighter. Still, aluminum frames are not as strong as steel frames of similar thickness, and they have been known to break with hard use over time. To compensate, aluminum frames are often made of thicker metal. This makes the bike much more durable but heavier and less sleek. A happy medium is reached through butted tubing, where the tube is thicker only where necessary.

Another advantage aluminum has over steel is that it absorbs shock well, which makes aluminum frames comfortable to ride. And where steel rusts, aluminum won't. It will, however, corrode from road salt or sweat.

Aluminum frames are a little more expensive than steel frames, but they have dropped in price as they've gotten more popular. Today, as new high-tech materials reach the market, aluminum frames provide an affordable middle ground between low-tech steel and new space-age fibers. However, many riders still swear by steel.

More than for its use in frames, aluminum is a popular choice of material for components due to its light weight. Strength is less of a consideration than weight for components that are not subjected to stress; and when strong components are needed, aluminum can be made thicker without sacrificing its weight advantage.

## Carbon Fiber and Composites

Among the high tech, nonmetallic composite fibers that have appeared in recent years, carbon fiber has attracted a lot of attention as the possible future of ultralightweight, ultrastrong, noncorrosive, and shock absorbent frame construction. This material is the product of complex chemical compounding and computer-age design. Like other composite materials, carbon fiber tubing is formed with epoxy resin, molded into shape, and bonded together, occasionally with the help of steel or aluminum lugs.

Sometimes, carbon fiber frames are made in entirely one piece, which makes them more aerodynamic.

At this point, carbon fiber frames are still quite expensive and generally appear on bikes that cost more than $1000, though prices have fallen quickly in recent years and may continue to fall in the future. While carbon fiber does make for a slightly lighter bike, the jury is still out on whether it will someday replace other materials as the best choice for bike frames. Some riders have found carbon fiber frames to be more breakable than steel or aluminum. Clearly, they've yet to be perfected.

## Titanium

Titanium is by far the most expensive of the common frame materials, but for good reason: it's rare and difficult to form and weld. But for riders willing to pay the price, titanium offers much less weight and at least as much strength as any other material currently available. What's more, it won't corrode. Besides price, the only disadvantage to titanium is that it's not as rigid as steel. However, a good frame design can usually overcome that shortcoming.

While titanium has yet to catch on significantly in the few decades since its introduction, it may still prove to be the future of bicycle frames. In the meantime, though, frames that use titanium alloy combined with other metals, such as aluminum, have become very popular and more affordable.

## Magnesium

Magnesium is lighter than any other material used to make bike frames and fairly inexpensive. It can also be cast to make a one-piece frame. But magnesium is also much weaker and less rigid than steel, even when it is strengthened through alloying. And the stronger magnesium frames are made, the heavier they become; by the time they can compare to steel in strength, magnesium frames weigh almost the same as steel frames.

# Ball Bearings

Though hidden from sight, tiny ball bearings are used in bicycles and play a crucial role in how bicycles operate. In fact, bicycles and ball bearings go way back. Those little hard steel spheres, used in countless applications throughout this century, were first invented for use in the bicycle back in the mid-1800s.

Ball bearings are used in the hubs of the wheels as an interface between fixed parts (the axles) and moving parts (the wheels). Because ball bearings significantly reduce the road resistance exerted on a bike and the friction between wheels and frame, these tiny metal balls play a larger role than any other bike part in making the bicycle an efficient vehicle.

In addition to their use in the wheels, ball bearings are used in the head tube to facilitate steering, in the crankset to allow the chainwheels to spin while they're held by the bottom bracket, and in the pedals to allow rotation around the pedal axle. So that ball bearings generate the least amount of friction and resistance, grease is used as a lubricant between the balls and the rolling surface.

While ball bearings are one of the more hassle-free parts of the bike, they occasionally become loose and must be adjusted. It's crucial to bike performance that ball bearings are set perfectly; they need to be secured well enough that they aren't loose or rattling inside their race (the area that holds the bearings), but they also need to be able to roll freely.

# Steering

The steering system is made up of the handlebars, the stem, the headset, and the fork. Unlike a car's steering system, a bicycle's steering system is not used simply for turning. It also plays a crucial role in balancing the bike. Steering and balance, in fact, are completely intertwined. The next time you make a wide turn on your bike, note how little you actually turn the handlebars. Most turning is simply a matter of shifting your balance and leaning to one side.

## The Headset

The headset uses ball bearings to enable steering. The handlebar stem locks into the head tube at the upper headset and connects with the fork shaft or steer tube inside the head tube. The fork shaft then exits the head tube at the lower headset, splits, and extends down to connect to the front wheel. While the head tube remains fixed, the steering system turns due to the ball bearings in both the upper and lower headsets.

## Steering Geometry

Built into the design of a bike are the angles and arrangements of the steering system, known as the *steering geometry*. The steering geometry determines how well a bicycle will handle—that is, how accurate and easy to maneuver steering will be. This is best indicated by a measurement called the *trail*.

The trail is the measure of the distance between the front wheel's point of contact with the road and the point where the steering axis, if extended beyond the head tube and fork, would touch the ground. In general, as the trail becomes larger, the bike becomes more stable but less responsive in steering.

The *fork rake* and the head tube angle determine the trail. The rake is the amount the fork slopes forward. It is measured as the distance between the line extended to the ground from the steering axis and a parallel line extending to the ground from the wheel axle. The larger the rake, the smaller the trail. So as rake increases, the bike becomes less stable and more responsive.

The head tube angle is another variable that affects trail. As long as the rake stays the same, a steeper head tube angle will make the trail smaller, while a shallower angle will make it larger. Thus, shallow angles encourage stability while steep angles bring more steering response.

To some extent, wheel size affects trail as well. While most wheels are large enough to leave a sufficiently large trail no matter what the rake, bikes with very small wheels (children's bikes, some folding bikes) should have small rakes to maintain the trail, and, thus, stability.

## TRACKSTANDING MADE EASY

 Is it possible to ride a bike without moving forward? Sure. It's called trackstanding, a little technique street cyclists practice to keep their bikes balanced and their feet off the ground while they're standing still. Trackstanding is a neat trick that can come in handy for folks who ride in traffic a lot. At the very least, it's a fun thing to do while you wait for the light to turn green.

To trackstand, it helps to be on a street that is slightly sloped sideways (for drainage purposes, most streets are), or else mildly uphill. As you come to a stop, instead of putting your feet down onto the ground, turn your front wheel toward the upward slope. This will usually be left, toward the center of the road. Position your pedals so that your inside foot (usually your left foot) is in a forward position, at around one o'clock. Exert forward pressure on the pedal to counteract the force of the slope pushing you backward. You'll end up rocking back and forth very slightly (a few inches), which will keep you balanced. To help more with balance, you may want to apply light pressure on the brakes and/or stand out of the saddle.

If it sounds easy, rest assured, it's not. Expect to put in lots of practice and have plenty of failed attempts before trackstanding successfully. Don't try trackstanding with clipless pedals until you get good at it, or you could end up lying in the street with a nasty road rash (or worse). Have patience—soon enough you'll develop a natural feel for it, and you'll be standing with the best of them!

# How Do Bicycles Stay Up?

How do bicycles stay up? is a good question. And, rest assured, there is an answer. But I'm not about to explain it here.

To the average rider how a bicycle stays up is something of a mystery. Anyone who's ever tried to walk a tightrope can attest to how difficult balancing on a one-inch-wide base can be. Quite often, we pedal around without even giving a thought as to why we're able to balance so easily on the thin tire underneath us.

One of the great ironies (and beauties) of bike riding is that, for all the bicycle's mechanical simplicity and energy efficiency, the scientific explanation for why a bicycle stays balanced is quite complex. Centrifugal force plays little role unless the bicycle wheels are turning. The motion of the bike has little to do with it either. It's amazing that anyone ever even attempted to make a bike—that anyone could imagine beforehand that a bike would actually work.

So what is it that keeps bikes up? Let's just say it has to do with steering. When we learn how to ride a bike, we train ourselves to shift our weight and turn the handlebars continuously in either direction to compensate for the forces that would cause the bike to fall. That explains why children learning to ride have erratic steering. And why skilled cyclists can balance their bikes while standing in place by deftly manipulating the handlebars. And why it's impossible for anyone to ride in a completely straight line. As we become more comfortable on a bicycle, this weight shifting and steering becomes automatic. And once we learn, we never forget.

As for an actual mathematical proof explaining it all? Let's just leave that to the physicists.

# Wheels and Tires

A bicycle wheel is made up of a rim, spokes, and a hub, with a tire and inner tube secured to the rim (see **Figure 2–4**). The bike wheel, which is light and yet supports heavy loads, is quite an engineering marvel. However, both wheels of a bike need to be perfectly true (flat and unwarped) and aligned to maintain balance and efficient handling.

## The Hub

The hub is located at the center of the wheel and surrounds the wheel's axle. While the axle is fixed and bolted to the bike frame (at the dropouts or fork ends), the hub turns the wheel around the axle through the use of ball bearings. At the sides of the hub, just inside of where the axle connects to the frame, hub flanges flare out to form flat disc surfaces that contain holes for the spokes.

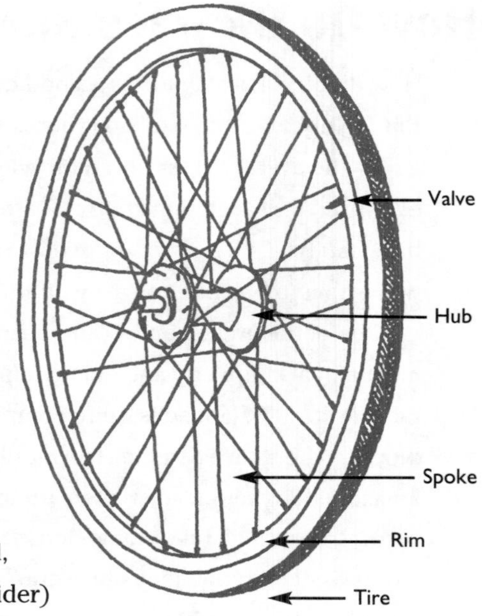

## Spokes

Spokes are needed on a wheel to connect the rim to the hub, to provide support for the wheel, and to absorb forces (of both the road and the rider) exerted on the wheel. However, unlike the spokes of a wagon wheel, bicycle spokes hold the wheel together through tension (by pulling in the rim) not through compression (holding the rim in place). Tighter spokes make for stronger wheels.

*Figure 2–3* THE WHEEL

Spokes are made of stainless steel and have nipple heads at the end for attaching to the rim and tightening. At the hub, spokes attach to one of the hub flanges, alternating between right and left sides. Wheels may have radial spokes, tangent or crossed spokes, or a combination of the two. Radial spokes simply connect a point on the rim to a point on the hub and do not cross each other, while the stronger tangential spokes wrap around the hub and connect to two points on the rim, crossing other spokes in the process. Most bicycle wheels have between 20 and 36 spokes.

Some aerodynamic wheels for racing do not use traditional stainless steel wire spokes. Instead, they may have two to eight blades made of steel or a composite material. Or, wheels may be solid disks with no spokes at all. While these aero wheels have less wind resistance, they are heavier and more difficult to make true if bent.

## The Rim

Rims are made of steel or aluminum (aluminum is better for bikes with rim brakes) and are generally flat on the inside with a concave groove or tire bed on the outside. The rim is lined with holes which the spokes run through. Spoke holes should be protected from the nipple head of spokes with small bushings or washers.

## Tires

The two main types of bicycle tires are clinchers and tubular tires. The vast majority of bikes use clincher tires, while some racing bikes use tubulars (see **Figure 2–4**). Tubular tires have the outer tire sewn around the innertube and then cemented onto a shallow concave rim. Clincher tires have metal or Kevlar wires along the edges that hook into a deep-bedded rim. A separate innertube, usually made of synthetic rubber, fits inside the tire.

Tubular tires were once popular with racers because they were much lighter and higher pressured than clinchers. With the availability of lightweight clinchers, however, that's no longer the case today. Tubulars are not as durable and are more expensive than clinchers, plus they're difficult to install and repair. For all these reasons, tubulars are far less common than clinchers.

Tires, of course, need to be properly inflated to work. Higher pressure tires generate less resistance against the ground. For suspension purposes, though, lower pressure tires provide a smoother ride. In addition, an effective tread pattern makes tires more stable on the ground and less likely to skid. While some racing bikes reduce friction by having no tread at all, off-road bikes perform better with large treads that grip the ground.

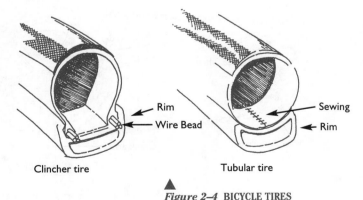

Clincher tire

Rim
Wire Bead

Tubular tire

Sewing
Rim

*Figure 2–4* BICYCLE TIRES

# Transmission

Transmission refers to the parts of the bike that make it go. Besides your own feet, the transmission includes the bike's drivetrain and the gear system. Refer to **Figure 2–5** while you read the explanations that follow.

## The Crankset and Pedals

The crankset consists of the chainwheels, which revolve around the bottom bracket by means of a spindle, and the cranks, which are the arms that turn the chainwheels. Pedals are attached to the cranks. The bottom bracket spindle uses ball bearings to turn the crankset in the fixed bottom bracket. Most bikes with variable gears have two or three chainwheels (a double- or triple-crankset). The chainwheels, or chainrings, are located on the right side of the bike (attached to the right crank) and increase in size as they move away from the bike. Each chainwheel has teeth on which the chain is threaded. As riders switch gears, the chain moves from one chainwheel to another.

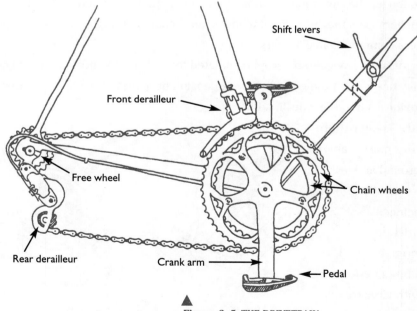

*Figure 2–5* THE DRIVETRAIN

Larger chainwheels are responsible for the high gears that are difficult to pedal and that move the bike fast, while smaller chainwheels engage the low gears that are used to climb hills.

Crankarms, or simply cranks, attach to the bottom bracket spindle. They are fairly standard, with slight variations in length (between 160 and 180 mm) and design. Most cranks are suitable as long as they contribute to a rider's proper bike fit (along with frame size and seat height), are strong enough to withstand pedaling force (which is exerted on the crank-spindle connection), and turn the chainwheels effectively. However, slightly longer crankarms will give the rider more leverage in climbing hills and more pedal power on level ground. There is a limit to how long crankarms can be, though. They must be short enough to allow ample clearance between the pedals and the ground at all times.

Crankarm ends attach to the pedals at the pedal axle, the midpoint on the inside of the pedals. Pedals rotate around the pedal axle through the use of ball bearings. The movements of the pedal independent to the crankarms enables riders to keep their feet planted on the pedals throughout the 360-degree pedal stroke and to get the proper leverage for maximum pedaling efficiency. A few different types of pedals are commonly found on bicycles. The ordinary flat pedals come in a variety of shapes and degrees of traction. They may also come with or without toe clips (and straps), cages which hold the feet on the pedal to provide more stability and power in the pedaling upstroke.

In recent decades, the clipless pedal has become popular, particularly with racers. Clipless pedals have neither platforms nor toe clips, but rather clamps (much like the attachments found on skis) that connect to specially designed shoes. Clipless pedals offer all the advantages of toe clips but do not restrict the feet because the clamps detach easily. The disadvantages of clipless pedals are their price and the need for special shoes (which are not comfortable for walking).

## The Chain

Chain design is virtually standard in all bikes and has remained unchanged for many years (see **Figure 2–6**). The tooth-and-link chain is made of two parallel sets of steel link plates with cylindrical rollers between them at the joints. The teeth of the chainwheels and rear cogs thread into the space between the rollers. A light oil or grease is needed to keep the chain lubricated and running smoothly, and the chain should be kept free of grime, dirt, and rust.

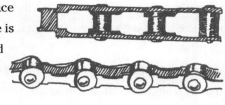

For the chain to run properly, chainwheels and cogs should be directly in line and centered. Gear settings that require the chain to deviate most (for example, a setting that uses the outermost chainwheel and the innermost cog) cause more wear on the chain and decreased pedaling efficiency.

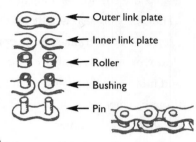

Outer link plate
Inner link plate
Roller
Bushing
Pin

*Figure 2–6* THE CHAIN

## Freewheel and Cogs

The freewheel is the mechanism attached to the rear axle that allows (with the help of ball bearings) the rear wheel to turn without the rider having to pedal (known as coasting) (see **Figure 2–7**). Coasting is accomplished when levers, or pawls, in the freewheel that engage the wheel during pedaling disengage (causing that familiar clicking sound) during coasting.

Usually installed around the freewheel are a series of cogs, or sprockets, similar in appearance to the chainwheels on the crankset but smaller in size and more numerous (typically there are five to eight of them). Like chainwheels, cogs are located on the right side of the wheel and progress in size, though cogs get smaller as they move away from the rear wheel. The chain, which is threaded onto the chainwheel in front, wraps around the teeth of a cog in the rear. As riders switch gears, the chain moves from one

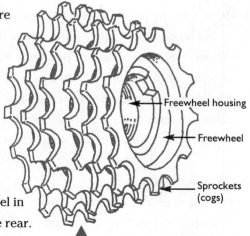

Freewheel housing

Freewheel

Sprockets (cogs)

*Figure 2–7* FREEWHEEL AND COGS

# GEAR DEVELOPMENT CHART

The numbers in the chart represent the distance in inches a bike will travel with different sizes of chainwheels and cogs. All calculations are based on a bike with 27-inch wheels.

**Gear development (inches)**

| Number of teeth in chainwheel | Number of teeth in rear cog | | | | | | | | | | | |
|---|---|---|---|---|---|---|---|---|---|---|---|---|
| | 12 | 14 | 16 | 18 | 20 | 22 | 24 | 26 | 28 | 30 | 32 | 34 |
| 28 | 63 | 52 | 47 | 42 | 38 | 34 | 31 | 29 | 27 | 25 | 24 | 22 |
| 30 | 67 | 58 | 51 | 45 | 41 | 37 | 34 | 31 | 29 | 27 | 25 | 24 |
| 32 | 72 | 62 | 54 | 48 | 43 | 39 | 36 | 33 | 31 | 29 | 27 | 25 |
| 34 | 76 | 66 | 57 | 51 | 46 | 42 | 38 | 35 | 33 | 31 | 29 | 27 |
| 36 | 81 | 69 | 61 | 54 | 49 | 44 | 40 | 37 | 35 | 32 | 31 | 28 |
| 38 | 86 | 73 | 64 | 57 | 51 | 47 | 42 | 40 | 37 | 34 | 32 | 30 |
| 40 | 90 | 77 | 68 | 60 | 54 | 49 | 45 | 42 | 39 | 36 | 34 | 32 |
| 42 | 95 | 81 | 71 | 63 | 57 | 52 | 47 | 44 | 41 | 38 | 35 | 33 |
| 44 | 99 | 85 | 74 | 66 | 59 | 54 | 50 | 46 | 42 | 40 | 37 | 35 |
| 48 | 108 | 93 | 81 | 72 | 65 | 59 | 54 | 50 | 46 | 43 | 40 | 38 |
| 50 | 113 | 96 | 84 | 75 | 68 | 61 | 56 | 52 | 48 | 45 | 42 | 40 |
| 52 | 117 | 100 | 88 | 78 | 70 | 64 | 59 | 54 | 50 | 47 | 44 | 41 |
| 54 | 122 | 104 | 91 | 81 | 73 | 66 | 61 | 56 | 52 | 49 | 46 | 43 |
| 56 | 126 | 108 | 95 | 84 | 76 | 69 | 63 | 58 | 54 | 50 | 47 | 44 |

cog to another. Unlike the chainwheels (which work in the opposite way), the larger cogs make pedaling easier while the smaller ones give more power.

## Gears

The gear of a bicycle simply refers to the position of the chain. It will always be threaded on one (of the two or three) chainwheels in front and one (of the five to eight) cogs in the rear. The number of gears or speeds a bike has is equal to the number of possible combinations of chainwheel and cog settings. It can be determined by multiplying the number of cogs by the number of chainwheels. For instance, a bike with six cogs and three chainwheels will have eighteen gears or speeds.

While the sizes of bike gears always increase relative to each other, the measurable size of chainwheels and cogs—and the range between the gears—will vary from bike to bike. Some bikes have extra small gears that are designed for hill climbing while other bikes lack smaller gears. Because the teeth on cogs and chainwheels are of a standard size in order to fit with standard chains, the size of a cog or chainwheel is often measured by the number of teeth it has. For instance, a 40T cog will have 40 teeth.

Difficulty in pedaling, however, is not a matter of the individual sizes of the cog and chainwheel used, but rather of the ratio of the two together. That is, the combined size of a midsized cog and chainwheel may be equal to the combined size of a small cog and large chainwheel, but the two settings will not provide equal difficulty in pedaling because the gear ratio of the latter is much greater than the former (and therefore makes the bicycle more difficult to pedal).

The number of teeth in a cog or chainwheel can be used to determine a standard measure for the size of a gear, which applies to any chain setting on all bikes. Gear size, also called *gear number*, is calculated by dividing the number of teeth on the chainring by the number of teeth on the cog to find the gear ratio, then multiplying the number by the diameter of the rear wheel (in inches or meters). For instance, a gear setting that uses a 36T chainwheel and an 18T cog on a 26-inch wheel will have a gear number of 52 inches ($36 \div 8 = 2; 2 \times 26 = 52$). To figure the distance a bicycle travels in that gear during each full turn of the pedals—called the *development*—multiply the gear ratio by $\pi$ (22/7 or roughly 3.14). In the example above, the bike would travel about 163 inches in each revolution of the pedals.

## Derailleurs and Shift Levers

Shift levers located on the handlebars or down tube regulate the switching of gears. Most bicycles have two levers—one that moves the chain between the chainwheels in front (typically the left lever) and one that moves the chain between the cogs in back (typically the right lever). The levers connect to the derailleurs (see **Figure 2–8**), which physically shift the gears through flexible cables that run along the bike frame.

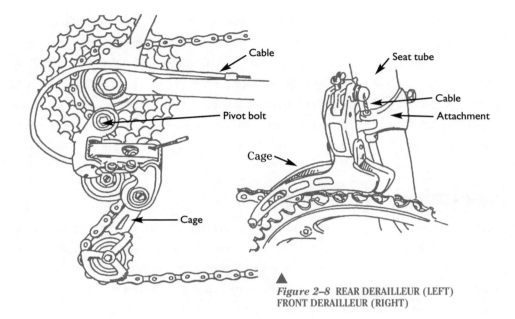

**Figure 2–8** REAR DERAILLEUR (LEFT) FRONT DERAILLEUR (RIGHT)

The rear derailleur, which hangs below the freewheel, is typically attached to the dropout (near the rear wheel axle) with a pivot bolt that allows it to move lengthwise along the rear drivetrain. Most rear derailleurs have two chain guide wheels through which the chain is threaded. Moving the gear levers causes the cables to be pulled or released, thus either pulling the derailleur in toward the wheel or allowing it to move farther away from the wheel. As the derailleur moves, it takes the chain with it, causing the chain to move to a larger or smaller cog—thus switching gears.

A spring mechanism causes the derailleur to swing backward, to pick up the chain slack as gears are shifted to smaller sprockets, and forward, to compensate for the additional chain needed as gears are shifted to larger sprockets. Therefore, how far the rear derailleur is able to swing back and forth determines the largest and smallest sizes possible for the chainwheels and cogs.

The front derailleur is located above the crankset and is typically attached to the seat tube. Much as with the rear derailleur, the chain runs through a piece of the front derailleur called the cage, which is responsible for physically pushing the chain from one chainwheel to another. Gear shifting on the front end is also accomplished by pulling or relaxing a cable connected to and manipulated by the gear levers.

While all derailleur gearing works on essentially the same principle, index derailleurs are preferable to conventional derailleurs because they offer more precision in shifting. For index shifting, the exact amount of cable pull needed to move the derailleurs (and chain) to each cog or chainwheel is preset, and gear shifters are clicked into each gear. Cables for index shifting are thicker and stronger so that they stay perfectly adjusted.

# Suspension

All bicycles need some form of suspension system to protect them and the rider from feeling every bump on the road or trail. Otherwise bikes would feel like the old bone-shakers of the nineteenth century. Good suspension protects the bicycle from the wear and tear of the road, increases traction by keeping the wheels on the ground, and also makes the rider more comfortable. Suspension can be built into a bicycle either directly through shock absorbers or indirectly through design.

Some bikes, particularly off-road bikes, have spring-loaded steel coils in the forks that absorb bumps and jumps and work like a car's shock absorbers. Other bikes have shocks built into the rear triangle of the frame, either on the seat stay or seat tube. Less often, bikes can be found with springs or other suspension systems built into the saddle or handlebars, though these create unwanted variables in bike fit. Fork shocks, the most common kind, have become a very popular component on mountain and BMX bikes in recent years.

Most bikes, especially road bikes, don't have shock absorbers. Instead, a milder form of suspension is built into the bike's design. Suspension is increased through a wider wheelbase; larger fork rake; and larger, fatter tires. In addition, the inflation of air in tires can be adjusted for ground conditions. While this kind of suspension is certainly not as effective as a shock absorber, it is certainly adequate for bikes in most circumstances.

There is one other method of suspension that riders use to ease the shock of surface bumps: movement of their bodies. By standing up as they go over bumps, they are essentially using their legs as suspension.

# Brakes

The two main types of braking systems used in bicycles today are *caliper brakes* and *cantilever brakes*. Both apply pressure on the rim of the wheel to stop the bike and are considered *rim brakes*. While calipers have been and continue to be the most common brakes found on bikes, the newer cantilevers are stronger and have become more popular in recent years (see **Figure 2–9**).

Rim brakes work through a system of levers and cables. Cables connect the brake levers (located on the handlebars) to the brake arms that surround the top of the wheels and are secured to the fork in front or seat stay in back. When the levers are flexed by hand, the cables pull, closing the brake arms around the rims. When the levers are released the brakes spring back to their original position.

The section of the brakes, called the *brake pad* or *brake shoe*, that comes into contact with the moving rim is usually made of rubber or leather to maximize the friction needed to stop. All other parts of the braking system—arms, cable, and levers—must be rigid and precisely positioned to transfer the relatively light force exerted by hands on brake levers to the high power needed in the brakes for effective braking.

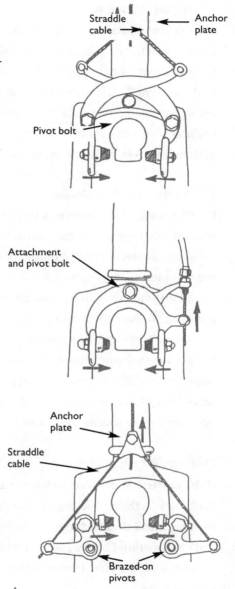

*Figure 2–9* BRAKES: CALIPER CENTERPULL (TOP); CALIPER SIDEPULL (CENTER); CANTILEVER (BOTTOM)

## Caliper Brakes

Most caliper brakes are sidepull, meaning the cable pulls the two brake arms (one on each side of the rim) from the same side of the wheel. Centerpull calipers, which are somewhat out of date and much less common, pull the brake arms from above the wheel. With centerpulls, the main brake cable forms an inverted Y shape with a second straddle cable, which connects to both brake arms separately on both sides of the wheel. Either method is effective for most bikes, but design considerations make sidepulls work better with thin wheels while centerpulls are more effective with wide tires.

## Cantilever Brakes

Cantilevers are also centerpull brakes (technically, they're also considered caliper brakes), but they do not function in the same way as calipers. The essential difference between cantilevers and traditional calipers is that with cantilevers the two brake arms are mounted separately and work independently, while with calipers the brake arms work together as a unit. As with centerpull calipers, cantilevers use a straddle cable to divide the brake cable's pull among the two sides.

Originally designed for use on tandem and BMX bikes, the high-power cantilever brakes have become quite common on mountain bikes and some touring bikes as well. Because they offer better stopping power, cantilevers are recommended for bikes that carry heavy loads or make steep descents. Most racers, meanwhile, stick with calipers because they're smaller and more aerodynamic.

## Other Brake Types

Older and less sophisticated bikes may use the coaster brake, which works by pressing backward on the pedals. Simply, the backward motion counteracts the forward spin of the rear wheel to slow and stop the bike. Other less common brakes include U-brakes and cam-operated brakes, both of which are variations on the caliper and cantilever designs, and hydraulic brakes, which use compressed liquid (usually oil) for stronger braking force.

Drum brakes and disk brakes are entirely different braking systems that use hand-activated cables but work at the wheel hub. Drum brakes use flexed cables to push brake pads against the inside of the hub shell to stop the turning of the wheel. Disk brakes use caliper-style brakes to clamp onto a small disk that turns along with the wheel and is located next to the hub.

### References

Chauner, David, and Michael Halstead. *Tour de France Complete Book of Cycling.* New York: Villard Books, 1990.

Ford, Norman D. *Keep On Pedaling: The Complete Guide to Adult Bicycling.* Woodstock, Vt.: The Countryman Press, 1990.

Matheny, Fred. *Bicycling Magazine's Complete Guide to Riding and Racing Techniques.* Emmaus, Penn.: Rodale Press, 1989.

Perry, David B. *Bike Cult.* New York: Four Walls Eight Windows, 1995.

Van der Plas, Rob. *The Bicycle Commuting Book.* San Francisco: Bicycle Books, 1989.

Van der Plas, Rob. *Bicycle Technology.* San Francisco: Bicycle Books, 1991.

**CHAPTER 3**

# BICYCLE TYPES

# Road Bikes

Road bikes are known by a few different names, most of which are not entirely accurate. They are often called *ten speeds*, though today's road bikes may have twelve, eighteen, even twenty-four speeds depending on how many chainwheels the bike has. Then, of course, there are the old fashioned roadsters that have only one or three gears. Road bikes are also somewhat inaccurately labeled racing bikes because their thin frame and drop handlebar design resemble bikes used for racing. While it's true that most racing bikes are road bikes, some (such as track bikes) are not meant for the road at all. And not all road bikes are good for racing, either. Sports bikes, for instance, look very much like racing bikes but are not made for competition.

What all road bikes have in common is that they are drop handlebar derailleur bicycles designed for paved surfaces only. Road bikes also have large wheels and thin tires (how thin depends on the type of road bike), and they tend to be more lightweight than other bicycles (twenty-four pounds or less). Beyond these common characteristics, though, road bikes have a great range of purpose and design. They're good bikes for racing, touring, staying in shape, or simply having fun.

## Racing Bikes

Racing bikes are designed, not surprisingly, to maximize speed (see **Figure 3–1**). That is, after all, how riders win races. Because slight details can make a great difference in a race, good racing bikes feature a precision design. To make the bikes as light and as aerodynamic as possible, frames are made very thin with strong, lightweight materials. Aluminum alloy or the newer and more expensive carbon fiber which is 30 percent lighter than aluminum, are popular choices.

Because small increments of speed and power can also make a difference in a tight race, racing bikes have closely spaced, precise gears. High gears, which increase speed, are emphasized. To allow racers to maintain speed as they pedal through turns, bottom brackets are raised higher off the ground than they are on other bikes. For increased control and turning speed, racing bikes have a steep head angle, steep seat angles, and a short fork rake, which together make for a shorter wheelbase. Very narrow high pressure tires minimize road resistance and also result in increased speed. Typically, clincher tires are used, though more expensive racing bikes use tubular tires.

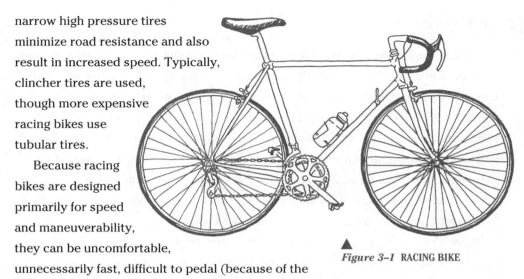

*Figure 3–1* RACING BIKE

Because racing bikes are designed primarily for speed and maneuverability, they can be uncomfortable, unnecessarily fast, difficult to pedal (because of the higher gears), and quite expensive. For these reasons, good racing bikes are not the best choice for most new or occasional riders who are interested in biking primarily for recreation or transportation. New riders who like the look and design of racing bikes may consider a sports bike. These are similar to racing bikes in every way—in fact, they can be hard to distinguish from racing bikes at first glance. But sports bikes are simpler and less expensive. They offer more comfort—through a less rigid frame geometry and longer wheelbase—and a wider range of gears, including low gears for easy pedaling. Because sports bikes are often more durable and have less of a precision design, they typically weigh a few pounds more than real racing bikes.

Racing bikes are also not the best choice for riders interested in touring. Their short wheelbase lacks the suspension needed for comfort on long rides and their thin tires may not be durable enough to survive many miles of rough road. Also, racing bikes' high gears make them harsh for riding over hills and bad for carrying loads.

If you decide you'd like to ride a racing bike, there are a number of racers available that you should be familiar with. Four types are described in the paragraphs that follow. The style you choose will likely depend on the type of racing you plan to do. Or, if you don't plan to race but would like a racing bike anyway, choose the style that best suits your riding needs.

*Criterium racer.* These bikes are designed for road competitions called criterium races, in which riders do laps through city streets. Criterium bikes typically have a higher bottom bracket—so the rider can pedal through sharp turns—and a short wheelbase—for faster turns. Like other racing bikes, criteriums are very lightweight and have a stiff, tight frame with a short fork rake for maximum responsiveness.

*Road racer.* These bikes are designed for longer road races during which a variety of riding surfaces are likely to be encountered. Road racers are sleek and lightweight, but in some ways resemble touring bikes (which are described later in the chapter). The longer wheelbase adds the comfort and suspension needed for long rides, while the high bottom bracket typical of short-distance racing bikes is not necessary because sharp turns and sprinting are less common.

*Time-trial bike.* These bikes are meant for sprinting against the clock, so a light, aerodynamic frame and components are most important. Unlike typical bicycle wheels, which have spoked rims and are of equal size in front and back, time-trial bikes may have spokeless diskwheels (usually on the back wheel) and a smaller front wheel for increased aerodynamics. Special handlebar attachments, *aerobars*, designed to reduce wind resistance by making the rider's body lower and thinner, are often used on time-trialers as well.

*Track bike.* Used only for racing on an enclosed bike track, these bikes are very lightweight—in part because there's nothing to them! Mechanically, track bikes are pretty close to the bikes designed over a hundred years ago. They have a fixed gear, which means riders can neither shift gears nor coast (in other words, the pedals move whenever the wheels move). And because track racers ride uninterrupted along a circular track, they have no need for brakes. Riders can stop only by slowing the pedals or by letting the bike drift to a stop. Of course, brakes are a necessity and gears are very helpful when riding in any situation other than on a track. In case you haven't figured it out, track bikes should never be used on the road.

## Touring Bikes

Strictly speaking, any bike can be used to tour. But as any experienced bike tourist will tell you, if you're going to put a bicycle through the rigors of long rides and heavy loads—and expect it to survive—you'll need a bike designed to accommodate the special needs of long distance road riding. Good touring bikes are designed to be comfortable, sturdy, and reliable. They should be strong enough to carry loads many times their own weight and efficient enough to handle the hills of country roads (see Figure 3–2).

Touring bikes can often be identified by how they are equipped. They have mounts or eyelets used to attach baggage (called *panniers*), extra water bottles, or other materials needed while touring. Mudguards, or fenders, around the tops of the wheels protect panniers and the rider from the spray of wet, muddy roads. Thicker tires and heavier tubes protect the wheels and provide greater comfort through added suspension. Additional suspension comes from a longer wheelbase—the result of longer chain stays, a sloping fork rake, and a shallow head tube angle (71 to 72 degrees).

Without touring equipment such as racks and panniers loaded on, a touring bike can look a lot like a road racing bike. Drop handlebars are necessary on tourers to allow riders a variety of positions on long rides (upright position is better for visibility in traffic, while the drop position is better for speed—and switching positions once in a while prevents riders from getting stiff). And a triple chainwheel makes for a wide range of gears, particularly very low gears, that allow easy pedaling on hills even when the bike is weighed down by bags and equipment. In exchange for greater comfort, strength, and pedaling ease, the touring bike has

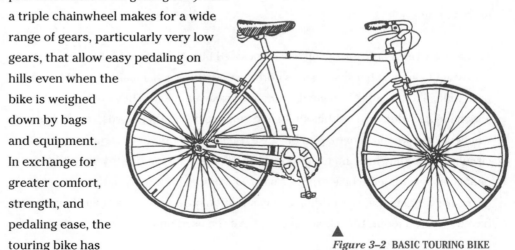

*Figure 3–2* BASIC TOURING BIKE

less speed and agility than a racer and usually weighs a bit more (thirty to thirty-five pounds).

Specific touring bikes are designed to accommodate the different kinds of touring—from short rides to camping trips to cross-country treks. Basic touring bikes are made for short trips where less equipment and baggage is needed, while long-distance bikes are better able to carry heavy loads in panniers or racks. Riders who plan to do any long-distance touring or bike camping should opt for the latter because even though it will weigh more and be more rigid, a heavy-duty tourer allows the best range of possibilities for touring.

Even riders who don't plan to tour should consider a touring bike for its rugged frame and ability to handle hills. Or, as a happy compromise for people who prefer the lighter weight and shorter wheelbase of a sports or racing bike but like the durability of a touring bike, there's the hybrid sports-touring bike. It tends to be equally good for long and short rides, though, as for all hybrids, its strength is also its weakness: versatility waters it down so it's neither as good for touring as a touring bike, nor as fit for sports use as a sports bike.

For lack of a better category, one other type of bike is classified as a touring bike: the *roadster*. Also known as an *English bike* or *utility bike*, the roadster predates the modern touring bike by many decades but has managed to remain in use despite its relative inefficiency. Roadsters have upright handlebars, thick tires, wide saddles, fenders, a chainguard, and a rack. Typically, these bikes are very heavy (weighing as much as forty-five pounds), often rely on only three speeds, and use coaster brakes (that is, pressing back on the pedals to stop). With some advancements from the balloon-tire roadsters popular in the 1930s, various styles of roadster remain in use in the United States, England, Germany, and France. But roadsters, which are the most inexpensive bikes in the world, are most common today in third-world countries.

# Mountain Bikes

Also known as *all-terrain bikes*, or *ATBs*, *mountain bikes* swept the country during the 1980s (see **Figure 3–3**). Since then, they have revolutionized the bike industry by vastly widening the possibilities for biking as a sport and activity. When mountain bikes first appeared in northern California in the late 1970s, they were like aliens from another planet; sleek ten-speed bikes were still the norm. ATBs brought back the balloon tires from roadsters and combined them with the knobby tread of BMX bikes (described in the next section). They also adapted the strong handlebar brakes of motorcycles and borrowed the derailleur and lightweight components from racing bikes. What resulted was an entirely new type of bike that enabled riders to go where they had never gone before: off-road. First introduced commercially in the early 1980s, mountain bikes were heavy at first, weighing as much as forty-five pounds. By the end of the decade, though, the weight had been cut down to around twenty-five pounds without sacrificing frame strength. ATBs began to attract legions of new riders who were drawn by the action and excitement of mountain biking.

Today, the mountain bike is by far the most popular type of bike sold in the United States. Of course, not all riders use their mountain bike for its originally intended purpose. Many riders have found ATBs quite useful on-road as well—some road riders even prefer them to road bikes! The reasons? First, mountain bikes tend to be more comfortable than racing bikes. Also, they are better able to handle roads that are not well paved or that have

*Figure 3–3* MOUNTAIN BIKE

obstructions. And finally, the mountain bike rider's upright position is good for seeing and being seen in traffic. Sure, mountain bikes are neither as fast nor as aerodynamic on the street as road bikes—and they're not as well equipped or as comfortable on long rides as a touring bike—but for many riders, the mountain bike is the best choice for all-around riding.

Mountain bikes are designed to keep the rider in control on rough and uneven terrain such as rocks, dirt, bumps, and twigs; they're also made to climb hills and withstand jumps. The best ATBs balance strength with comfort and light weight. Frames have a sturdier geometry, tending to be thicker and more compact than road bikes. Shorter chain stays and a steeper seat angle put the rider's weight over the back wheel for better traction and control, while a steeper head angle and large fork rake make for better handling and suspension. Some mountain bikes have actual spring shocks for improved suspension.

Fat, knobby tires that are highly pressurized provide traction, strength, and cushion. A straight handlebar creates the upright riding position preferable for off-road riding. A sliding seat post allows riders to make quick adjustments for hills (lower seats are best for descents, higher seats for climbs). A triple chainring enables a wide range of gears, including low gears for climbing hills and mountains; an easily-accessible gearshift makes it possible to shift gears without taking either hand off the handlebar. Cantilever brakes, sometimes with the addition of hydraulic brakes, provide the needed extra-strength stopping power.

## BMX Bikes

*BMX*, or *bicycle moto-cross*, began in the 1970s as an adaptation of moto-cross motorcycle racing. When kids wishing

▲
*Figure 3–4* BMX BIKE

to experience the competition and action of moto-cross began to race specially designed dirt bikes, BMX was born. Moto-cross bicycles are in many ways the forerunners of mountain bikes, and they remain popular with children. These bikes typically have knobby tires with smaller wheels (20 to 24 inches), straight forks, and a high bottom bracket (see **Figure 3–4**). Like other track racers, BMX bikes often have only a single speed; though unlike the track racing bike, they have a freewheel to enable coasting. Rubber grips, extra suspension, and a padded handlebar and top tube make the ride more comfortable and safer.

## City Bikes

Strange as it seems, city bikes are essentially modified mountain bikes. As mountain bikes became more popular and people began to use them for street riding, attempts were made to iron out the mountain bike's shortcomings on the road. While the city bike retains the mountain bike's heavy-duty design and upright positioning, other characteristics have been changed to better suit the needs of city riders. For instance, fenders and chainguards are often added to protect the clothes of commuters. And because hills are not as much of an issue in cities (unless you're in San Francisco, of course!), there is less range in the gears (the lowest chainring is sometimes removed, leaving two). Tires remain thicker than they are on most road bikes but have become somewhat thinner than they are on mountain bikes. And to make riders more upright and visible in traffic, city bike handlebars are raised slightly higher than they would normally be on mountain bikes.

As you might expect, city bikes are popular in cities where the roads are filled with potholes and countless other obstacles. Bike messengers especially find city bikes useful in their endless dodge through traffic.

# Hybrid Bikes

Hybrid bikes that offer a mix between mountain bikes and road bikes have become extremely popular in recent years. With less-bulky tires and a thinner frame, they are faster and more aerodynamic on roads than are mountain bikes. And with a triple chainring, upright handlebars, and sturdy frame, hybrids can also take on mountains. Note, though, that the hybrid is neither as well suited to the road as a road bike, nor as fit for off-road riding as a mountain bike. But for a compromise that offers more versatility, hybrids can't be beat.

# Tandems

Tandem bikes are easy to distinguish from other bikes because they are made for two riders sitting in line (see **Figure 3–6**). Though tandems—as well as other multi-bikes made for multiple riders—have been around since the early days of bicycles, they have received renewed interest since the 1980s and may now be more popular than ever. Why? Because tandems are fun. They're a great way for couples, friends, or a parent and child to work together in a physical activity. And because tandems combine the effort of both pedalers into a single energy output, they're especially well suited for duos with different abilities—those partners who may have trouble riding at the same pace on separate bicycles.

Tandems are especially good for riding with children. While it's not advisable to put a very young child on any bike, kids who can ride a bicycle on their own will do well riding on the back seat

*Figure 3–5* HYBRID

## UNICYCLES

Ever heard of the U.S.A.? No, it's not the United States of America, but rather the Unicycling Society of America. It's the main organization of those somewhat eccentric folks who scoot around on one-wheelers.

It may surprise you to find out that unicycling is not just for circus performers anymore. In fact, the range of unicycling activities almost rivals that of bicycling. There's unicycle track racing, with events ranging from 100-meter sprints to 1600-meter competitions. There are unicycling marathons for endurance unicyclists. For dirt track one-wheelers, there's even UMX, unicycle moto-cross. And of course there's still plenty of trick riding.

While unicycling is a bit harder to learn than bicycling, riders as young as three and well into their sixties have mastered it. So can you. For more information, get in touch with the U.S.A. (www.unicycling.org/usa/). After all, who ever said you needed two wheels to be a cyclist?

of a tandem. This is a perfect opportunity for children to experience a long or briskly paced bike ride without having to work too hard. By riding behind an experienced adult they can learn teamwork, safe biking techniques, and important riding skills. If your child is too small to reach the pedals or handlebars of an adult bike, tandems can be found with an adjustable low seat tube and handlebars for kids. It's also possible to get a Kid Back attachment that raises the crank and makes it easier for kids to reach.

The rider in front on a tandem is called the *captain*, while the rider in back is the *stoker*. On a traditionally designed tandem, the captain is in control. Steering, braking, gear shifting, and balancing the bike are all the front rider's responsibility. The stoker's handlebars don't steer; rather, they are attached to the back of the captain's seat or seat post. The back rider's main responsibility—beyond sharing the pedaling—is to refrain from shifting body weight or leaning too much. Either action could throw the captain off balance.

Because tandems are longer than single-rider bikes and must carry a heavier load, designing the two-person bike is a real challenge. Tandems must be sturdy and well balanced. There are many different tandem frame designs, each with its advantages and disadvantages. Some perform better for riders with unequal pedaling power; others are

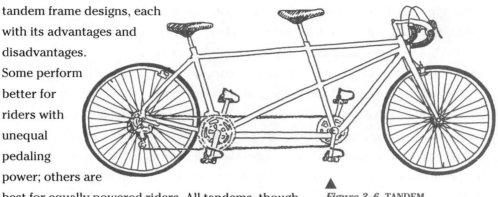

▲
*Figure 3–6* TANDEM

best for equally powered riders. All tandems, though, should have thick tubes for strength (many add on a lateral tube for support); wide handlebars for better balance; high-pressure, wide tires to support the weight and give cushion; tight spokes (often forty-eight spokes instead of the usual thirty-six) and strong rims. In addition, tandems need low gears to help the heavy bike climb hills and a higher bottom bracket so the bike can clear hill crests without the pedals scraping against the ground. Tandem riders often prefer to use heavy duty mountain bike components to add strength to their bikes.

The most apparent design challenge for tandems is in integrating the two cranksets—that is, turning the pedal power of two into a single transmission. There are a few different possibilities for tandem drivetrains. The most common involves two chains, one that connects the cranks to each other (usually on the left side) and another that connects the cranks to the wheel. Tandem chainrings tend to be larger than normal to handle the added force of two pedalers. The two sets of pedals do not need to be aligned. In fact, setting them a half-turn out of line with each other makes for a strong, continuous pedaling force and smoother movement (though the bike will be harder to mount).

As you'd expect, the combined weight and pedaling force of two riders has a clear effect on a tandem's performance. Tandems bring out the extremes in riding: riding uphill is harder due to the heavier weight, while riding downhill is faster due to weight as well as greater pedaling power. Even riding on level ground is noticeably faster than on a single bike. A wide range of gears (up to twenty-four) and special chainrings are needed to keep the bike in control and to accommodate these extremes of weight, speed, and pedal power. And, because the bike is heavier and moves faster, brakes need to be stronger. Cantilever brakes are typically fixed to both wheels, plus an additional drum or disk brake may provide extra stopping power for the rear wheel.

Though a well-designed and properly maintained tandem shouldn't require much more attention and repairs than other bikes, problems such as bent rims and broken spokes occasionally arise due to weight overload. These are fairly routine and can be fixed the same way you'd fix them on any other bike. However, for repairs that require the replacement of special tandem parts, there may be some difficulty finding shops that carry the needed materials. Thankfully, though, as tandems become more popular, parts are becoming increasingly available.

Two other factors can cause potential tandem owners to think twice before buying. First, a tandem's large size makes it difficult to handle, store, and transport. It's too long to fit on a car's bike rack—and good luck getting it on an airplane or on public transportation. Second, quality tandem bikes can be quite expensive. Due to the heavy duty materials required, tandems typically cost more than two single-rider bikes of a similar quality.

Still, as tandems become more available, new developments are keeping them up to speed with single-rider bikes. Though tandems have traditionally adopted a touring bike framework, newer models have taken on other designs. Recently, a tandem mountain bike has become available. While hardcore mountain biking is impractical and even dangerous on a tandem, the mountain bike design is good for tandems on the road because of the mountain bike's comfort, durability, increased suspension, and better handling.

# Recumbent Bikes

Recumbent bikes are those funny looking, long, thin vehicles that riders pedal while lying back on a backrest (*recumbent* means "lying down"). Beyond that one requirement recumbents come in many designs (see **Figure 3–7**). Most of them are supine, which means riders lie on their back, though some are prone, which means riders lie on their stomach. While recumbent bicycles, by definition, have two wheels, other recumbents use three wheels for greater balance (but significantly less handling). Recumbents are typically foot-powered, though certain designs use hand-cranks instead of or in addition to foot pedals. Recumbents can have either above seat steering (ASS), which tends to be easier for beginners, or under seat steering (USS). Like upright bikes, recumbents are usually rear-wheel driven for increased power, though front-wheel drives have a shorter wheelbase and chain. Some recumbents have just a bare framework like other bicycles, while others have weatherproof enclosures that make them look more like a one-person car.

Called *bents* for short, recumbent bikes have been around as long as other bikes, if not longer. Their speed and comfort advantages over upright bikes have been well documented; as far back as 1934 a bent set the bike speed record, though it was deemed unfair competition for regular bikes and the record was disallowed by the racing commission. In recent decades, attention has focused on recumbents—particularly those that have been fashioned into human-powered "cars"—as the future of individual transportation. For now, though, the recumbent bike remains at the center of a small cult of riders and enthusiasts and has not yet caught on in the general public.

The recumbent's lack of popularity is somewhat surprising considering its benefits. When compared to an upright bike, recumbents are more comfortable and tend to produce less saddle soreness, neck strain, and wrist pain. Admittedly, the unusual positioning and balance of a recumbent takes some getting used to, but once a rider's body has become accustomed to using different muscles, the recumbent will often prove more aerodynamic and a good deal faster than an upright.

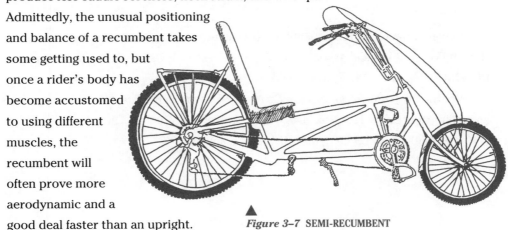

▲

*Figure 3–7* SEMI-RECUMBENT

Recumbents are not the perfect vehicles, of course. They can be slow and difficult to pedal up hills. Plus, the recumbent position makes it more difficult for riders to be seen by others on the road (though riders can easily solve this problem by attaching a tall, bright flag to the bike). And, recumbents tend to be significantly more expensive than uprights.

The following are descriptions of the three main categories of recumbent bikes.

1. *Long wheelbase* (LWB). These are between 65 and 70 inches long, with the front wheel positioned in front of the pedals. While LWBs tend to be less maneuverable, they are more comfortable than bents with shorter wheelbases. A low bottom bracket means they use similar muscles as upright bikes.
2. *Short wheelbase* (SWB). Between 33 and 45 inches in length, SWBs locate the pedals in front (or sometimes over) the front wheel. They offer good handling, maneuverability, and increased speed, plus they are easier to transport and store. The shorter wheelbase makes for less suspension, though, which means less comfort.
3. *Compact long wheelbase* (CLWB). At between 45 and 65 inches, CLWBs can be a good medium between the comfort of LWBs and the handling of SWBs. Higher seats (which technically qualify some of them as semirecumbent) make CLWBs more visible, though smaller wheels can make them slower.

More information on recumbent bicycles can be found by contacting the International Human Powered Vehicle Association. Their address is: P.O. Box 51255, Indianapolis, IN 46251. Their Web site: www.ihpva.org.

Also, the magazine *Recumbent Cyclist News* keeps up on the latest bent developments. Its mailing address is: P.O. Box 2048, Port Townsend, WA 98368. Or, it can be reached at this website: www.recumbentcyclistnews.com.

# Other Special Bikes

## Folding Bikes

Though it may sound like a very modern invention, folding bikes have been around for at least a hundred years. They were used by French and Italian soldiers—who carried them on their backs—in World War I. Everyday use of folding bikes rose in the 1950s, and the bikes became increasingly popular in the 1960s. Today, with the rise of bicycle commuting and interest in space economy, folding bikes have experienced some renewed interest.

The main benefit of a folding bike is its ease of transport. Commuters can simply bring their folded bikes into the office and store them in a closet. Folders are also very convenient on planes, where checking a full-size bike can be expensive, and on public transportation, which may have limits on bike transport. Some are even small enough to fit in suitcases.

Some folding bikes require tools to disassemble, while others use levers and hinges (such as around the seat post, top tube, and handlebars) that make them easier to collapse. Bikes that disassemble are generally stronger but can take up to thirty minutes to take apart, while true folders require as little as one minute to collapse. A few folding bikes do both; they offer riders a choice between folding (which is quicker) and disassembling (which makes the bike more compact).

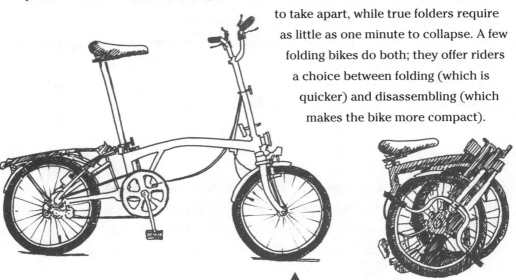

*Figure 3–8* FOLDING BIKES

For storage reasons, many folding bikes have small wheels (sometimes only 12 inches in diameter), but their wheel size makes them less efficient than regular bikes. Small wheels also provide less suspension and produce more friction, which can cause the rims to overheat. Folding bikes with full-size wheels are available. While these offer better handling and more efficient pedaling, they don't fold as compactly (which may defeat the purpose of getting a folding bike in the first place).

Buyers of folding bikes should look for one with the best balance of size, ease of collapsing, and riding efficiency. Manufacturers such as Montague, Dahon, Bike Friday, Brompton, Slingshot, and Moulton offer many models with varying degrees of quality. These companies sell directly over the phone and through catalogs. In some cases, folding bikes can be bought in stores, though they usually cost a lot more that way.

An organization called The Folding Society is dedicated to providing information on folding bikes. It puts out a bimonthly magazine called *The Folder*. The group can be contacted at: 19 West Part, Castle Cary, Somerset BA7 7DB, England.

## Multibikes

Multibikes are simply an extension of the idea that led to the tandem bike. They are bicycles designed for three, four, or more riders in line (the most ever recorded on one bike was forty riders!). Obviously, each added rider creates more design problems with regard to weight, balance, suspension, gearing, and so on. It's not surprising, then, that even the smallest multibikes are extremely rare. Still, when they can be found—and when they actually work—multibikes are great fun for the same reasons tandems are so enjoyable.

## Lowrider

Lowriders were developed and popularized in the late 1960s and early 1970s in Los Angeles's Hispanic community. A small cult around lowrider bikes still exists today that includes special manufacturers and enthusiasts (there's even the publication *Lowrider Bicycle Magazine*). In the spirit of lowrider motorcycles (*choppers*) and automobiles (*muscle cars*)—and adapted from balloon-tire roadsters—the lowrider bike's most identifying features are its banana seat, longhorn handlebars, excessive

## FUTURE BIKES

 Since their creation, bicycles have gone through highs and lows, booms and busts; but through it all they've always stayed around. What's more, they've stayed pretty much the same all along.

There's no reason to expect anything less in the future. As we head off into cyberspace, you can still count on your old reliable pedal-powered two-wheeler to remain at your side. As always, though, there will be technical improvements that enable you to ride faster and farther, with less effort and less trouble.

Look for bikes of the future to be virtually maintenance free. You'll have tires that don't get flats and a drivetrain that uses a clean, easily replaceable, lightweight belt instead of that old greasy chain you use now.

For the technically minded training rider, new bicycle computers will be infinitely more sophisticated than the speedometers and heart rate monitors used today. Your computer will collect data on every aspect of your riding (including body temperature, braking intensity, and suspension travel) and present it to you in easy-to-understand charts that indicate your progress. And—bad news for bike coaches—it'll even make suggestions for how to improve your riding.

suspension, small (20-inch) frame, and low-to-the-ground ride. Traditionally, lowriders are decorated with flags, fringes, glitter, colored spokes, or anything else that will bring out the personality of its rider (which tends toward the eccentric). Some lowriders have even been known to have windshields! The recent revival of interest in all things from the 1970s has caused the reemergence of the banana seat lowrider as a symbol of hip weirdness.

## Hand Cycles

Usually recumbent, hand cycles (which may have two or three wheels) are most often designed for people who have little or no use of their legs. They employ either a hand crank or rowing mechanism, and hand brakes. Some hand cycles make use of both hands and feet; in those cases, the added pedaling power can make them move very fast.

## Children's Bikes

Traditionally, children's bikes have been very simple, often just one speed with a coaster brake. Parents are hesitant to buy an expensive bicycle that their child will outgrow in a matter of years. But with the low cost of good children's bikes today, there's no reason not to buy kids bikes that are as complex and as well made as adult bikes. In fact, starting kids off with good bikes encourages them to ride more often and to develop into better bicyclists.

Children's bikes should be sturdy and safe, with a lightweight, tight frame and strong (preferably cantilever) brakes. One chainring with a wide range of gears is often good enough to start, at least until the child begins to venture out on country roads. Saddles and stems should be adjustable so the bike can grow with the child for a few years. For kids from ages four to six, start off with a 16-inch wheel; seven- to twelve-year-olds can upgrade to a 20-inch wheel. After that point, there's no reason not to go with a small-framed adult bike (26-inch wheels).

Trailer bikes, which attach to the rear of adult bikes and create a tandem (or attach to a tandem to make a multibike), are another way to expose kids (from ages five to eleven) to safe riding. Because the trailer bike has no connected chain, the child can pedal as much as he or she wants.

## References

Ballantine, Richard, and Richard Grant. *Richard's Ultimate Bicycle Book.* New York: Dorling Kindersley, 1992.

Chauner, David, and Michael Halstead. *Tour de France Complete Book of Cycling.* New York: Villard Books, 1990.

Ford, Norman D. *Keep On Pedaling: The Complete Guide to Adult Bicycling.* Woodstock, Vt.: The Countryman Press, 1990.

Nye, Peter. *The Cyclist's Sourcebook.* New York: Perigee Books, 1991.

Perry, David B. *Bike Cult.* New York: Four Walls Eight Windows, 1995.

Van der Plas, Rob. *The Bicycle Commuting Book.* San Francisco: Bicycle Books, 1989.

Van der Plas, Rob. *Bicycle Technology.* San Francisco: Bicycle Books, 1991.

CHAPTER 4

# BUYING
# A BICYCLE

# Deciding on the Type of Bicycle You Want

As for any large purchase, the first step in buying a bicycle is to figure out what kind you are looking for. Chapter 3 outlines the various types of bicycles—including the racing bike, touring bike, mountain bike, hybrids, and tandems—and discusses each style's special uses, strengths, and weaknesses. Be sure you understand what each bike offers so you can decide what bike is best for you. Do not underestimate the importance of getting the right bike for your needs. You're not likely to get excited about riding an uncomfortable bike that can't take you where you want to go. A well-chosen bike, though, will make you want to ride.

## Your Biking Needs

Think about what you'd like to do with the bike. Will it be strictly for exercise and recreation? For long-distance touring? For off-road riding? Would you like to get into racing? If you are shopping for your first bike and don't know exactly what sort of biking activity you'll enjoy most, it's best to get a versatile bike, such as a hybrid, that is suited for a number of different kinds of riding. Remember though, while hybrids are good for general use, their middle-of-the-road design means they won't be as well-suited for any one purpose as a bike designed specifically for that type of riding. For instance, hybrid wheels are apt to warp if subjected to the rigors of the trail. For that reason, many riders find mountain bikes even more versatile than hybrids.

As you discover what kind of riding you like best, you may want to trade up for a bicycle more closely designed for one specific activity, whether it be touring, racing, or mountain biking. Or if you find you like them all, you may decide to splurge and get a separate bike for each type of riding. This will cost you a lot more, of course, but it will also best satisfy you when it comes to riding comfort and efficiency. No matter what kind of bike you get, be prepared to care for it properly so that you can enjoy it as long as possible.

### Bike Brands

There are hundreds of reputable bicycle manufacturers—large and small—to choose from. Usually, though, a bike's brand name is not as important as the makers of its individual parts. After all, a large percentage of bike frames are made in Japan or Taiwan and sold to U.S. companies who simply put their name on them. And as large American companies consolidate the industry by buying out smaller bike manufacturers, brand names are becoming even more confusing and irrelevant. Keep in mind, as well, that large manufacturers produce bikes in a wide variety of quality levels, from mass market toys to highly crafted top-of-the-line machines. The only time brand names count in determining quality is when you're dealing with high-end specialty companies that make custom frames and parts for their bikes.

More important than buying a particular brand is considering the quality of the bike's components and the workmanship of the frame. When shopping, compare a few different brands of bikes in the same price range to determine which offers the best value. Look into which manufacturers offer the best warranties; many companies still guarantee their lower- and midrange aluminum frames for life (though this has become less common as off-road biking's popularity has made life harder on frames). Some bikes have a limited five-year warranty, and other warranties become void if the bike is used for racing. While you should always remain open to a better brand or a better-suited style of bike, try to narrow your choices before you begin to shop seriously for a new bike.

# Where to Look for a Bicycle

### Bike Shops

Before you start visiting bike shops to look at specific bikes, do a little preliminary research—particularly if you don't know much about bicycles. Though a good bike shop and a helpful salesperson can teach you a lot about bikes, brushing up on some bike basics beforehand will only make you better able to distinguish a sales pitch from legitimate advice. Start by asking the advice of experienced riders or by flipping through some cycling magazines to find product reviews and consumer reports.

When you begin checking out bike shops, pay close attention to what each store offers. Buying from a good shop can make a huge difference in your bike riding experience. Don't just settle for the shop closest to your house; a good bike shop is worth traveling a bit farther to find. Ask friends and other riders to recommend a good shop, and if you can, bring them along with you to help. And don't just go to one shop. Visit as many stores as you can to compare quality, selection, and price; and take the time to find out as much about each store as you can. Spending a little extra time looking for the best bike shop will pay off in the long run if it means you purchase the best possible bike.

Only visit bike shops that have a good reputation with experienced bikers. Many of the best bike shops are small Mom and Pop businesses that offer more personal attention, have a friendly atmosphere, and sometimes carry the best brands. Depending on where they are located, some small shops are geared toward a specific customer. Shops in college towns, for instance, cater to the needs of students and may not be the best places to find family bikes. You'll have an easier time finding your bike in a large store that has a wide selection of quality bikes, though you may not get the same customer service. But of course, any bike shop, big or small, that carries the kind of bike you want could be the right bike shop for you. Look for shops that have a decent selection of accessories and a clean, well-stocked repair area. Not too clean and well-stocked, though, because that could be a sign the shop doesn't get any business!

Salespeople should always be friendly and helpful; avoid those shops where employees look down on beginners. Beware of salespeople who work on commission because they may encourage you to buy a higher priced bike or a part you don't really need. Also watch out for sales advice from serious bikers who have a prejudice for or against certain brands; though they probably give honest opinions, they may not look out for the best interests of beginners. Above all, look for salespeople who can answer all your questions about the bikes on display.

Good bike shops will offer repair and maintenance service, including a free tune-up and adjustment after thirty days (very important because bikes have a period of breaking in), and regular free checkups at least through the first year. Buying from a small shop can be an advantage. In order to compete with the big stores, many small shops draw buyers by offering great service plans, including free labor for bikes under warranty. By all means, take advantage of these offers. Some shops offer a warranty for parts and service in addition to the warranties provided by the manufacturer. When you buy a bike, shops may also throw in extras such as a water bottle or a new seat or stem. And if they don't make such offers, it never hurts to ask.

## Department Stores

From lack of experience, many first-time bike buyers find themselves shopping in a department store. They are attracted by the seemingly large selection and the low prices. Certainly if you are looking for the cheapest bike you can find—and will be happy with anything that has two wheels and a seat—department store bikes are perfectly fine. But anyone in search of a quality bike that will last and provide a smooth, efficient ride will find most department store bikes lacking. Most of these bikes are mass-produced and improperly assembled using cheap metals. They therefore lack the precision, strength, and quality of bikes found in shops. Also, department stores will not offer repair and maintenance service and probably will not even let you have a test ride. Add to that the fact that many bike shops won't repair department store bikes because they feel it wastes parts and effort (repairs often cost more than the bike!), and the low prices of department stores no longer seem so appealing.

## Mail-order Catalogs

When you already know exactly what you want, buying a bicycle through a mail-order catalog can be a bargain. Mail-order companies usually charge less than stores because they don't have the overhead costs of salespeople and rent. Buying directly from a manufacturer's catalog can be even cheaper because the middle person (in this case, the shop) is eliminated. Catalogs can also be convenient: there's no bike shop hunting, no sales pitch to hear, and no need to leave your house.

But unless you are 100 percent sure what you want—and most bike buyers aren't—shopping from catalogs can be like shooting in the dark. Catalogs offer no sales assistance, no test rides, no fitting, no adjustments, and no repairs or maintenance afterward. Bike shops provide very important services, without which finding the right bike can be nearly impossible. Beginners should make sure they know what they're getting—and what they're getting into—before they buy through mail-order catalogs.

## Used Bikes

Like used cars, used bikes are much cheaper than new ones. If you can find a used bike in very good condition, which may not be difficult to do, you may have a real bargain. Good bikes that haven't been misused by their previous owners tend to stand up pretty well. There are two potential disadvantages, though, to buying older bikes: first, they may lack the latest developments and materials, and second, spare parts may be difficult to find if the bike is no longer being produced. You could find yourself needing to replace a whole group of components just to fix one broken part. Fortunately, most bike components are widely interchangeable, so it is unlikely that you would experience too much of a problem.

Closely inspect used bikes when shopping. For the most part, you can use the same techniques you use for finding a new bike: look for the right type of bike, take it on a test ride, make sure the bike fits your body, look for a quality frame and components. But also look for signs of wear and tear: rust, bends or dents in the frame or wheels, loose nuts and bolts, frayed cables, worn out chainrings. As you take the bike for a test ride, listen for any squeaks, creeks, or pops that could indicate worn or loose parts. Beware of frames that are cheaply made or have a limited life span. Before you buy, ask the shop to replace any parts that look worn out, and make sure you have a guarantee on any work done or new equipment added to the bike. Some problems can be hard to detect initially, even for experts. Have a qualified bike mechanic (preferably someone who doesn't work for the shop) do a complete inspection of the bike for you. And once you've purchased a used bike, be even more careful to take care of it and tend to any problems as they arise. At the same time, don't be too paranoid. Bicyclists who are constantly fixing bikes never get to enjoy riding them.

Used bikes sold by individuals, such as at yard sales or through an ad in the newspaper, are even cheaper than used bikes from bike shops. However, you will probably not be able to have any repairs done or parts replaced before buying, so be even more careful when you inspect the bike. Any work you'll need to put into the bike should be reflected in a lower buying price. Beware of individuals who offer very good bikes at what seem like extremely low costs or who seem to have a number of different bikes for sale. Unless a seller can show you a receipt for the purchase of a bike or an official bike registration, there's no way to know for sure that the bike isn't stolen. Do everything you can to avoid buying a stolen bike. It not only encourages criminal activity, but it could cost you if the rightful owner recovers the bike.

For a complete reference to buying used bikes, including information on specific models and their worth, Louis Deeter's *Used Bike Buyer's Guide* is a great source.

# What to Look for in a Bike

## Frame

Frames should be made of a material that combines strength with light weight. Though more rugged frames tend to weigh more, it is certainly possible to find a good balance between the two considerations. Steel frames are most common on low-end bikes, while the lighter-weight aluminum and chromoly frames are the best choice for good midlevel bikes. Less common materials such as carbon fiber and titanium offer lighter weight but are extremely expensive (usually reserved for bikes over $1000).

Frames should feel sturdy and have a comfortable frame geometry. A tight frame, with a larger angle between the head tube and the ground, is stiffer and has a short wheelbase. Tight frames handle better but provide less cushion for riders. They perform better through turns, though not as well downhill or at high speeds. A loose frame geometry has a smaller angle between the head tube and the ground—it is shallower with a longer wheelbase. This geometry provides more suspension but less control at normal speeds.

More than any other consideration, the bike frame should fit your body (see Finding the Right Fit on p. 75).

## Handlebars

Like the frame, handlebars are made of a variety of materials, ranging in strength and weight from steel to aluminum to titanium. On mountain bikes, there's not a whole lot of variation in handlebar types. Positioning is the most important consideration. Handlebar specifications come into play more with road bikes. Road bikes should have drop handlebars, about as wide as your shoulders, for more aerodynamic riding.

## Stem

While stems do not allow a lot of room for adjustment, they are easily interchangeable. Shops commonly replace uncomfortable stems for free before you even buy the bike. It's most important to have a stem with the correct height (see Reach, Stem Length, and Stem Height on p. 78 for details). Like materials for other bike parts, stem materials vary in strength and weight. Get a durable stem if you plan to ride off-road, otherwise find one that is lightweight. Some stems are designed for better aerodynamics, though usually that's only a concern for serious racers.

## Wheels and Tires

The quality of the wheels and tires you get depends on the price you are willing to pay. Aluminum wheels are better than steel but will cost you more. There's even a large variation in price and quality of different aluminum rims, depending on whether or not the metal has been heat treated. Higher-end wheels may offer details such as a double-wall rim or reinforced eyelets, which add strength and responsiveness. On any wheels, be sure to look for rust free stainless steel spokes.

There are two main types of tires: clinchers and tubulars. Most bikes, particularly beginner's bikes, use clinchers. Because they fold over the rim and need no further fastening, clinchers are relatively easy to install with the right tools. They're also less expensive and require little maintenance. Tubulars, on the other hand, are sewn and then glued onto the rim. They are more expensive than clinchers and can be difficult to change. Though they can be repaired (instead of replaced like clinchers), the hassle of resewing the tires leads many riders to buy a new one every time one gets a flat. At one time tubulars were preferable to clinchers because they could withstand a higher air pressure; now stronger clinchers have matched the strength of tubulars. While some cyclists, still claiming that tubulars are more durable and offer a more responsive ride, continue to use them faithfully, most cyclists today only use tubulars for road racing.

Assuming that most bikes you encounter in shops use clincher tires, a more important consideration will be tread. Some tire treads are better designed for riding on certain surfaces than on others. Make sure the tires on the bike you buy are equipped with a tread that is appropriate to the kind of roads or trails on which you plan to be riding. If they are not, ask the shop to replace them with tires that have a suitable tread.

## Seats and Seat Post

While seats should not be too wide, they need to be wide enough to provide support and comfort. Seats with Lycra covers and gel cushioning provide the most comfort, though some riders find them too soft and too heavy. Lycra also soaks up water, which can make riding after a rain shower quite unpleasant. Vinyl saddle covers, with either foam or gel cushioning, are a more common choice. Leather seats are more durable, though also expensive and otherwise unnecessary.

A seat post made of an aluminum alloy offers a good balance of strength and light weight. A large number of bikes, except perhaps those designed for city use, have adopted the quick release levers of mountain bikes. These enable riders to adjust the saddle height without using tools or even getting off the bike. Make sure these levers are easy to reach and work properly. Don't worry if the bike you wish to buy doesn't have a quick release lever; they're easy to install if you choose to do so. Caution, though: quick release makes saddles easier to steal.

## Gears and Derailleurs

Most new bikes have at least twelve gears, some as many as twenty-four. Keep in mind, though, that more gears on a bike may not mean a wider range of speeds. Instead, bikes with more gears tend to offer closer gears with more subtle differences between them. The best way to determine the range of gears is through a test ride. Try out all the gears, most importantly the highest and lowest. Buy a bike with a wide enough range of gears to allow you a comfortable ride wherever you plan to ride. If you live in an area with a lot of hills, look for a bike with lower gears. While all-purpose mountain bikes may be fine, bikes specifically designed to conquer steep mountain trails may be too slow for riding flat roads.

Look for derailleurs that shift smoothly and don't rub against the chain. Be aware of the various quality and price levels, and make sure you are getting what you pay for.

## Brakes

Because they're cheaper and easy to install and maintain, sidepull brakes are still common on less expensive bikes such as cruisers, and department store brands. Racing bikes often use sidepulls because they weigh less than other brakes. The newer style of cantilever brakes, though, have become standard on most quality bicycles.

Cantilevers are centerpull brakes with an independent brake mechanism on each side of the wheel that attaches directly onto the frame. Designed originally to provide more brake power for tandem bikes, cantilevers were so successful they caught on with single-rider bikes as well. They are easy to adjust and largely maintenance free. On some bikes, though, cantilevers work too well—road bikes can be more apt to skid with extremely strong brakes.

For high-end bikes, hydraulic brakes are even stronger and more maintenance free than cantilevers. Though they can be too heavy for road bikes, hydraulics offer better control in stopping. Another new type of brake, the V-brake, is essentially a variation on the cantilever. It performs better than regular cantilevers and tends to be more expensive as well.

## Crankset

As usual, aluminum is better and more expensive than steel. The most important variable in cranksets is in the chainrings. Get removable chainrings—they'll save you a lot of money and hassle. You should be able to replace each ring individually. Without removable chainrings, a bend in one ring will require replacement of the entire crankset.

## Pedals

Though they are less expensive, avoid bikes with plastic pedals. While plastic may weigh a little less, it is not nearly as durable as metal. Get pedals with at least a metal outer cage, and preferably pedals made completely of metal.

Beyond materials, the main consideration when it comes to pedals is deciding whether or not you want toe clips. Toe clips and straps serve to keep feet on the pedals. While they are certainly not necessary for casual road riding, toe clips become more useful when it comes to racing, long-distance touring, and mountain biking. Still, they are largely a matter of personal taste. Some people like the support and stability toe clips offer, others feel confined by them. If you decide you want toe clips but the bike doesn't have them, they can usually be installed. Be sure the pedals are designed to accept clips, though, before you buy the bike.

The latest advancement in pedals is the clipless pedal. These require riders to wear special cleated shoes that attach to the pedal. Essentially clipless pedals serve the same function as toe clips, but they allow more movement and better performance. While they are very popular with racers, their high cost (which includes the price of special bike shoes) makes them impractical for most recreational riders.

## Forks and Shocks

With midrange mountain bikes, chromoly forks are your best bet. They are lighter and stronger than steel and less expensive than aluminum. Aluminum forks, though, are more common on road bikes (particularly those with aluminum frames).

Forks with shock absorbers can add immensely to a rider's comfort, particularly on trails and rough terrain. And with the poor quality of many city streets, shocks can even add comfort to bikes used mainly on the road. In case your shocks end up needing repairs—and they very well may if you ride them hard enough—buy quality shocks made by one of the larger manufacturers so you can be sure to get replacement parts easily.

## Other Details

If you plan to use your bike for touring, make sure the mounts for panniers have been brazed on with high-temperature soldering. Bikes not made for touring should at least have mounts for a water bottle, and possibly an air pump. Also look for a bike with a good paint job, although, unfortunately, it's often impossible to determine until the paint actually chips.

Also keep an eye out for other areas where quality can be difficult to determine. Things such as the bottom bracket, hubs, headset, and spokes are where companies can trim their costs by using less than top-of-the-line parts. Here's where shopping with experienced riders can really pay off. Have those with experience closely inspect all the fine points. When looking for a bike, leave no stone (and no gear!) unturned.

# Finding the Right Fit

Finding the right size bike is crucial to your performance and comfort. Too small a frame will feel cramped and be difficult to pedal, while too large a frame will stretch you out and be too tall to straddle. However, a frame slightly smaller than the ideal fit is better than one that is slightly larger because smaller frames provide more control and better handling (though larger bikes can be faster and more comfortable). Still, perfect fit—with maximum comfort, control, efficiency, and aerodynamics—is the ultimate goal.

Because most bikes are sized in two-inch increments, getting the perfect size can be difficult. Unless you decide to pay a lot more for a custom-made bike, you will probably have to settle for something less than perfect. However, with proper adjustment (or replacement) of the seat, stem, handlebars, and cranks, any bike frame that is within a few inches of the ideal size can be made to suit your body. Have the bike shop make all the fittings and adjustments before you buy the bike. Keep in mind, though, that even after fitting and adjusting the bike in the shop, a truly perfect fit will come only after a long process of fine-tuning. Each person is built differently and may prefer slight variations of standard bike fitting formulas. As you begin to ride you will become better able to determine the settings your body feels most comfortable with. Make slight and gradual readjustments as you find your own style of riding.

A popular method for determining bike fit was developed by cycling coach Bill Farrell. Called *Fit Kit*, the system uses charts based on the bike sizings of top perfor-mance riders to determine appropriate measurements for frame, saddle height, stem length, and other sizings. Fit Kit, along with other similar systems, can be found in many bike shops. Salespeople, either with or without the help of Fit Kit, should be able to help you determine the proper bike size for you.

## Frame Size

Bike frames are measured by the length of the seat tube, from the center of the bottom bracket to the top of the seat lug, with most frames ranging from 18 to 26 inches. For a frame to fit your body, its length should be about 10 inches less than the length of your inseam (the length from the floor to your crotch). Mountain bike frames should be slightly smaller relative to your body—about twelve inches less than your inseam.

*Method for determining proper frame size.* For the most basic method of measuring frame size without the aid of a ruler, simply straddle the bike (preferably barefoot or wearing thin-soled shoes) with your feet close together. There should be about 2 to 3 inches of space between your crotch and the top tube.

## Seat or Saddle Height

Seat or saddle height is the most important factor to consider for bike efficiency. Improperly set seats can cause any number of problems. If the seat is too high you can overstretch your muscles and possibly pull them. If it is too low you may cramp your muscles and strain connective tissue. In either case, you will not get the most out of your pedaling power.

*Method to determine proper saddle height.* Wear thin-soled shoes—preferably the pair you plan to wear when you ride—and sit on the bike. Adjust the seat so that when you extend your heel to the pedal, your leg is almost fully extended at the bottom of the stroke. For a little more pedaling power on short distances, you may want to make the saddle slightly lower, but be aware that the lower position increases the risk of knee injury. On the other hand, making the saddle too high diminishes power.

*Alternate methods.* Measure the length of your inseam and the distance from the top of the seat to the center of the bottom bracket (along the seat tube). Your inseam should be 3.5 to 4.5 inches longer. Or, for a more precise measure, multiply your inseam by .88 to get the proper seat height.

When taking measurements, keep in mind a few factors that can effect your fit and make adjustments accordingly. Besides the thickness of your shoes, take into account the length of the crankarms (long cranks will call for a slightly lower adjustment) and the length of your feet (long feet will need a higher seat setting).

## Saddle Horizontal Position and Tilt

Besides their height adjustment, seats can also be set back or forward slightly for better pedaling and control. Sometimes known as your *setback* or your *fore-and-aft positioning*, your horizontal seat adjustment will determine where you sit in relation to the pedals. Setting the seat too far back may cause back soreness, while setting it too far forward will put added weight on the front wheel to create less control and pedal power.

*Method for determining proper horizontal seat position.* Sit on the bike and turn the pedals so the cranks are parallel to the ground. With your feet properly positioned on the pedals (typically with the ball of your feet on the pedal axle), a correct seat position will mean that the line from your kneecap down through the pedal axle is perpendicular to the ground. To see the line better, drop a weighted plumb line from your knee down to the pedal.

Your knee need not line up exactly with the pedal axle—if it lines up within an inch or so, it is fine. In fact, a line that falls slightly behind the axle is better for distance and climbing, while a line slightly forward is good for increased speed. On bikes with more shallow angles, knees tend to line up slightly behind the axle; on bikes with steep seat tubes, they are more likely to line up perfectly. However, if a frame is too steep it may be impossible to adjust the seat far enough back to enable optimum pedaling.

*Method for determining proper saddle tilt.* Adjusting the seat tilt will change the angle at which the saddle meets the seat post. For the most part, saddle tilt should be level to the ground—in other words, at a 90-degree angle to the seat post. Some riders, though, prefer to tilt their seat slightly upward to shift weight toward the back for more control.

## Reach, Stem Length, and Stem Height

Reach is the amount your body will have to reach on a bike in order to stretch from the seat to the handlebars. In concrete terms, reach is defined as the length of the top tube and the stem extension. Bikes with proper reach will distribute the rider's body weight efficiently over the bike. A proper length will mean a rider's elbows will bend at a comfortable angle when leaning on the handlebars (though this depends somewhat on the rider's preference). When in racing position, the rider's elbows and knees should almost touch.

*Method for determining proper reach.* While standing to the side of the bike, butt your elbow against the tip of the saddle so your forearm runs above and parallel to the top tube. On a bike with an appropriate reach for your body size, your fingertips will extend to roughly the middle of the stem. This measurement varies somewhat among riders and doesn't need to be precise.

*Method for determining proper stem length.* Make sure you are in an area with no traffic (an empty parking lot, for instance). On a bike with curved drop handlebars, ride with your hands on the drops and then look down at the bars. On a bike with a proper length stem, the handlebars are visually in line with the front hub. If they are not, the only solution is to replace your stem with one that is a more appropriate length. Don't try to adjust your seat position to compensate—that will only throw off other, more important measurements.

*Stem height.* The top of the stem should be about 2 to 3 inches lower than the top of the saddle, although you may want to make adjustments for personal preference. A lower stem is more aerodynamic and distributes weight better over the length of the bike—that's why they're more common on racing bikes. But, because a higher setting is more comfortable, stems are typically raised on touring bikes. If you adjust the stem height, be sure not to raise the stem above the maximum height line. If the stem is unmarked, leave at least 2 inches in the head tube, otherwise you risk breaking the stem off.

## REELS ON WHEELS

 There have been many films made about or featuring bicycling. The following list includes some of the most popular ones. Notice how many of them either won or were nominated for an Academy Award. It must've been the bicycles.

*The Bicycle Thief* (*Ladri di Bicicletta*). Winning the Academy Award for best foreign film in 1948, this famous film by director Vittorio de Sica is one of the all-time classics, bicycles or not.

*Breaking Away*. Another Academy Award nominee, for best picture, it's the quintessential film about bike racing. In 1979, it helped put the sport back into the consciousness of America.

*Birdy*. An eccentric film about a disturbed war veteran who thinks he can fly, and uses a bicycle to try. From 1984, starring future Oscar-winner Nicholas Cage.

*Quicksilver*. An otherwise forgettable film about bike messengers starring Kevin Bacon. From 1986.

*The Wizard of Oz*. A true American classic from 1939. Remember Miss Gulch (Margaret Hamilton) riding on her old clunker bicycle? An Academy Award nominee in a year of great films (*Gone With the Wind* won that year).

*E.T.: The Extra Terrestrial*. Yet another Academy Award nominee, this 1982 story of a cute alien is one of the most popular movies of all time. The climax: an action-packed bicycle chase through the suburbs to get E.T. back home.

*Butch Cassidy and the Sundance Kid*. Classic western tale of train robbers, complete with a memorable bike ride. It earned an Academy Award nomination for best picture in 1969.

*The Sound of Music*. Maria (Julie Andrews) and the Von Trapp family playfully sing and dance—and at one point bicycle—through Austria. This movie won the Oscar for best picture in 1965.

*Pee-Wee's Big Adventure*. Definitely not an Academy Award winner, but lots of fun nevertheless. Great bike, too.

### Handlebar Width and Position

Handlebars typically range in length from 15 to 18 inches. They should be about the same width as your shoulders. Narrower handlebars are slightly better for aerodynamics but provide less comfort and make it harder to breathe. On the other hand, handlebars that are too wide can be dangerous because they're more likely to get in the way of others.

In addition to width, handlebars vary in other ways, such as in the size of the drop and in the length of the drop handles. Except for their relationship to reach, these factors are a matter of personal preference. The angle in which handlebars are held in the stem should be set so the drop bars are parallel with the ground. Typically, the drops will hang a few inches lower than the top tube, close to where the down tube meets the head tube. Some riders prefer their handlebars tilted up slightly, though it may be less comfortable. Set the brake levers halfway down, on the curve of drop handlebars.

# Getting the Right Price

After you've determined what kind of bike you want, you're ready to shop more seriously. As you compare features on different bikes of a similar model, also compare prices. What do more expensive bikes offer? While you generally get what you pay for, a slightly higher price may not mean a better quality bike. Consider less expensive bikes unless there is a good reason to pay more. It may not make sense to spend extra money on a top-of-the-line bike if you plan to ride only occasionally. As you test ride bikes and compare designs, the subtle differences that make some bikes more expensive than others will become more apparent.

It's possible to get a very good beginner's bike for around $500. As prices increase, quality increases more or less proportionately. Once you get up to $1000, though, the differences between more expensive bikes will only be noticeable to experienced riders (that's even more true of bikes between $2000 and $3000). Such bikes may be a touch lighter or use more high-tech components, but unless you are a serious rider, they're probably not worth the extra cost. On the other hand, anything significantly below $500 will be less durable and less well crafted. A $250-bike may not even be half as good as a $500-bike.

Midrange bikes costing between $350 and $500 may have less precision and fewer top-notch components than more expensive bikes, but they can nevertheless be quite solid. These bikes, which are often mass-produced in Japan, Korea, or Taiwan, have increased in quality in recent years. For beginners who may find themselves upgrading their bikes as they get more into bicycling, these bikes can be an excellent choice.

# Bicycle Manufacturers

There are more than 100 bike companies out there competing for your business. Some offer low-end bikes, some high-end, and others sell bikes in a wide variety of price categories. Most bike companies, except for the specialty manufacturers, make more than one type of bike. Here's a list of the companies (most of them, anyway) that have had bikes on the market in recent years.

### Road Racing Bikes

Aegis, American Flyer, Beyond Fabrications, Bianchi, Bilenky, Cannondale, Carbonframes, Cicli Francesco Moser, Co-Motion, Corima, Crankin, Croll, Curve, DeRosa, Dean, Diamondback, Eddy Merckx, Ellsworth, Fat Chance, Fuji, Giant, Giordana, GT, Guru, Hampton, Hotta, Jamis, Kestrel, KHS, Klein, Kona, Land Shark, LeMond, Lifespeed, Lotus, Mandaric, Marinoni, Masi, Merlin, Mondonico, Mongoose, Otis Guy, Performance, Peugeot, Pinarello, Quintana Roo, Race Team Ross, Rhygin, Schwinn, Scott, Serotta, Signature, Sling Shot, Softride, Spectrum, Steelman, Ti Cycles, Titus, Tommasini, Torelli, Trek, Univega, Waterford Precision Cycles

*Track racing bikes.* Bilenky, Corima, KHS, Romic, Spectrum, Waterford Precision Cycles

### Sports Bikes

Bianchi, Bilenky, Boulder Bikes, Diamondback, Giant, GT, Jamis, KHS, Klein, Mongoose, Performance, Peugeot, Raleigh, Romic, Ross, Schwinn, Softride, Specialized, Terry, Trek, Univega

### Touring Bikes

Bianchi, Bilenky, Bruce Gordon, Cannondale, Diamondback, Fuji, Marinoni, Mikado, Novara, Romic, Softride, Trek, Waterford Precision Cycles

### Roadsters

Aerofast, Breezer, Gary Fisher, Jamis, KHS, Kona, Research Dynamics, Ross, Saintropez, Schwinn, Trek, Univega

### Mountain Bikes

Aegis, Alpin Stars, American Flyer, Amp Research, Balance, Barracuda, Battle, Beyond Fabrications, Bianchi, Bilenky, Bontrage, Boulder Bikes,

Breezer, Bruce Gordon, Caloi, Cannondale, Catamount, Cherry, Cignal, Co-Motion, Coneja, Crankin, Croll, Curve, Dan/Ed, Dean, Diamondback, Dirt Research, Ellsworth, Fat Chance, Fuji, Gary Fisher, Giant, Gonzo, GT, Guru, Hampton, Hanebrink, Haro, High Zoot, Ibis, Iron Horse, Jamis, KHS, Klein, Kona, Land Shark, LOCOmotion, Marin, Merlin, Mongoose, Motiv, Mountain Cycle, Mrazek, MTN TEK, Nashbar, New Sense, Nishiki, Norco, Novara, Oryx, Otis Guy, Parkpre, Performance, Peugeot, Proflex, Python, Quintana Roo, Raleigh, Research Dynamics, Rhygin, Ritchey, Rocky Mountain, Ross, Saintropez, Santa Cruz, Schwinn, Scott, Serotta, Signature, Sling Shot, Softride, Specialized, Spectrum, Steelman, Supergo, Terry, Ti Cycles, Titus, Trek, Trophy, Univega, Valley Cycles, Ventana, VooDoo, Waterford Precision Cycles, Yellow Mushroom, Yeti, Zerobike

*City bikes.* Aerofast, Electra, Pashley

*Cyclo-cross.* Bilenky, Ellsworth, Merlin, Redline, Steelman, Ti Cycles

## Hybrids

Bianchi, Cignal, Diamondback, Fuji, Gary Fisher, Giant, Jamis, Marin, Mikado, Mongoose, Nishiki, Norco, Novara, Parkpre, Peugeot, Raleigh, Ross, Schwinn, Scott, Signature, Softride, Terry, Trek, Univega

## Tandems

Bilenky, Boulder Bikes, Burley, Cignal, Dirt Research, Ibis, KHS, Pashley, Research Dynamics, Santana, Ti Cycles, Trek, Two's Day, Univega

## Recumbents

Ace Tool and Engineering, Advanced American Bicycle Concepts, Advanced Transportation Products, Angle-Tech, DH Recumbents, Easy Racer, Kingcycle, Lightning, Linear, Quadracycle, Rans, ReBike, Rotator, Ryan Recumbents, S&B Recumbents, Vision

## Folding Bikes

Bike Friday, Bilenky, Brompton, Co-Motion, Dan/Ed, Fuji, Montague, Moulton, Ross, Worksman

## Children's Bikes

Cignal, Diamondback, Fuji, Gary Fisher, Giant, Haro, Iron Horse, Jamis, Marin, Nishiki, Novara, Raleigh, Research Dynamics, Ross, Saintropez, Specialized, Trek, Univega

# Top 100 Bike Shops

Each year, the bike industry trade magazine Bicycle Dealer Showcase (BDS) surveys representatives of bicycle manufacturers to determine the best bike shops in the country. Shops are judged based on criteria that include store presentation, selection, personnel, industry reputation, and integrity. The following shops were, according to BDS, the top bike shops of 1996.

*Alabama:* Cahaba Cycles (Birmingham)

*Alaska:* The Bicycle Shop (Anchorage)

*Arizona:* Domenic's Cycling (Tempe); Racer's Edge Bicycles (Tucson); Rage Bicycles (Tempe)

*California:* Berkeley Cycle (Berkeley); The Bicycle Factory (Petaluma); The Bicycle Outfitters of Los Altos (Los Altos); Bikecology, Inc./Supergo Co. (Santa Monica); Cambria Bike Outfitters (Cambria); City Cycle of San Francisco (San Francisco); Cycle Scene (Ventura); Goodtime Bicycle (Sonoma); Helen's Cycles (Santa Monica); I. Martin Imports (Los Angeles); Jax Bicycle Center (Long Beach); Los Gatos Cyclery (Los Gatos); La Mesa Cyclery (La Mesa); Mulrooney's Sea Schwinn (Santa Ana); Off Ramp (Mountain View); Robinson Wheel Works (San Leandro); Talbots Toyland, Inc. (San Mateo); Walt's Cycle & Fitness (Sunnyvale); Wheel Away Cycle Center (Campbell); Wheelsmith, Inc. (Palo Alto)

*Colorado:* Criterium Bike Shops (Colorado Springs); Self-Propulsion (Golden); Turin Bicycles Ltd. (Denver); Wheat Ridge Cyclery (Wheat Ridge)

*Connecticut:* Central Wheel/All Wheel Corp. (Farmington); Newington Bicycle (Newington); Scott Cyclery (Wilmington); Zane's Cycles, Inc. (Branford)

*District of Columbia:* Bicycle Pro Shop

*Florida:* Orange Cycle Works, Inc. (Orlando)

*Georgia:* Atlanta Cycle (Atlanta)

*Illinois:* The Bike Rack (Saint Charles); Bikes Plus Ltd. (Arlington Heights); Kozy's Cyclery & Fitness (Chicago); Mike's Bike Shop, Inc. (Palatine)

*Indiana:* Bicycle Garage Indy (Indianapolis)

*Iowa:* Bike World (Des Moines); World of Bikes (Iowa City); Michael's Cyclery (Ames)

*Kansas:* Harley's Cycle Supply (Hutchinson)

*Louisiana:* Bicycle Sports, Inc. (Shreveport)

*Maryland:* The Bicycle Authority (Cockeysville)

*Massachusetts:* Belmont Wheel Works (Belmont); International Bicycle Center (Allston)

*Michigan:* Brick Wheels (Traverse City); Livonia Schwinn Bicycle (Livonia); MGM Bicycles & Fitness (St. Claire Shores); Penn Cycle (Richfield); South Lyon Cycle (South Lyon)

*Minnesota:* Bennett's Cycle, Inc. (St. Louis Park); Erik's Bike & Fitness (Minneapolis)

*Montana:* The Spoke Shop (Billings); The Touring Cyclist (Bridgeton)

*New Jersey:* Beacon Cycling & Fitness (Northfield); Cranford Bike Shop (Cranford); Cyclesport (Park Ridge); Danzeisen & Quigley (Cherry Hill); Marty's Reliable Cycle (Morristown)

*New York:* Bicycle World (Mount Kisco); Brands Cycle & Fitness Center (Wantagh)

*North Carolina:* Cycles De Oro (Greensboro); Liberty Bicycles (Asheville)

Ohio: City Bike (Cleveland); Eddy's Bike Shop (Stow); Montgomery Cycle (Cincinnati)

*Oregon:* The Bike Gallery (Portland); Bike 'N Hike (Beaverton); Bob's Bicycle Center (Portland); Collins Cycle Shop (Eugene); River City Bicycles (Portland)

*Pennsylvania:* Bike Line (Paoli); Gatto Cycle Shop (Tarentum); Genesis Bicycles (Easton); Keswick Cyclery (Glenside); Vitulli's Cycle-Fit (Stroudsburg)

*Rhode Island:* East Providence Cyclery (East Providence)

*South Dakota:* Two Wheeler Deeler Cycle & Fitness (Rapid City)

*Texas:* Bicycle Sport Shop (Austin); Bike Barn (San Antonio); Freewheeling Bicycles (Austin); Richardson Bike Mart (Richardson); Texas Racing Works (Richardson)

*Utah:* Jan's Mountain Outfitter (Park City); The Sportsman (Logan)

*Virginia:* The Bicycle Exchange/Bikes USA (Alexandria); HDK Cyclery (Hampton); Metropolis Bicycles (Arlington)

*Washington:* Bicycles West (Seattle); Gregg's Greenlake Cycle (Seattle); Kulshan Cycles (Bellingham); Wheel Sport (Spokane)

*Wisconsin:* Budget Bicycle Center (Madison); Wheel & Sprocket (Glendale); Yellow Jersey Ltd. (Madison); Williamson Bicycle Works (Madison)

## References

Deeter, Louis. *Used Bike Buyer's Guide*.

Ford, Norman D. *Keep On Pedaling: The Complete Guide to Adult Bicycling*. Woodstock, Vt.: The Countryman Press, 1990.

LeMond, Greg, and Kent Gordis. *Greg LeMond's Complete Book of Bicycling*. New York: G. P. Putnam's Sons, 1990.

Matheny, Fred. *Bicycling Magazine's Complete Guide to Riding and Racing Techniques*. Emmaus, Penn.: Rodale Press, 1989.

Nye, Peter. *The Cyclist's Sourcebook*. New York: Perigee Books, 1991.

Perry, David B. *Bike Cult*. New York: Four Walls Eight Windows, 1995.

# CHAPTER 5

# BICYCLE MAINTENANCE AND REPAIR

# Tools for Bicycle Maintenance and Repair

The tools needed for bike maintenance and repair vary somewhat depending on the make and model of your bike. The number of tools you have will depend on how much work you want to do yourself. While all cyclists should know how to fix a flat tire and have the materials to do so, not everyone will want to undertake routine maintenance and more complex repairs. That's what bike shop mechanics are for. However, if you are interested in bike maintenance and repair and willing to do a good job, by all means stock up on the whole spectrum of available materials.

Make sure you have all of the tools needed to do all the bike work you want to handle yourself. Don't try to squeeze by with a minimum of tools—you'll only make your job a lot harder. Most bike tools can be found in any hardware store, while some are designed especially for use with bicycles and may be more difficult to find. A well-stocked bike shop should have all the tools you need. Buy only quality tools from reputable manufacturers, and make sure the tools fit your bike (most bikes use European components that are sized according to the metric system).

## Bike Tool Set and Materials

Bike stand

Screwdrivers: Phillips, flathead, and miniature

Adjustable wrench and/or socket wrench

Wrench set with sizes ranging from 8 to 17 millimeters and/or three-way wrench with sizes ranging from 8 to 10 millimeters

Allen wrench set (also called allen keys or allen bolts) with sizes ranging from 4 to 7 millimeters

Spoke wrench (to fit spoke-nipple size)

Pedal wrench or flat wrench, sized 13 to 16 millimeters

Replacement bolts of various sizes

Headset wrench

Lubricant

Chain remover

Needlenose pliers

Cable cutters

Spare cable

Crank and crankarm bolt remover

| | |
|---|---|
| Freewheel remover | Spare inner tubes |
| Tire patch kit | Replacement spokes |
| Tire irons | Air pump and tire gauge |

# Inspection Before the Ride

Before you get on your bike to take a ride, particularly a long ride, it's important to give a quick look to check that all bike parts are tight, well adjusted, and working properly. Assuming you don't find any problems, this inspection should take no more than a few minutes. Any problems you find, though, should be tended to immediately. The following is a discussion of things to check.

*Check the frame.* Most frames are strong enough to easily handle normal riding. But, if you have a mountain bike and take it off-road a lot, you should check the frame closely for cracks and dents before (and after) you take it out on the trails.

*Check quick-releases.* Depending on your bike, you may have quick-release levers on the seat tube or front and back wheel hub. Make sure these are locked and secured tightly.

*Check seat.* Seat tilt should be in the correct position and fastened tightly. It can come loose from hard riding, particularly off-road.

*Check tires.* Tires should be properly inflated to the recommended pressure, which is usually written on the side of each tire. Use a tire gauge to measure the air pressure. If necessary, inflate the tires with an air pump. Also, check the surface of the tires for worn-down tread or cuts.

*Check wheels.* Spin each wheel to see that it is properly centered in the frame and completely flat (called true). If the wheels look wobbly when they spin, they may need to be trued (or the hub bearings may need adjustment). Also, try to move the wheels side to side with your hand to make sure that they are secure and don't touch the brake pads. In addition, make sure the spokes are tight by moderately plucking them.

*Check brakes.* Squeeze each brake lever independently as you push the bike forward. The levers should activate the brake pads to press securely around the wheel rim and stop the wheels completely. Check that the pads are not worn down and also make sure the rims are clean and dent free.

*Check the cables.* Inspect the entire length of brake and derailleur cables for any breaks or loosening, particularly at the mounting points.

*Check the crankset.* Both the pedal screws and the chainwheel bolts tend to come loose over time. Feel for play in these areas.

*Check the headset and forks.* The headset should be sturdy and tight, but turn smoothly. Make sure headset bearings do not rattle. If you have a mountain bike with suspension forks, check that all fork bolts are secure. Push down on the handlebars to test whether the suspension works properly.

# Maintenance

## Schedule

Any maintenance schedule will vary depending on how much you ride and how hard you ride. The following information is intended for cyclists who ride just about every day. If you only ride once a month, you certainly don't need to check your bike every week. But to keep your bike in the best possible condition, try to stick as closely as possible (and practical) to the schedule.

*Things to do every week.*

Clean your bike completely—particularly lights, reflectors, and wheels—with a
damp rag.
Check reflectors and lights for cracks, and check the batteries on your lights and
computer.

*Things to do every month.*

Check the bike's lubrication. If necessary, lubricate the chain, cables, and pivot points (on
brake levers, shift levers, brake arms, and derailleurs) with a recommended lubricant.
Check that all nuts and bolts are secure.
Check that all the joints housing ball bearings are secure.
Check all spokes closely for tightness.

*Things to do every three to six months, as necessary.*

Clean the bike thoroughly and wax the frame finish.

Clean the chain, sprockets, and derailleurs completely and relubricate.

Have your wheels trued if you ride off-road a lot (otherwise only when needed).

Replace brake pads if worn and readjust brakes.

Test gear shifting and readjust derailleur cables if necessary.

Closely inspect tires, remove any debris lodged in the tread, and replace tires if they are cracked or badly worn.

Clean and lubricate the tubes of your suspension forks, and replace any worn parts or seals.

*Things to do once a year.*

Take your bike into the shop for a tune-up. (Even if you're an expert mechanic, it's always good to get a second opinion. Another mechanic may notice something you missed.)

Overhaul all component systems. Remove all ball bearings; clean them, repack them, and relubricate. Unless you are experienced in bicycle maintenance, this should be done at a bike shop by an experienced bike mechanic.

Remove the seat post and relubricate it (be sure to mark the seat post height so you can reinstall it correctly).

Remove the stem and relubricate it (be sure to mark it so you can reinstall it to the correct height).

Clean the cable and replace it if it is at all frayed or damaged.

Check the pedals for damaged teeth and grinding bearings. Replace or repair pedals if necessary.

Replace the tire patches and spare tube you carry in your repair kit if you haven't used them all year.

Unload your bike's tool bag and home tool box to check that all tools and equipment are in good condition.

If you have suspension shocks and use them frequently, take your bike in to a bike shop for a suspension check (include it in your yearly tune-up).

## Cleaning

Your bike should be thoroughly cleaned on a regular basis—either every week or every few months depending on your riding habits. If you ride off-road, chances are good your bike will get dirty quite frequently. You may need to wash your bike after every ride. More than following any particular time-table, it's important to clean your bike as often as necessary—and as soon after it gets dirty as possible (before the dirt dries and hardens). A grinding sound or feel in any of the bearing joints will indicate dirt is stuck inside and an overhaul is needed. Clean bikes look better, but, more importantly, they're safer. A build-up of dirt and other particles can quickly affect the performance of the brakes, chain, and other components.

To clean your bike, first get it completely wet with a sponge or low pressure water hose (don't wipe dried dirt off the bike because you could scratch the finish). Then get a bucket of soapy water and a soft rag to further scrub the bike and wash away any dirt or grime from the frame and wheels. To wash the wheels, start at the hub and axle and work your way outward by wiping the spokes and rims. Do not use an oily cleaning product on the rims or the rim brakes will become ineffective. Remove any dirt, tar, or stones lodged in the treads. When you've finished, rinse all dirt and soap away completely.

The most important part of the bike to keep clean is the drivetrain. Dirt or particles that get into the chain or bottom bracket can grind and wear down the parts. Short of disassembling the drivetrain and cleaning the parts individually, you can wash the area thoroughly with a brush and water or with special chain cleaning equipment available at bike shops. Loosen any debris from the chainwheels, pedals, cranks, and derailleurs. Avoid spraying water directly into areas where there are ball bearings, though.

To clean the chain, spray or wipe it with degreaser, then run the chain through a wet, soapy rag (or chain-cleaning device) until all the oil and grease is removed. A good method to do this is to hold the rag around one part of the chain, then turn the cranks backwards to pull the chain through the rag. Once the chain is clean, relubricate it with a light coating of a recommended lubricant, and run a dry rag over the chain to remove excess lubrication.

After cleaning, inspect your bike closely to make sure all the parts are clean and working properly. Allow your bike to dry completely before you ride it.

# Brakes

## Brake Testing

To test the effectiveness of brakes, follow this procedure.

1. While sitting on the bike, coast moderately on a flat surface at about five miles per hour (be sure there's no traffic around).
2. Squeeze tightly on the brake lever that operates the front brake. If the rear wheel feels like it is lifting off the ground slightly, then the front brake is adequate. If not, the brake may need to be adjusted.
3. Repeat step 1.
4. Squeeze tightly on the brake lever that operates the rear brake. If the rear wheel skids slightly, brake pressure is adequate (too much skid could mean the tire tread is worn). If there is no skid or you feel a slow response, the brake may need to be adjusted.
5. If either brake has not performed adequately, check to make sure the levers, brake arms, and cables are pulling properly. Also check that rims are clean and dry.

## Brake Cable Adjustment

If the brake is properly centered around the wheel and the brake pads are positioned perfectly on the rim, any further brake adjustments you may need to make will likely involve tightening the brake cable. To do this, follow these steps (see **Figure 5–1**).

1. Loosen the locknut where the cable connects to the brake levers.
2. Turn the adjusting barrel in the desired direction. It will be located either next to the locknut or near the rim brake itself. If the brakes are too tight (the wheels squeak while riding or rub against the brake pads), loosen the cable. If the brakes are not tight enough (insufficient breaking), tighten the cable.
3. When you have turned the adjusting mechanism to the proper point, the brake pads will be at an optimum distance from the wheels, the point at which they

don't rub the wheel when at rest but brake effectively when the lever is squeezed (a few millimeters is good). With perfectly adjusted brakes, the brake levers will only need to be pulled a short distance to stop the bike.

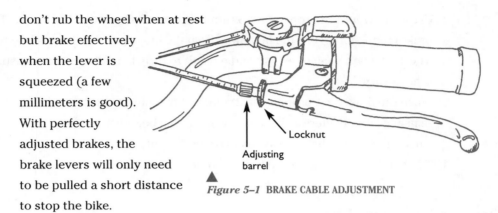

Locknut

Adjusting barrel

*Figure 5–1* BRAKE CABLE ADJUSTMENT

4. Retighten the locknut while making sure not to turn the adjusting barrel.

## Brake Centering

If your rim brakes are not properly centered, one brake pad will rest closer to the wheel than the other, possibly rubbing the tire. To re-adjust their position, take the following steps (see **Figure 5–2**).

1. Many newer bikes have a small screw on top of the brake arms for centering the brakes. Turning the screw to make fine tune adjustments will often center the brakes properly. If more adjusting is needed, continue to step 2. *Note:* Cantilever brakes may also have a small centering screw on each brake arm. However, since cantilever brake arms work independently of each other, the problem can usually be fixed by adjusting the distance between the brake pads and the wheel.

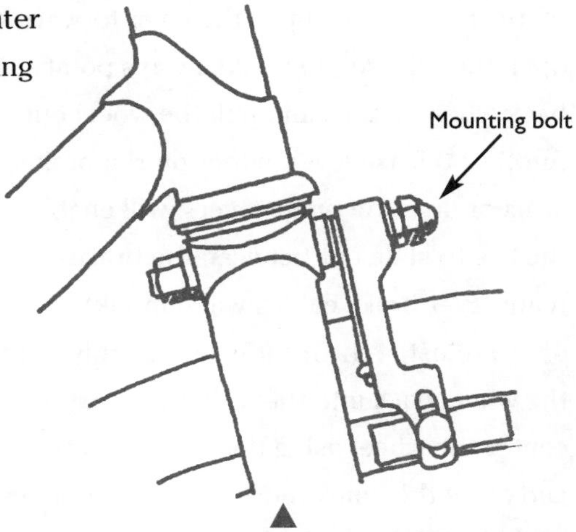

Mounting bolt

*Figure 5–2* BRAKE CENTERING

2. Use a flat wrench of proper size to turn the mounting bolt, which attaches the brakes to the fork. Turn the bolt away from the brake pad that is too close to the wheel. The bolt should be tight and difficult to turn, but only a slight adjustment is necessary.

3. When the brakes are properly centered, test them by flexing them. If they do not remain centered afterward, adjust the mounting bolt further, overcompensating if necessary, until the brakes remain properly centered.

4. Tighten the mounting bolt so it does not fall out of center.

# Wheels and Tires

## Wheel Removal and Installation

To do most repairs and maintenance on the wheels and tires, you'll first need to know how to remove them from the bike and reinstall them.

*Front wheel.* Nearly all quality bikes have a quick-release lever on the front wheel hub that makes front wheel removal easy (see **Figure 5–3**). No tools are needed. The quick-release mechanism holds the hub and axle on the fork. Simply push the lever forward to open the release (it should always point back when locked) and pull the wheel out. Another release lever, either on rim brake arms or near the brake levers, will enable the tire to slide out between the brakes (cantilever brake cables will unhook).

To reinstall the front wheel, simply put the wheel back into the fork dropouts, center the wheel using the adjusting nut, and close the quick-release lever by pulling it back tightly. Close the brake release as well

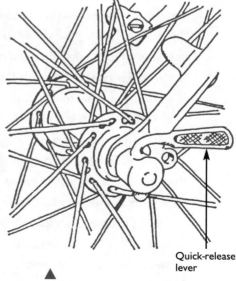

Quick-release lever

*Figure 5–3* FRONT WHEEL REMOVAL

(or re-attach the cantilever cables), and check the brakes to make sure they're properly adjusted.

If the bike does not have a quick-release front wheel, you must unscrew the nuts at the hub until the wheel comes loose. If the brake pads are too close to allow the tire to slide through, you may need to deflate the tires (of course, that won't be necessary if the tire is already flat). To reinstall the wheel, put it back into the fork slots, center it, and tighten the hub nuts. Then reinflate the tires.

*Rear wheel.* Rear wheel removal and installation is a little more complicated. To remove the rear wheel, do the following (see **Figure 5–4**).

1. While turning the pedals, shift the gears so the chain rests on the smallest cog and smallest chainwheel.
2. Release the rear brake arms, using the lever provided, to allow the tire to slide out. With cantilever brakes, squeeze the brake arms in and then unhook the transverse cable. This will open the arms wide enough to remove the tire.
3. If the wheel has a quick-release lever, open the lever to release the wheel. If there is no quick-release lever, unscrew the hub nuts until the wheel is released.
4. Pull the rear derailleur back and up to remove the chain from the rear wheel cog.
5. Pull the wheel out of the dropouts and away from the bike.

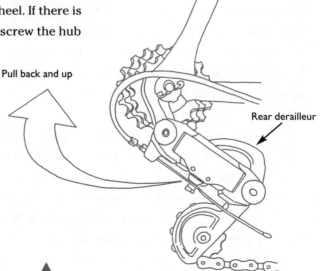

Pull back and up

Rear derailleur

*Figure 5–4* REAR WHEEL REMOVAL

To install the wheel, follow these steps.

1. The gear should still be set on the smallest chainwheel (and smallest cog if it was present), and the brake arms should still be released from the removal procedure.

2. Pull the rear derailleur back and up.

3. Move the wheel into position so the axle fits into the dropouts and the wheel is centered on the frame. The chain should come to rest on the smallest freewheel cog.

4. Close the quick-release lever or tighten the hub nuts to secure the wheel in place.

5. Restore the brakes to their position near the wheel. Test the brakes to make sure they are properly adjusted and the brake pads meet the rim.

6. Spin the wheel to ensure it is properly centered and doesn't rub against the brake pads.

## Flat Tire Repair

If you only learn one bicycle repair procedure, make it this one (see **Figure 5–5**). Flat tires are the most common problem and they can make riding dangerous or impossible. The procedure is quick and easy if done right. If you carry with you the necessary equipment (and you should!), tire repairs can be made on the side of the road (safely away from traffic) as well as at home. Have a tire repair kit, three tire irons (or tire levers), a spare tube, and an air pump with you whenever you ride. The following directions describe how to fix a flat tire.

1. Inspect the flat tire to determine, if possible, where the flat has occurred. If you can see any sharp object that has punctured the tire, carefully remove it and mark the spot.

2. Remove the wheel from the bike (follow the procedure in the previous section) and lay the bike on its left side (the side without the chain).

3. Deflate the remaining air from the tire by depressing the air valve or pin.

4. Wedge one of the tire irons (levers) between the tire and rim, a few inches away from the valve. Pull the lever down to pry the tire bead over the rim, then hook

the opposite end of the lever onto a spoke to hold it in place.

5. Repeat step 4 with a second tire iron, inserted a few inches away from the other tire iron.

6. If necessary, repeat step 4 again with a third tire iron, inserted a few inches away from the other irons.

7. Once the bead has come loose from the rim, use the tire irons to pry the entire side of the tire off the rim. Or, you may be able to do it with your hands. It is not necessary to remove the entire tire from the rim unless you detect a problem with the tire. Otherwise leave one side of the tire on the rim.

8. Reach under the tire and pull out the innertube. Begin at the side opposite the valve, and remove the valve last by pushing it through the valve hole.

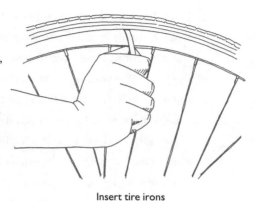

Insert tire irons

▲
*Figure 5–5* FLAT TIRE REPAIR
▼

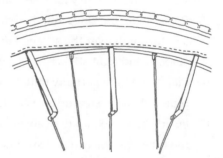

Hook tire irons to spokes

9. Locate the puncture. If you previously marked the tire (step 1), the innertube puncture should correspond to the mark. If not, inflate the tube partially and squeeze it. Listen to where air escapes or try to feel it with your hand or face. If that doesn't work, wet the tube with water and look for where a bubble forms when air escapes (dry the tire before repairing it). There may be more than one hole, so check the entire tube even if you've already found one puncture.

10. If you did not find any sharp objects in the tire in step 1, go back now and check the area of the tire that corresponds to the innertube puncture. Look for what might have caused the puncture and make sure you remove it from the tire.

11. If you have a spare innertube with you, use it. It's easier to replace the tube than to repair it, particularly when you are out on a ride. If you want to reuse the punctured tube, take it home and repair it later at your own convenience, then use it as your spare tube (make sure it works). If the tear is larger than one-half inch, it cannot be repaired and must be replaced. To install a spare tube, skip to step 16. However, if you must repair the punctured tube using a repair kit, continue with the next step.

12. Find a patch from your repair kit that will cover the hole.

13. Use the scraper or sandpaper in the patch kit to roughen the area of the tube around the puncture. Scrape an area slightly larger than the size of the patch you will use.

14. Apply a thin, even film of rubber glue (from the patch kit) to the scraped surface and let it dry for a few minutes.

15. Remove the backing from the patch and, with the adhesive side down, carefully lay the patch over the scraped area. Press down on the patch to ensure a smooth and tight stick. Hold it for a minute.

16. Inflate the tube partially until it begins to take shape (if the tube has been repaired, make sure no air is leaking).

17. Insert the valve into the valve hole on the rim, then carefully insert the rest of the tube into the tire and around the rim without twisting the tube.

18. Use your hands to lift the tire bead back onto the rim (using irons may repuncture the tube). Make sure the tube is not pinched by the tire at any point. If necessary, deflate the tube to make reinstallation of the tire easier.

19. Inflate the tube fully with a hand pump as you check that the tire is centered on the rim, the bead is in the proper position, and the tube has not been pinched.

20. Replace the wheel onto the bike (see directions in previous section).

## Spoke Replacement

If a spoke breaks while riding, it will send your wheel out of true and may make riding difficult and unsafe. While it's difficult to make your bike completely true again without spending a good deal of time—and without experience in truing wheels—replacing the spoke immediately will help stabilize any wheel problems until you can get your bike into the shop. To replace the spoke, follow these steps (see **Figure 5–6**).

1. Get a replacement spoke that is exactly the right length. Bikes often use a variety of spoke lengths, depending on where the spoke is located. If you buy replacement spokes to carry with you, make sure they fit your bike.

2. If the replacement spoke is the same gauge (thickness) as the broken spoke, use a spoke wrench to unscrew the spoke nipple (which sticks out of the rim bottom) and release the spoke.

   If the new spoke is not the same gauge as the old, you will not be able to reuse the nipple. Instead, remove the tire from the rim in order to replace the nipple with one that fits the new spoke (always buy spokes and matching nipples together). Once the new nipple is in place, complete steps 3–5 and then replace the tire as explained in the previous section.

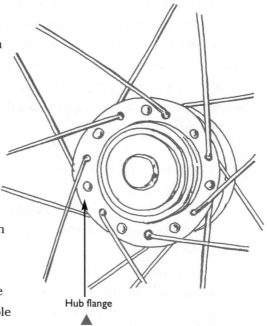

Hub flange

*Figure 5–6* SPOKE REPLACEMENT

3. Thread the new spoke through the hole in the hub flange, exactly as the broken spoke was threaded. If the spoke is on the rear wheel, you will first need to completely remove the freewheel before you can slide the spoke through the flange. This will require a lot more work, but it is a necessary step.

4. Slide the end of the spoke into the nipple.

5. Turn the nipple until the spoke catches and tightens. Continue screwing in the spoke until a proper spoke tension is achieved. Do not screw the spoke in too far, or it may protrude into the rim and puncture the innertube.

## Wheel Truing

Truing wheels is like tuning an instrument; most people can do it with experience and practice, while some people never will get it right. The best way to get your wheels perfectly trued without a lot of hassle is to take them to a bike shop. But for those who are determined to do their own bike repairs (and are willing to chance really messing up their wheels) the following explains the basics of wheel truing. Take your time the first few tries, and practice on an old rim that you no longer use. As you become more experienced, wheel truing should become much easier and quicker (see **Figure 5–7**).

1. Completely remove the tire and innertube from the wheel.
2. Replace any broken or missing spokes exactly as they were originally arranged.
3. Tighten the spokes until all the spokes on each side of the wheel have the same tension. Equally tense spokes will make the same musical tone when plucked. If you don't have an ear for music, estimate equal tension through the resistance of the spokes when plucked.
4. Using a repair stand to elevate the bike, reinstall the wheel onto the bike without replacing the tire. The rim should rest between the brake pads.

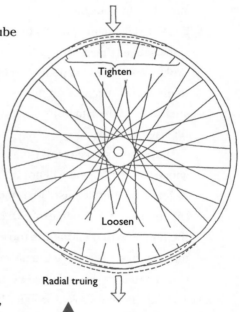

*Figure 5–7* WHEEL TRUING

5. Check for warps both side-to-side (laterally) and up-and-down (radially). To see lateral warps, stand directly in line with the wheel (in front of the front wheel or in back of the rear wheel) and spin the wheel. A laterally true wheel rim will remain exactly the same distance from the brake pads at all times. To see radial

warps, stand to the side of the wheel as you spin it. A radially true wheel will be a perfect circle and always run parallel to the brake pads. The wheel will not have any humps or dips in the rim.

6. Locate any spots where the wheel warps. Mark these spots by holding a felt marker close to the rim and spinning the wheel. Only the warped spots will rub against the tip of the marker.

7. Tighten or loosen the spokes in the warped areas to eliminate the warps. If the rim warps laterally to the right side, tighten the spokes that connect to the left flange while loosening the spokes connected to the right flange. Do the opposite for warps to the left side. If the rim warps radially up to create a hump, tighten the adjacent spokes (both on the right and left flanges) appropriately. Loosen the area spokes if the rim dips below true.

8. After adjusting the spokes, check that they are stretched and secured in the wheel by squeezing sets of parallel spokes together.

9. Repeat steps 5–8 until all the warps are have been eliminated and the wheel is completely true.

# Derailleurs and Freewheels

There are a number of reasons why derailleurs may not shift the chain properly between sprockets. First, the derailleur may have been knocked out of alignment by a fall or hit. If that's the case, the derailleur will need to be bent back into proper alignment with the sprockets. Beyond that, incomplete or improper shifting is likely the result of either a poorly adjusted derailleur or too much slack in the derailleur cables.

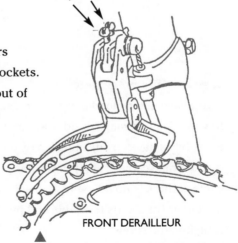

Stop screws

FRONT DERAILLEUR

*Figure 5–8a* DERAILLEUR ADJUSTMENTS

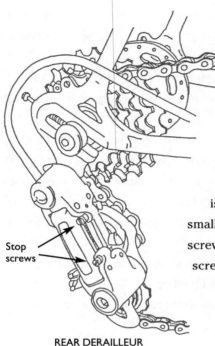

Stop
screws

REAL DERAILLEUR

▲
*Figure 5–8b* DERAILLEUR ADJUSTMENTS

## Derailleur Adjustment

Both front and rear derailleurs (see **Figures 5–8a** and **b**) have a pair of stop screws that regulate chain travel. One stop screw controls the amount the derailleur moves in (toward the wheel) and the other controls the derailleur's outward movement (away from the wheel). If the derailleur's range of motion is not sufficient to move the chain from the smallest sprocket to the largest sprocket, the stop screws need to be adjusted. Use an allen key or a screwdriver (depending on the type of stop screws) to turn the appropriate stop screw the amount necessary to allow full movement in the derailleur. Make small adjustments as you test the shift levers (the rear wheel must be elevated and the pedals turning to shift levers). Be sure you don't overadjust the screws. This will cause the derailleur to carry the chain entirely off the chainwheels.

## Cable Tightening

If you have determined that the stop screws are properly adjusted and the derailleur has an adequate range of sideways motion, you may need to tighten the derailleur cable. Some bikes have an adjusting barrel near the shift levers, similar to the adjusting barrel on the brake cable. If so, turn the barrel to tighten and eliminate any excess slack in the cable. If there is no adjusting barrel, though, you will need to unscrew the bolt on the derailleur that holds the cable and pull the cable taut by hand. Once the cable is taut, retighten the screw.

# Saddle and Seat Post

## Seat Post Adjustment

If your seat post has a quick-release lever, follow these steps to make adjustments (see **Figure 5–9**).

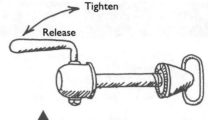

*Figure 5–9* QUICK RELEASE
SEAT POST ADJUSTMENT

1. Turn the lever to loosen the seat post.
2. Holding onto the seat, slide the seat post up or down to set it in the proper position.
3. Holding the seat in place with one hand, turn the lever to secure the seat post.

If your seat post does not have a quick-release lever, follow these steps to make adjustments.

1. Use an allen key or wrench to loosen the seat post bolt.
2. Holding onto the seat, slide the seat post up or down to set it in the proper position.
3. Holding the seat in place with one hand, firmly retighten the seat post bolt to secure the seat post.

## Fore-and-aft Adjustment and Seat Angle Adjustment

Both the fore-and-aft position and the angle of the seat are governed by the same bolt or bolts, located underneath the seat. To make adjustments, follow these steps.

1. Unscrew the bolt or bolts with a wrench or screwdriver until the seat loosens from the seat post.
2. To change fore-and-aft position, slide the seat forward or backward. To alter the seat angle, tilt the seat up or down.
3. Holding the seat in the desired position with one hand, firmly retighten the bolt or bolts until the seat is secure.

## CYCLING MUSEUMS AND HALLS OF FAME

There are two major cycling halls-of-fame in the United States.

U.S. Bicycling Hall of Fame
34 E. Main St.
Somerville, NJ 08876
800-BICYCLE
www.usbhof.com

Mountain Bike Hall of Fame and Museum
P.O. Box 1961
Crested Butte, CO 81224
303-349-7280
www.mtnbikehalloffame.com

In addition, there are some smaller museums dealing with bikes and cycling, including the following.

American Bicycle and Cycling Museum (Santa Fe, New Mexico)
Antique and Classic Bicycle Museum of America (Ann Arbor, Michigan)
Bicycle History Museum and Gift Shop (Boise, Idaho)
Bicycle Museum of America (Chicago, Illinois)
National Bicycle Museum and Education Center (Baltimore, Maryland)

# Handlebars and Stem

## Handlebar Adjustment

Most handlebars are held in the stem by a binder bolt. Newer models may have a design with two bolts. These make the handlebars easier to remove from the stem by enabling the handlebars to be lifted straight off as opposed to slid out from the side.

To adjust handlebar position, follow these steps (see **Figure 5–10**).

1. Use a wrench or allen key to loosen the bolt or bolts that hold the handlebars in the stem.

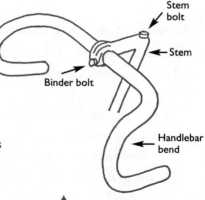

*Figure 5–10* HANDLEBAR AND STEM ADJUSTMENT

2. Adjust the handlebar angle by turning the handlebars up or down as needed.

3. Holding the handlebars in place, firmly retighten the bolt or bolts until the handlebars are held securely in place.

### Stem Adjustment

To adjust the stem, follow these steps.

1. Holding the bike firmly in place, loosen the stem bolt using a wrench or allen key.

2. Adjust the stem height by sliding it up or down into the head tube. Make sure the handlebars remain perfectly centered and straight relative to the frame.

3. Holding the adjusted stem in position, retighten the stem bolt until the stem is held securely in the head tube.

# Sprockets and Chain

### Sprocket Maintenance

Check the sprockets occasionally for damage and wear (see **Figure 5–11**). Like wheels, sprockets should be true. If sprockets appear to wobble as they turn, they may have been bent in a fall. Even slightly bent sprockets may not catch the chain properly or may cause undue wear on the chain. While it's possible to repair a bent sprocket yourself by banging it back into shape with a hammer, you're just as likely to damage it as to fix it. Your best bet is to take your bike into the bike shop for sprocket repair or replacement.

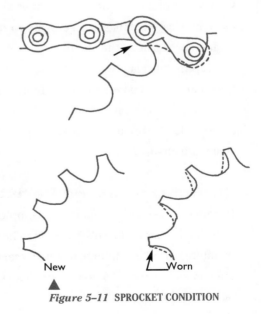

*Figure 5–11* SPROCKET CONDITION

A worn chain is the most common cause of worn sprockets. Chains that have been stretched will not fall precisely between the sprocket teeth. Over time the chain will wear down the sprocket teeth on one side, causing the sprocket teeth to deform into a wave shape. The only way to prevent excessive wear on the sprockets is to replace your chain before it becomes stretched. Once a sprocket becomes worn it must be replaced.

Use sprocket or freewheel removers to pull a sprocket off the freewheel. If the sprockets on your freewheel or crankset cannot be removed individually, you may need to replace the entire set of sprockets. To avoid replacing a complete set of sprockets, it's best to have individually removable sprockets. This way you'll only need to replace those that are more susceptible to bending (outside sprockets) and wear (small sprockets).

## Chain Lubrication

Whenever your chain starts to squeak or feel dry (every hundred miles or so) you will need to relubricate it. Check lubrication regularly by touching the chain lightly with your finger or a rag. If little oil or grease comes off, the chain probably could use some more lubrication. It is also necessary to relubricate the chain whenever you have cleaned or replaced the chain.

A spray lubricant will create the least mess and ensure that the correct part of the chain is lubricated. Spray the lubricant lightly and evenly onto the roller pins of the chain. Be very careful not to get any lubricant onto the spokes or rims because oil could make the brakes unworkable. Use a rag to wipe any excess lubricant off the chain and chain stay.

## Chain Removal and Reinstallation

To replace the chain or to clean it completely, you will need to remove it from the bike. Single-gear children's bikes often have a master link that easily comes undone. On multigear bikes, though, it is necessary to remove one of the pins that holds the chain links together. To do this, you'll need a chain remover or rivet extractor (see **Figure 5–12**).

Extracting a pin from the chain may ruin the pin, so make sure you have a replacement pin to take its place. Some chains are easier to undo than others—higher quality chains with special high-tension links tend to be more susceptible to damage. Be careful not to damage the links while extracting the pin.

To remove the chain, follow these steps.

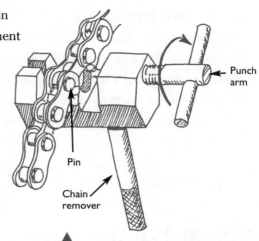

Figure 5–12 CHAIN REMOVAL

1. Shift gears so the chain rests on the smallest chainwheel and smallest cog.
2. Align the chain remover so the chain runs through the tool and one of the pins is in line with the punch screw.
3. Screw the punch arm into the pin and push it through the chain links until the links come undone. Try not to push the pin all the way through; leave it sticking out the other side.
4. Retract the punch arm to release the chain links.
5. Slowly turn the pedals as you pull the chain free of the drivetrain.

When you reinstall the chain it's a good idea to put it back on inside out to switch the side that gets worn. To reinstall the chain, follow these steps.

1. Lay the unattached chain onto the smallest chainwheel and smallest cog, then weave it through the derailleur wheels.
2. Reconnect the end links at the bottom of the chain run. The extracted pin should be sticking out to the right, away from the bike. Hold the links in position while you set the chain tool in place around the link.
3. Screw the punch arm into the extracted pin to push it back into the chain. Continue twisting the arm until the pin returns to its original position.

### Chain Maintenance

Under stress, chain links become slightly stretched and no longer thread smoothly onto the sprockets. In extreme cases, chains start to skip sprocket teeth, causing a harsh crunch sound during heavy pedaling. Replacing the chain every few thousand miles ensures the chain remains the proper length and the sprockets don't become worn.

To test the chain for wear, try to lift the links off the chainwheel. If the chain does not lift, there is no need to replace the chain. If, however, you can lift the chain off the chainwheel even a few millimeters, it should be replaced. If the chain has worn to that point, chances are good some of the sprockets will need to be replaced as well.

# Tandem Maintenance

Because tandems tend to be built stronger, they may need less maintenance than other bikes. However, the greater load put on a tandem, plus the greater weight of the bike itself, can take its toll by causing bike parts to wear faster. Pay even closer attention to your tandem than you would to a one-person bike. Follow these maintenance guidelines.

*Before each ride.*
> Because brakes work harder on a tandem, they wear down quicker. Check brakes and brake pads each time you ride.
> Keep tire pressure slightly higher than you would on a solo bike. Check tire pressure and inflate if necessary.

*Once a month.*
> Check to make sure the wheels are true. Spokes should be wound tightly and the rims should have no warps.
> Check the cranks to ensure they are tight and the crankset turns smoothly.

*Every three to six months, as necessary.*
> Check the chains and the sprockets for wear. Adjust or replace parts as necessary.

## References

*Bicycling Magazine.* Jan. 1995–July 1996.

*Bicycling Magazine,* eds. *The Most Frcequently Asked Questions about Bicycling.* Emmaus, Penn.: Bicycling Books, 1980.

Chauner, David, and Michael Halstead. *Tour de France Complete Book of Cycling.* New York: Villard Books, 1990.

Ford, Norman D. *Keep On Pedaling: The Complete Guide to Adult Bicycling.* Woodstock, Vt.: The Countryman Press, 1990.

Honig, Daniel. *How to Bike Better.* New York: Ballantine Books, 1985.

LeMond, Greg. *Greg LeMond's Pocket Guide to Bicycle Maintenance and Repair.* New York: Perigee Books, 1990.

LeMond, Greg, and Kent Gordis. *Greg LeMond's Complete Book of Bicycling.* New York: G. P. Putnam's Sons, 1990.

*Mountain Bike.* August 1996.

*Schwinn ATB Owner's Manual.* Chicago: Schwinn Bicycle Company, 1998.

Staff of *Bicycling Magazine. Women's Cycling.* Emmaus, Penn: Rodale Press, 1996.

Van der Plas, Rob. *The Bicycle Commuting Book.* San Francisco: Bicycle Books, 1989.

Van der Plas, Rob. *Bicycle Technology.* San Francisco: Bicycle Books, 1991.

CHAPTER 6

# RIDING
# TECHNIQUES

FOR CASUAL OR OCCASIONAL USE, IT'S VERY EASY TO RIDE A BICYCLE FUNCTIONALLY. You need only be able to balance and pedal—to perform the same skills you perfected when you first learned to ride. But for cyclists who wish to get more out of their bicycles—whether competition, exercise, or just fun—mastering a little more cycling technique is important.

But before you attempt to learn any techniques that will enhance your riding, it's absolutely crucial your bike is properly sized and adjusted to fit your body. Without the proper bike and the proper fit, none of the advice in this chapter will do you any good—it may even hurt you. Make sure you have first read and followed the directions offered in Chapter 4.

# Body Posture and Position

The reason good cyclists adhere to well-founded principles of body position and form is to maximize their cycling efficiency. They do this by getting the most power and leverage possible in pedaling, while minimizing wind resistance. And of course, they want to be as comfortable as possible to avoid injury and to enjoy more intense cycling. Because it's so easy to get by with only the basic skills you learned as a child, it may surprise you to find how much better you can ride—and with less effort—when you follow correct cycling form.

That said, it's also important to note that there's no such thing as a universally perfect form. Riders need to find what's right for their own specific body dimensions, strength, and comfort, within the general guidelines of proper cycling.

Bicycles with drop handlebars allow riders three main riding positions. When pedaling for long periods, cyclists need to periodically switch positions to avoid soreness or numbness in the hands, arms, and upper body. And because each riding position offers its own advantages (and disadvantages), the best all-around bike form involves a combination of all three positions.

## Top Bar Position

The most common (and not coincidentally the most comfortable) bike posture is the top bar position (see **Figure 6–1**). For riders of straight-handlebar bikes (mountain bikes, hybrids), the top bar position is the only choice. Its upright orientation enables riders to keep their backs straight and neck muscles relaxed. This is the ideal position for casual riding and riding in traffic. Also, the top bar position enables cyclists to ride back in the saddle for more power uphill.

*Figure 6–1* TOP BAR POSITION

However, the top bar position puts hands far from the brakes on road bikes and therefore creates a slow braking reaction. Some road bikes have brake extenders that can be easily reached from the top bar, though these offer much less braking power than the main levers. And because riders in the top bar position trap the most wind, it's the least efficient aerodynamically.

## Drop Position

While riding in the drop position, with hands on the bottom handlebar extensions (called *drops*), riders experience the least amount of wind resistance and the greatest pedaling and braking power (see **Figure 6–2**). Also, riders distribute their weight more evenly across the bike, which eases the load directed on the saddle. But because the position requires riders to hunch over to reach the drops, maintaining the posture for an extended time can cause back, shoulder, neck, and arm strain.

*Figure 6–2* DROP POSITION

Drop position is best for sprinting and for riding against the wind, but the body fatigue and numbness it can cause makes it difficult to sustain for long periods. While drop position typically involves sliding hands into the curves of the handlebar, riders can achieve better leverage for climbing by sliding their hands back toward the ends of the handlebars.

## Brake Lever Position

For some, the brake lever position offers a happy medium between the top bar and drop positions (see **Figure 6–3**). By resting hands on the tops of the brake levers, riders will have less wind resistance than in the top bar position and more comfort than in the drop position. This posture provides easy access to the brakes for safety, particularly on descents, and good leverage for hill climbing and riding out of the saddle. Its all-around appeal makes the brake lever position the standard long-distance racing posture.

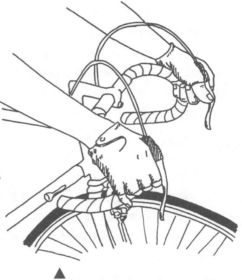

*Figure 6–3* BRAKE LEVER POSITION

## Good Posture

Correct cycling posture ensures that you stay as safe and as comfortable as possible while best utilizing your body for optimum pedaling efficiency. Good posture, though, goes hand in hand with proper bike fit. Make sure your bike has been properly sized and adjusted before you even attempt to ride with a healthy posture (see Finding the Right Fit in Chapter 4 for complete information on bike fit). No matter in what position you ride, the following main points for proper bicycle posture stay the same.

Maintain a firm but easy hold on the handlebars that will keep arms relaxed and provide better control of the bicycle. Keep your wrists straight and grip the bars tighter when riding on rougher surfaces.

Keep your arms in line with your body; keep your elbows comfortably bent to absorb road bumps and to maintain steering flexibility.

Keep your back flat for better comfort, strength, flexibility, and aerodynamics. Lean forward from the hips at an angle of at least forty-five degrees in the top bar position, more for the drop position.

Keep your upper body relaxed, particularly your back and shoulder muscles.

Always keep your head facing straight ahead, while varying your neck position to ease muscle strain.

Rest your rear on the saddle cushions, but shift your weight and seating position slightly whenever necessary to maintain comfort and to get better leverage while climbing.

# Pedaling

While it's natural and tempting to stamp down or chop at the pedals for extra power in the downstroke, the jerky pedaling motion this creates is actually counterproductive to efficient riding. The key to effective pedaling is maintaining a smooth form that utilizes all of your leg muscles, not just the thighs. Your feet and legs should turn the cranks in a continuous motion that applies equal energy throughout the rotation, not just in the downstrokes (see **Figure 6–4**). Knees should point straight ahead, close to the bike frame, and move up and down in a fluid motion.

Each pedal stroke involves four movements, strung together in one unified action: (1) the forward push that begins to extend your knee, (2) the downward push that almost fully extends your knee and hip, (3) the backward pull that bends

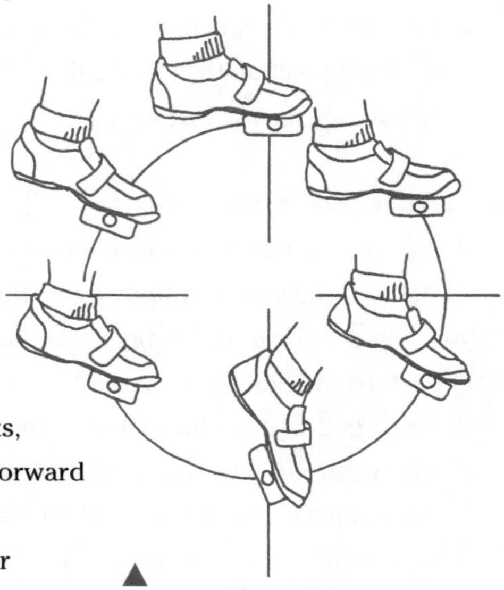

*Figure 6–4* PEDALING MOTION

your knee again, and (4) the upward raise that bends your hip and raises your knee. Of course, the first and second segments of the stroke provide the majority of force on the pedal.

In order to keep pedaling force equal throughout the stroke, the downstroke leg must compensate for the upstroke leg. Evenly balanced pedaling is accomplished when both legs apply equal power on the pedals. That is, the left leg's downstroke is equal in force to the right leg's downstroke. Concentrate particularly on pedaling smoothly through the dead spot at the top of the stroke (during the forward push), where the force shifts from the upstroke to the downstroke.

The use of toe clips or clipless pedals adds tremendously to pedaling efficiency because it allows the feet to exert much more force on the pedals in the weakest part of the stroke—the upward raise. To allow comfort and efficiency in the upstroke, though, clips and attachments need to be perfectly adjusted.

## Cadence and Spinning

*Cadence* in bike riding is the equivalent of revolutions per minute in cars. But rather than measuring the revolutions per minute of an automobile engine, cycling cadence refers to the revolutions per minute that your human-powered bike engine—that is, the pedals—makes. For instance, a pedal cadence of 80 means you are turning the pedals 80 full revolutions per minute. To determine cadence, simply count the number of complete turns your pedals make in a minute (or better yet, count for ten seconds and multiply the number by six).

On smooth, level ground, and in a suitably low gear, recommended pedaling cadence is between 80 and 100. While that may raise to 120 on descents or decrease to 60 on hills, switching gears as needed helps you stay in the proper range. Pedaling evenly in this range is known as *spinning*. Spinning is preferable to pedaling slower in a higher gear, which takes you the same distance but requires a lot more effort and causes more fatigue and soreness. When spinning, cyclists experience the greatest pedaling efficiency with minimal fatigue in the legs, and they gain the most cardio-vascular health benefits. Slow, difficult pedaling, on the other hand, strengthens thigh muscles but damages knees and has only minimal health benefits.

Riders who aim for efficient pedaling need to learn how to spin properly. While the relatively high cadence may be difficult for new riders to maintain, effective spinning can be achieved through practice and conditioning. If necessary, use lower gears to make fast pedaling easier.

# Braking

Most bikes use rim brakes that have a brake mechanism on both the front and rear wheels, each operated by one of two hand brake levers. While two-wheel braking provides the best stopping power, riders must know how to combine both brakes efficiently. Too much pressure on the rear brake could cause skidding or less effective braking. Too much on the front brake could send riders toppling over the handlebars as their bike flips forward.

Usually the right brake lever controls the rear brake while the left lever controls the front brake. Riders should know which lever corresponds to which brake and how to best apply the brakes. Good braking should be instinctive because in an emergency, you won't have time to think about how to use your brakes. Be prepared to brake at any time by keeping your hands as close to the brake levers as possible. Some handlebar positions make it easier than others to reach the brake levers. See the earlier discussion of body position.

The most common braking technique for normal road conditions is to squeeze slightly harder on the rear brake at first, then to gradually put more pressure on the front brake as the bike comes to a stop. This will distribute the decelerating force evenly for the smoothest stop. Avoid applying any sudden, intense pressure on the brakes if possible. Instead, apply firm but moderate pressure on the brakes. On downhills, apply light pressure at regular intervals (called feathering) to avoid speeding faster than you'd like. Feathering will keep brake pads from overheating from friction. To stop during a descent, squeeze the rear brake slightly harder than the front, because you are more susceptible to flying over the handlebars during downhills.

Be especially cautious applying brakes when your wheels are wet. Because brakes will be much less effective and more prone to skids when the rims are wet, be sure to brake earlier and more gently than usual. Exert caution, as well, if you must brake while turning, particularly on loose ground. Too much brake pressure in a turn can easily cause your bike to skid or topple over. To brake while turning, apply light pressure, with more emphasis on the rear brake. Whenever possible, brake before entering the turn.

To make an emergency stop in dry conditions, squeeze both brakes firmly, with more pressure on the front brake (which has more braking power). To keep yourself from flying over the handlebars, slide back in the saddle as far as possible and get your body into a low riding position before you begin braking (see **Figure 6–5**). Also, brace your arms to hold your body back against the forward momentum. If you can tell in advance that emergency braking will not be enough to avoid a collision, try steering out of the way. Or, when

▲
*Figure 6–5* EMERGENCY STOP POSITION

there is a possibility of serious injury, you may need to intentionally take a spill off your bike (expect some cuts and bruises). If you're wearing the proper safety gear, injuries can be held to a minimum.

# Shifting Gears

The first rule of gear shifting on a derailleur bike is, as many already know, to keep pedaling forward. Continuous pedaling ensures a smooth transition as the derailleurs move the chain from one sprocket to another. But, on most bikes it's also a good idea to ease up slightly on the pedals as the gear is shifted to avoid any chain slippage.

Most bikes have two gear shift levers: one that controls the rear derailleur (usually on the right) and one that controls the front derailleur (usually on the left). Just as you must become familiar with which brake lever corresponds to which brake, so too should you learn your way around the gearing system. You should be able to immediately distinguish between the two shift levers and know automatically which direction to move the levers in order to raise and lower the gears.

Though it's okay if you need to look down at the drivetrain once in a while to check what gear you're in, taking your eyes off the road can be dangerous and should be avoided. If you ride a road bike you may also need to remove one hand from the handlebars in order to shift. While this is necessary, avoid riding one-handed over rough or loose terrain and replace your hand as soon as possible. To maintain balance and control during one-handed riding, move the hand that remains on the handlebars toward the stem in the center.

Choosing the right gear in a given riding situation is purely a matter of experience. As you ride, you'll learn to recognize which gears are best suited for certain inclines or descents. While there is no such thing as an absolutely correct gear for a certain road condition, any gear that allows you to maintain spinning cadence (60–120 r.p.m.) is suitable. In general, low gears (smaller chainwheel and larger cog) make pedaling easier and are used for climbing hills or riding against wind, while high gears (larger chainwheel and smaller cog) make pedaling more difficult and are used on level ground or for riding fast down hills. To better understand how the gears work, refer back to the section on transmission in Chapter 2.

Anticipate hills by shifting early; in doing so you will avoid losing pedaling momentum and causing unnecessary wear on the chain and sprockets. Unless your

## BMX JARGON

BMX is partly a sport and partly a subculture. Predictably, there is a whole glossary of slang that surrounds BMX racing and that separates the true BMX insiders from the *trickstars*.

| | |
|---|---|
| *berms:* | Banked gravel corners for turns. |
| *catch air:* | To jump with both wheels off the ground. |
| *leathers:* | Race clothing (usually synthetic, not leather). |
| *holeshot:* | A fast start or quick lead. |
| *mains:* | Race finals. |
| *motos:* | Qualifying race heats. |
| *pimp:* | To block or cut off another rider. |
| *six-pack:* | Series of six jumps. |
| *snap:* | To get a good start. |
| *stylin':* | To perform tricks during a race. |
| *table tops:* | Mounds in the course for jumping. |
| *trickstar:* | Poser; rider with good equipment but no skills. |

bike has indexed gearing, you will need to listen and feel for signs that you have shifted the chain properly. If the chain rattles after shifting, it could mean you have shifted too far or not far enough. In that case, move the lever until the rattling stops.

The last rule of gear shifting is to always downshift before stopping. It's much more difficult to start riding again from a high gear, especially if you are on level ground or on a descent.

# Turning and Steering

While you might think that handlebars are designed for steering, they're actually used primarily for balance. Most of the turning on a bike is accomplished by the leaning of the rider, while handlebars play a lesser role. Simply, to turn right you lean the bike to the right; to turn left you lean to the left (see **Figure 6–6**). The amount a rider leans the bike determines the arc of the turn or how sharp the turn will be. More leaning makes the turn sharper (too much causes you to fall!), while subtle leaning causes wide turns. Riders must deftly balance gravity's downward pull with the outward centrifugal force of a turn. But leaning into bike turns need not be overanalyzed. With only a little experience, most riders instinctively know how far to lean in each situation.

Before entering into a turn, riders must determine the necessary arc of the turn and a safe speed at which to travel. The arc of the turn often depends on the rider's surroundings: the terrain, the size of the roadway, the angle of the road intersection, or any obstacles on the road or trail. Whenever possible, opt for a wider turn over a sharp turn. Wider turns are easier and safer to make and require less reduction in speed. Because you need to brake more before making a sharp turn, you lose riding momentum and pedaling efficiency. To reduce the angle of your turns, it is sometimes necessary to veer away from the turn at first and then cut back into it (see **Figure 6–7**).

*Figure 6–6*
TURNING POSITION

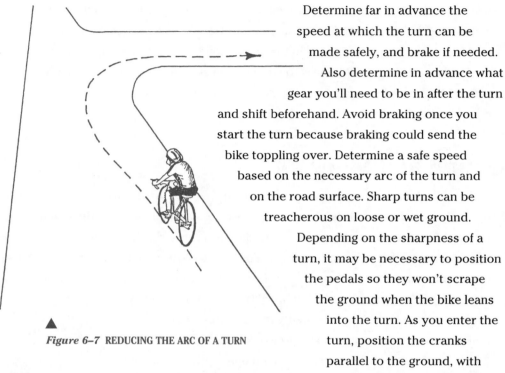

Determine far in advance the speed at which the turn can be made safely, and brake if needed. Also determine in advance what gear you'll need to be in after the turn and shift beforehand. Avoid braking once you start the turn because braking could send the bike toppling over. Determine a safe speed based on the necessary arc of the turn and on the road surface. Sharp turns can be treacherous on loose or wet ground.

Depending on the sharpness of a turn, it may be necessary to position the pedals so they won't scrape the ground when the bike leans into the turn. As you enter the turn, position the cranks parallel to the ground, with the pedals at three o'clock and nine o'clock. For sharper turns, position the outside pedal down—at six o'clock—and center most of your weight on the outside pedal. This will help keep you anchored and balanced, as will pointing your inside knee toward the turn. Unless the arc is wide enough to allow pedaling, it's best to cruise through turns.

To enter the turn, lean your hips and push the inside handlebar gently downward in the direction of the turn. Whenever possible, maintain the arc you've chosen throughout the entire turn. Steering during a turn—particularly in a turn that is sharp, fast, or on hazardous ground—can cause a fall. A safe and effective turn has a steady, fluid motion. As the turn is completed, gradually raise your bike back to an upright position. As soon as it is safe to resume pedaling, do so.

On loose surfaces such as trails, where leaning too much can be dangerous, steering with the handlebars may be necessary. To steer, direct your weight toward the inside of the turn and turn the handlebars in the direction you wish to go. Try to keep your body and bike as upright and stable as possible.

When riding in traffic, be sure to signal each turn far in advance and watch for approaching vehicles. It's even more important to turn safely in traffic because a fall would not only cause road rash but could also put you in the hospital.

# Hill Climbing

For casual and serious riders alike, hill climbing is the one most dreaded aspect of cycling. It is slow, physically difficult, and mentally frustrating. If it weren't for the downhills and straightaways that follow hills, no doubt there would be fewer cyclists in the world. On the other hand, some riders thrive on hill climbing. They welcome the challenge hills provide, have learned to handle them, and no longer find them loathsome. In order to get the most enjoyment out of riding, it's recommended that you learn to love hill climbing as well.

The first key to successful uphill pedaling is making sure you're in a suitable gear. Don't be afraid to shift into an extremely low gear if that's what it takes to make pedaling comfortable and to keep a brisk cadence (at least 60 r.p.m.). On hills, the steady, smooth pedaling described earlier is most important—and most difficult— to maintain. The momentum needed to get a bike uphill is lost when riders jab at the pedals. If you ride in very hilly areas, buy a bike with very low gear ratios or have a smaller chainwheel installed on your bike. Anticipate hills and shift down as soon as you begin to lose momentum. That way you won't get stuck in too high a gear during steep climbs.

For a little extra leverage on hills, many riders slide back slightly on the saddle, lean forward, and pull the handlebars back with each stroke. If you try it, be sure not to jerk and bob your body. And by all means, use toe clips or clipless pedals—they'll improve your hill climbing immensely. A trick to try on very steep hills, where you have no momentum from the start and cannot get into a suitable gear, is to lessen the incline of the hill by riding in a zig-zag pattern. Make sure you have enough room to maneuver and no traffic is approaching before you attempt this.

As important as using any climbing technique is having the right attitude when climbing. Instead of going into a climb with dread, set yourself a goal you can look forward to achieving. If the hill is long, mentally divide it into smaller, more manageable parts. Keep your mind occupied: take in the view or think about something else. Whatever you do, don't let yourself get discouraged or impatient.

## Riding Out of the Seat

The best way to get extra pedaling power on steep hills is to raise your body off the seat and stand as you pedal—a technique sometimes called honking (see **Figure 6–8**). This puts all your body weight onto the pedal during each stroke, which helps push the pedal forward and down. Because the rider must actually stand on the pedal with each stroke, the motion is somewhat similar to climbing steps (and it uses the same quadricep muscles). While standing, riders should shift their weight from the right side (as they push the right pedal down) to the left (as they push the left pedal down). This motion creates a rhythmic rocking effect that puts the descending pedal directly under the rider's entire body weight. The direction of the bike should remain straight at all times.

▲
*Figure 6–8* RIDING OUT OF THE SEAT

In addition to the extra power you get, riding out of the seat is a good way to utilize different muscles and give your seated climbing muscles a break. To make honking worthwhile, it may be necessary to shift into a higher gear for more pedal resistance. It'll be difficult, however, to preserve a steady, continuous pedaling motion and maintain an efficient cadence while standing. And honking is also much more physically demanding than seated spinning. Your legs tire more quickly and you need a greater oxygen intake. Therefore, out-of-seat riding should only be used for a limited time, on short hills, or when you can't find a gear low enough to get you up a hill comfortably. Honking is also useful when you need a quick burst of power for acceleration.

# Descending

For obvious reasons, most cyclists prefer zipping downhill to trudging uphill. Clearly, it's much more exciting—and a lot easier. But as easy as it seems, there is a technique to descending that will get you down the hill safely and quickly.

Take advantage of descents to build up speed and momentum, particularly when you know there's another hill up ahead. First, switch into a high gear that will allow you to continue pedaling. You can also help maximize your speed by minimizing wind resistance. Ride low on the bike, position your hands on the drops (if you have drops), and keep your back straight. Keep your hands close to the brakes while riding downhill, especially at high speeds. On straight descents, riders can become even more aero-dynamic by moving their hands closer together, near the stem. However, this will also give you less control and balance.

Rather than putting more weight on either one of the wheels as you would when pedaling uphill, distribute your weight evenly across the bike on descents to reduce the load on each tire. Down steeper hills, shift weight toward the back to help you maintain control. If by pedaling you can continue to push yourself faster, you may want to continue spinning. If not, coast with the crankarms parallel to the ground ·(pedals at three o'clock and six o'clock). When coasting, apply part of your weight on the pedals and the rest on the saddle.

Because of the natural acceleration caused by gravity, effective braking is necessary to keep you in control during descents. While some riders feel more comfortable at higher speeds than other riders do, any speed at which a cyclist feels out of control is too fast. It's very important that you stay relaxed while descending. If you need to slow down during a straight descent (though not while turning), apply a light and even pressure on the brakes—with more pressure on the rear brake—until you have regulated your speed.

Because dangers approach faster at high speeds, be especially alert to road conditions when flying downhill. Make sure your visibility is adequate to enable you to spot and avoid obstacles or to slow down.

# Mountain Bike Riding

While the vast majority of riding techniques apply to both on-road and off-road riding, the rough and unpredictable terrain of mountain biking requires a few more techniques for safe and effective riding. First and foremost, when faced with a number of potentially dangerous obstacles on a trail, it's very important to plan your path as far in advance as possible. Riders should scope the terrain constantly and always think about how to best handle the course.

The following is a list of some important tips for off-road cycling.

*Riding position.* Keep your weight low to make riding more stable.

*Pedaling.* Use toe clips or clipless pedals to keep your feet from sliding off the pedals on bumpy terrain.

*Braking.* Use the rear brake more than the front brake on loose terrain.

*Shifting gears.* Shift more often to better deal with the variety of inclines and terrain off-road.

*Downhills.* Slide back in the saddle and stay low on steep descents. Remain loose, but hold your position firmly. On steep descents, stand on the pedals with knees bent for better shock absorption.

*Uphills.* Stay low and close to the handlebars while pulling the handlebars back to keep the rear of the bike planted on the ground. Slide up in the saddle.

*Traction.* Increase traction by letting a small amount of air out of the tires. Underinflating the tires increases the amount of tire tread in contact with the ground.

# Speed

In the same way that speeding cars get lower gas mileage, cycling too fast can be an inefficient use of your body's energy—even if it gets you where you're going quicker. This is especially true for people who use their bicycles for transportation. Burn out too soon and you won't get to where you want to go. Even for fitness cyclists, too much emphasis on speed riding is not good. Cycling too fast provides less health benefits than riding at a manageable, steady pace.

There are times, of course, when riding fast is desirable or necessary. During a race, you need to sprint if you have any hope of winning. And for exercise cycling, combining sprinting with more moderate riding can make for a well-balanced workout. Besides, riding fast can be fun!

Whatever the reason for high speed cycling, there are two main methods to make a bicycle accelerate. First, riders can shift to a higher gear while keeping the same pedal cadence. Because higher gears have larger developments, they move the bike farther with each turn of the pedals. The other method for accelerating is simply to pedal faster. The faster the cranks turn, the faster the wheels will move. Pedaling faster is a better way to accelerate without tiring yourself out.

Other methods to a more limited degree can help increase speed. An aerodynamic position in which you lean forward—keeping low, narrow, and steady—reduces the wind resistance that can slow you down significantly. Conversely, when you're fortunate enough to ride with the wind, your speed may increase naturally. Drafting behind other willing bicyclists or vehicles also reduces wind resistance significantly.

Riding out of the saddle is a good way to build up speed in a short time. Honking, as described earlier in the section on hill climbing, can also be used on level ground for quick acceleration, such as when you need to cross an intersection quickly. It tires you out quickly, though, so use it sparingly. The best way to increase speed is to maintain a steady, even acceleration. For that, all you need is the fit body and strong muscles that come naturally with regular cycling.

# One-Handed and No-Handed Riding

Cycling safely means riding with both hands securely on the handlebars at all times. In the real world, though, that's not always possible. After all, safety rules also dictate that cyclists must signal turns in traffic by pointing their arms in the direction of the turn (try doing that with two hands on the bars!). Every now and again riders also need to let go of the handlebars in order to shift gears, take a drink, adjust their seat, tighten their helmet, wipe their tires, remove their jacket, or do any number of other things to make their ride more comfortable.

Still, the fact remains that riding with anything less than two hands on the bars puts you in some degree of danger. Your position is less stable and more vulnerable to bumps in the road. Riding with no hands is even more risky than one-handed riding. Not only are you more unstable and unbalanced, but also you have no control over steering and must ride in an upright position that makes you more sensitive to wind resistance. Avoid no-handed riding whenever possible.

Make one-handed riding as safe as possible by keeping your eyes open for obstacles or rough terrain. Make sure the road is smooth, straight, and free of traffic, and that you will not need to perform any complex maneuvering while your hand is away from the bars. Level ground and mild downhills are easier to handle one-handed than uphills or steep descents. Before you remove one hand, move the other hand close to the center of the handlebars, near the stem. Never remove a hand from the bars if you are in any position other than the upright, top bar position. Once you begin to ride one-handed, try not to make any jerky, awkward motions as you do whatever you have to do with the other hand. Move smoothly and deliberately in order to keep your balance.

The only time no-handed riding may be unavoidable is while eating during long rides. If you need to peel a banana or break open the package of your energy bar, you will probably need to let go of the handlebars for a short time. As much as possible, do all your peeling and opening before your ride. Don't attempt no-handed riding on the road unless you have first perfected it in an empty parking lot. Even after you've become comfortable with it, avoid no-handed riding on curved or bumpy roads. Always remain cautious and ready to grab onto the handlebars if you begin to lose your balance.

# Riding with Groups

Sometimes group riding is involuntary, such as if you are racing in a pack or if you encounter a bunch of other cyclists on the road. One of the most enjoyable cycling activities, though, is the organized group ride. Cycling with friends or teammates is great for recreation and training. While it doesn't take any special knowledge to go out riding with some friends, group rides with experienced and motivated cyclists involve a few techniques that aren't needed when you're out riding alone. To become an active, safe group rider, you'll need to be familiar with these cycling techniques.

## Drafting

It's a well-established fact in cycling that a rider can reduce wind resistance significantly—and thus ride more easily and faster—by following closely behind another vehicle. For that reason, in some track racing, a pace vehicle usually blocks the wind, while the cyclists who follow—or *draft*—the vehicle can increase their speed by as much as 30 percent without expending any more energy.

Even in situations where there is no pacing vehicle, cyclists practice drafting anyway; they draft each other (see **Figure 6–9**). Drafting is a major part of bike racing strategy, and it plays a large role in group riding as well. When a number of cyclists ride close together, drafting is unavoidable. If the group is organized, however, it can use drafting to raise the pedaling efficiency and speed of the entire group.

Unless riders are extremely careful, though, drafting can be very dangerous. Because it requires a cyclist to ride very closely behind another cyclist—sometimes as close as a few inches away to maximize the benefits of drafting—any sudden, slight change in speed by either rider can cause the two to collide and crash to the ground. When drafting or pacing, always ride predictably and know what to expect from the

*Figure 6–9* DRAFTING

other riders. Watch the rider in front of you, but also watch the road so you can anticipate any changes that might occur. Keep your hands on the brake levers at all times. Drafting must be perfectly orchestrated to ensure safety. For that reason, cyclists should never draft a vehicle in traffic and, if there is no traffic, never draft a vehicle without the knowledge and consent of the driver.

Before you venture out with a group of experienced drafters, practice with others at slower speeds and with greater distance between bikes. Practice riding very close to others, even bumping them lightly to prepare yourself for what might happen in a collision.

## Riding in Pacelines and Echelons

The standard formation for a group of riders who are drafting each other is called a *paceline*. A single paceline consists of a single-file line of cyclists riding about a foot apart, while a double paceline consists of two single-file lines riding closely side by side (see **Figure 6–10**). The leader of the paceline has no one to draft and must therefore pedal harder. To ensure one rider isn't stuck as the leader the whole time, riders in a paceline typically rotate positions. Usually, a cyclist will lead the pack for about a minute. This will require hard pedaling to keep up the pace of the other cyclists. After a minute, the leader moves out of the line (usually to the left in a single paceline, after first checking for traffic) and slows down to join the back of the line, while the cyclist who is next in line takes over as leader. In double pacelines, the leaders move to opposite sides of the group. This process is repeated throughout the entire ride.

In addition to setting an appropriate and consistent pace, the lead cyclist is responsible for keeping a close eye on the road, pointing to or calling out major obstacles, and directing the line away from dangers. The rear cyclist is responsible for notifying the group of approaching cars. The riders in between should concentrate on keeping their cadence at the right pace to maintain a well-spaced line and watch the road as well.

Another common group cycling formation, similar to a paceline, is called an *echelon* (shown in **Figure 6–10**). Riders use an echelon formation when a strong wind hits them at an angle. Instead of riding in a single-file line, they form a staggered line pointing away from the wind, with each rider behind and to the side of the rider in front. This enables riders to more effectively shield themselves from wind resistance. Because echelons take up more room than pacelines do, they can be dangerous (or impossible) on busy roads. Only experienced riders should participate in an echelon.

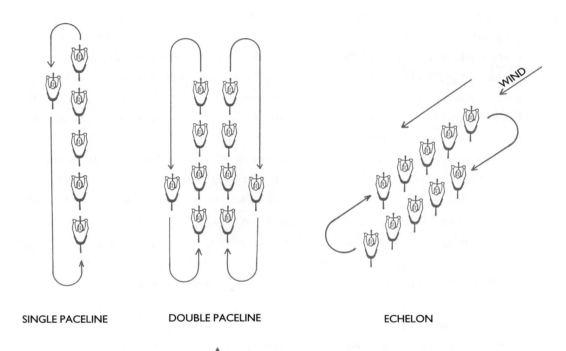

SINGLE PACELINE          DOUBLE PACELINE                    ECHELON

▲
*Figure 6–10* PACELINE AND ECHELON

# Jumps and Wheelies

## Jumps

Jumps and wheelies are often categorized as bike tricks—things hot-shot riders do to show off. Maybe so, but of all the stunts a cyclist could pull, wheelies and jumps (also called a *bunny hop*) are the two with the most practical application to everyday riding.

Jumps may be necessary to avoid running into obstacles or to lift the rider onto a higher surface (such as a curb). They are useful for riding both on-road and off-road. To jump you must actually raise both wheels off the ground—the front first, then the rear—while riding. If you lift the rear wheel before the front wheel lands, you have succeeded in jumping the bike. To lift the front wheel off the ground, shift your weight back as you pull back on the handlebars and push down strongly on the forward pedal to increase your speed. Once the front wheel is lifted, shift your weight forward and pull up with your legs to lift the rear wheel.

Jumping is a lot easier if you use toe clips or clipless pedals because you can actually pull the bike off the ground with your feet. By applying force in the right directions, though, clips are not necessary. Begin by practicing small jumps, then increase the size as you become more comfortable. Never jump so high that you lose control. Pulling too hard could flip your bike and knock you off. Also, timing is just as important as technique when jumping. In order to jump over an obstacle you must perform the maneuver at exactly the right time. With some practice, this will become natural.

## Wheelies

Wheelies are useful for smaller bumps or ridges where it is not necessary to lift the rear wheel. They are performed the same way as the first half of a jump. Shift your weight toward the rear as you pull back on the handlebars and pedal hard forward. To maintain a wheelie and actually ride for some time on one wheel, you must be able to keep your weight back as you balance the front wheel in the air. Do not try to raise the front wheel too high if you have toe clips or clipless pedals. If you pull too far and fall back, you'll need your feet to land safely on the ground—otherwise you'll fall flat on your back.

# Teaching Kids to Ride

Before you can teach your children to ride, they have to want to ride. If you've taken your children riding with you since they were young, using a bike trailer or baby seat, that shouldn't be a problem. They probably already have a sense of the fun and excitement that goes with bicycling. And once they learn how to ride, continue encouraging them by taking them out on family rides.

There's no definite age at which kids should learn to ride. They can start as soon as they demonstrate the balance and coordination needed; and though that can come as early as four years old, it should not be rushed. When they're ready, it's best to start children on bikes with training wheels. These bikes enable young children to balance easily while they become accustomed to the feel of a two-wheeler.

Make sure your children learn on bicycles that suit their body size. It's important that they learn correct posture and riding techniques from the start, and they can only do so on a properly sized bike. Single-speed bikes with coaster brakes are generally adequate; there's no sense getting beginners confused by gears and hand brakes.

Around age six, children may be ready to ride without training wheels. It may be many years, though, before they are ready to venture out on their own. In the meantime, keep an eye on their riding. They should stay close to home and on the sidewalks at first; later they may ride only on quiet streets. Keep them out of traffic until they fully understand the rules of the road. Before children are ready to ride unsupervised on the street, they should understand all the points discussed in Chapter 7, Bicycle Safety, possibly not until they are eleven or older.

When it comes to actually teaching your children to ride a bike, you'll be surprised at how little you need to do. Riding is simply a matter of learning to balance and control the bike. It will take some time, but most of it will happen naturally. As a parent, your job is to guide and encourage. Teach the basics of how to pedal, steer, and stop the bike. Then walk beside the bike to help keep the children balanced and upright; but don't hold on too tightly or they won't learn to balance alone. Have patience, and make sure your children have patience as well. Learning to ride is a gradual process, so congratulate your kids every step of the way.

Once children have learned the basics you can move on to more advanced riding techniques. Take it one step at a time, though, and always emphasize the fun. If children feel like riding is a chore, they may not develop any enthusiasm for the sport. While it's important to challenge your children and teach them correct riding techniques, it's also very important that they're successful in what they do and enjoy themselves.

## References

*Bicycling Magazine.* Jan. 1995–July 1996.

*Bicycling Magazine*, eds. *The Most Frequently Asked Questions about Bicycling.* Emmaus, Penn.: Bicycling Books, 1980.

Chauner, David, and Michael Halstead. *Tour de France Complete Book of Cycling.* New York: Villard Books, 1990.

Ford, Norman D. *Keep On Pedaling: The Complete Guide to Adult Bicycling.* Woodstock, Vt.: The Countryman Press, 1990.

Honig, Daniel. *How to Bike Better.* New York: Ballantine Books, 1985.

LeMond, Greg, and Kent Gordis. *Greg LeMond's Complete Book of Bicycling.* New York: G. P. Putnam's Sons, 1990.

Lieb, Thom. *Everybody's Book of Bicycle Riding.* Emmaus, Penn.: Rodale Press, 1981.

Matheny, Fred. Bicycling Magazine's *Complete Guide to Riding and Racing Techniques.* Emmaus, Penn.: Rodale Press, 1989.

*Mountain Bike.* August 1996.

Van der Plas, Rob. *The Bicycle Commuting Book.* San Francisco: Bicycle Books, 1989.

# CHAPTER 7

# BICYCLE
# SAFETY

# Rules of the Road

Like any vehicle on the road, bicycles can be perfectly safe or they can be extremely dangerous. How safe or dangerous they are depends on how closely you and the people around you adhere to the rules of the road. While you can't account for everyone else on the road, making sure you know the safe and legal way to ride will drastically reduce your chances of becoming involved in a bike accident.

## Is It a Car's World After All?

Undeniably, motor vehicles are the masters of the roadways. They're bigger, faster, stronger, and more numerous than bicycles. It's only natural that many drivers have come to think that roads were made specifically for cars and other motor-powered transportation—and that roads are no place for bicycles.

The truth is, though, that bicyclists have the same legal rights to the road as motorists. Just as a bicyclist cannot interfere with a driver's right of way (and wouldn't want to!), a driver cannot legally get in the way of a bicyclist's path either. Of course, with these rights come responsibilities. All road laws that apply to cars and other motor vehicles also apply to bikes, and there are a number of additional rules that pertain specifically to bikes.

When cars and bikes share the road, it's literally and figuratively a two-way street. Each vehicle must be on the lookout for the other. But because a car-bike collision stands to hurt the cyclist much more than the motorist, the cyclist needs to be even more cautious. Many bike-related accidents, as it turns out, are at least partly caused by the mistakes of cyclists.

Don't let bicyclists' status as underdogs on the road discourage you, though. Bikes have one large advantage over cars: they're more compact and maneuverable, so they're better equipped to react quickly to avoid accidents.

## What the Laws Say

In some cases society's pro-motor vehicle bias has created laws—such as mandatory sidepath laws—that seem like they're simply designed to keep bicycles as far out of the way of motorists as possible. Most traffic laws, however, are based on sound safety principles and have cyclists' best interests in mind. It's important to know those laws—those directed at all vehicles as well as those particularly for bicycles—before riding the streets. While specific laws vary from state to state, most general rules apply throughout the country. For information on bike safety laws in your state, contact your state's Department of Transportation, Department of Motor Vehicles, or your local bike shop. The rest of this section contains an overview of common bike-related traffic laws that may be in effect in your state.

*Obey all rules, signs, and procedures required of motor vehicles when riding on public roads.* Compliance includes respecting stop signs, stop lights, speed limits, one-way streets, turn lanes, and other directions.

*Always ride in the direction of traffic.* Inexperienced cyclists sometimes think riding against traffic is safer because it allows them to see approaching cars. But in reality, they are less visible and they put themselves at great risk for the most fatal kind of road accident: the head-on collision.

*Ride on the far right side of the street.* Slower traffic—no matter what vehicle—should keep to the right, and because bicycles are usually slower than cars, it's only logical they should be farthest right. Sometimes, however, moving too far right can expose bicyclists to other dangers such as the curb, parked cars, and pedestrians. To be safe, follow this rule of thumb: in wide lanes, ride just outside of normal traffic, a few feet to the right of

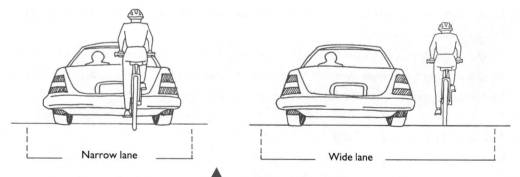

*Figure 7–1* POSITION IN TRAFFIC LANE

passing cars; in narrow lanes, ride just inside the path of traffic so that cars must move partially into the adjacent lane to pass.

*Pass on the left side when overtaking other vehicles in traffic, except if the other vehicle is turning left.*

*Ride in special bike lanes and bike paths where they are present, safe, and usable.* This law can be problematic, however, because it is subjective enough to be unenforceable (what constitutes *usable*?), thus often making the use of bike routes optional.

*Do not ride on limited-access expressways or other roads with high-speed traffic (over 50 mph) if restricted by state law.* Bicycles are sometimes permitted to ride on the shoulders of these roads, if there are any.

*Do not ride on pedestrian sidewalks where bicycles are prohibited.* While child bicyclists are encouraged to stay on the sidewalks, adults should avoid them. If sidewalk riding is allowed, watch out for people on foot, and follow pedestrian street-crossing rules.

*Do not ride through tunnels or over bridges unless they are specially equipped for bicycles.*

*Yield to pedestrians whether on sidewalks, on bike paths, or in the street.*

*Use standard hand signals to convey any intention to turn or merge.* They are shown in **Figure 7–2**. Make signals early (100 feet in advance is safe). Be clear and deliberate, and

Left turn or merge

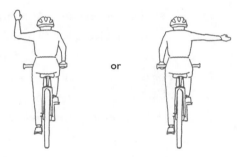

or

Right turn or merge

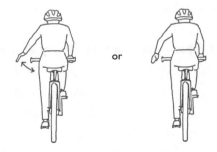

or

Stop or slow down

*Figure 7–2* HAND SIGNALS

repeat the signals regularly until you make the turn, merge, or stop. Signaling alone does not guarantee you will be able to maneuver safely, so continue to use caution.

*Stop for emergency vehicles and school buses just as you would in a motor vehicle.*

*Do not hitch onto a motor vehicle in traffic.* While some cyclists hitch on to move faster on the street, the practice is not only very dangerous but also inconsiderate to drivers.

*Do not ride with more people than the bike is equipped to carry.* One person belongs on a single-rider bike, two on a tandem.

*Do not carry anything that obstructs your steering, hold, or balance.*

*Keep at least one hand on the handlebars and your feet on the pedals at all times.*

*Wear a helmet that provides proper protection.* Though wearing a helmet is not the law in many states, helmets are extremely important because head injuries are the most common cause of bike-related fatalities. (For more information on helmets, see Chapter 8.)

*Do not wear headphones or earphones while riding in traffic.* Bicyclists must be able to hear other vehicles as well as their own bike in case problems arise. (Some states allow an earphone in one ear, though.)

*Have a horn or a bell loud enough to alert nearby cars.*

*Have a front headlight and rear reflector to see and be seen at night.*

*Use a specially designed child seat and child helmet if you ride with a child on board.* Even in a child seat, babies who cannot yet sit unsupported do not belong on bicycles.

*Do not, of course, ride while under the influence of alcohol or drugs, including prescription medications that cause drowsiness or irritability.*

## Other Smart Riding Principles

Safe bicycling is not simply a matter of following the law. Many safety principles are not covered in traffic regulations but are important nevertheless.

For bicyclists, defensive riding is key. If you ensure you'll be seen by others on the road, you've gone a long way toward avoiding an accident. It's equally important to remain in control of your bicycle at all times. Ride predictably; don't swerve or turn suddenly. Ride in a straight path and plan each move far in advance. Always be alert for potential hazards.

The following list includes some other tips to keep you safe on the road.

*Be courteous to others.* Let cars and bikes pass whenever possible, and don't lean on stopped or parked cars.

*Don't ever tailgate a motor vehicle—a sudden stop could spell trouble.* While following another bicycle closely (called *drafting*) has its advantages, it should only be done under specific circumstances, with the permission and knowledge of the other cyclist.

*Always check your bicycle for mechanical trouble before riding.*

*Move quickly and completely off the road to check a mechanical problem you may have with your bike.*

*Don't race on public roads.*

*Ride in single file when biking with other cyclists, unless space permits riding abreast.*

*Be especially careful riding at night, and don't ride at night unless your bicycle is properly equipped.*

*Wear bright colors so you will be more easily seen.*

*Carry some form of identification with you when riding, in case of an emergency.*

*Help others when you see they are in need.*

# Rules of the Trail

Roads are not the only place bicyclists experience traffic and other hazards—the trail has its own set of dangers and safety guidelines. The following are some of the most important tips for safe off-road biking.

*Ride only on trails where biking is allowed.* Don't trespass on private land; do respect trail closures and get permission from the proper authorities if you are not sure cycling is legal on a particular trail.

*Obey the speed limit on trails and remain in control of your bicycle at all times.*

*Don't ride alone, particularly in remote areas.* In case someone is injured, it's best to be with at least two other people, one to get help and one to care for the injured rider.

*Be well prepared.* Have enough food, water, and equipment to last in case of emergency. Carry a first aid kit and bicycle repair kit as well.

*Be familiar with an area before venturing out.* Bring a map and compass to guide you.

*Yield to hikers on the trail.* Anticipate people around every turn; keep your speed down and make your presence known to others by using a bell or horn.

*Stay away from hunting areas.*

*Wear a helmet and brightly colored clothing.*

*Respect the trail and the inhabitants of the woods.* Don't create new trails or otherwise leave evidence of yourself behind. And, don't disturb the animals or plants in any way—it's not only dangerous, it might be illegal as well.

# Road Hazards

Collisions with cars and other bicycles account for only about one-third of all bike accidents. That means there are plenty of other things to look out for when riding. While many road hazards won't cause more damage than a flat tire or a skid, some can cause more serious harm. The worst hazards knock riders off their bike or cause serious injury, even death. Be ready for anything: keep your head up, your eyes on the road, and stay alert at all times. Slow down whenever hazards are around.

A bicycle should be in excellent shape to safely and quickly react to unexpected occurrences. Brakes should be tight and tires cleaned frequently of the debris that accumulates on them. Carry a spare tire tube or patch kit as well in case sharp objects prove unavoidable.

Getting away from a road hazard is often simply a matter of swerving to the side or braking. Always keep in mind the traffic around you, though. It defeats the purpose to avoid broken glass if you end up colliding with a passing car. Look before you deviate from your path, then swerve right to avoid hazards. Move just enough to avoid danger.

Be especially wary at night or when the sun is blinding, times at which you (and others) are least likely to see danger approaching. Be careful, as well, of dangers at intersections and around corners, and keep an eye out for the road hazards described in the following lists.

## Damaged and Unsafe Roads

Potholes, particularly in winter and spring when they're most likely to form.

Loose debris from potholes, often lying near the pothole.

Metal sewer gratings, which can catch bike tires if they are wide enough.

*Avoidance techniques.* Slow down, check approaching traffic, and safely swerve out of the way.

## Sharp Materials

Glass, which often accumulates at the corners of intersections.

Gravel, particularly sticky bits from newly paved roads.

Twigs, thorns, pine cones, cactus spines, or other debris that has fallen from plants and trees.

*Avoidance techniques.* Slow down, check approaching traffic, and safely swerve out of the way. In addition, brush off tires frequently to keep sharp pieces from digging into them. You may also want to install a tire-saver device above your wheels that will clear away sharp materials before they cause flats.

## Slippery Surfaces

Ice, water, and mud, which make brakes less effective.

Oil slicks, which can be difficult to see and may stick to bike tires, making riding treacherous.

Leaves, especially when wet and newly fallen.

Painted streets and pavement, especially when wet and new.

All metal surfaces, including manhole covers, railroad crossings, and bridge expansion joints.

*Avoidance techniques.* If it is impossible to safely avoid slippery areas, drift through them slowly and smoothly. Ride straight; do not swerve, brake, jerk, or pedal until you are out of the area. Ride over metal tracks perpendicularly or, if you can do it safely, jump them.

### Fellow Travelers

Pedestrians, who are not bound by traffic laws and can be unpredictable (watch especially for children).

Parked cars, particularly doors that swing open in front of you.

Wind created by fast moving vehicles as they pass, which can throw you and your bicycle off balance.

Animals.

*Avoidance techniques.* Notify pedestrians of your approach with a horn, a bell, or a vocal warning, and give them time to get out of the way. Stay a few feet to the left of parked cars and as far from high-speed vehicles as possible.

### Beware of Dog

When you come upon an unleashed and barking dog, don't overreact. Usually the dog means no harm and will lose interest as you pass. But, if a dog is aggressive and begins to chase, you will need to take action. Try to either turn around or speed up to outrun it. While taking care to avoid a collision with the dog, don't let the animal distract you from the road. Firmly and loudly yell "Stay!" or "No!" at the dog. If that doesn't work, raise your hand as if to throw something at it (but don't actually throw anything). As a last resort, spray some water from your water bottle into the dog's face (some cyclists use a temporarily blinding ammonia solution, though that's usually not necessary). If you must get off your bike, use the bike as a barrier between you and the dog. If the dog's harassment becomes a regular occurrence, speak to the dog's owner or report the dog to the police.

# Handling Road Traffic

As discussed earlier in the chapter, riding a bicycle in traffic is not all that different from driving a car because most of the same rules apply. The key is to become a part of traffic, not a hindrance to its normal flow. While some motorists believe bikes don't belong on the road, remember your rights and earn your place in the streets through safe and competent riding.

## Avoid Traffic Whenever Possible

Cycling in traffic is not dangerous if proper riding techniques are followed. But even for the most cautious riders, traffic is always more dangerous than no traffic, so avoid riding in traffic whenever you can. Take roads less traveled, even if they make for a slightly longer route. Quiet streets are not only safer, they can make the ride quicker by circumventing traffic jams.

If you must ride on congested streets, stay to the right and keep away from motorist traffic whenever possible. If the road has a clear and well-paved shoulder, use it.

## Passing

Because bicycles generally move slower than cars on the road, you will probably be passed more often than you pass. While cars approaching from behind cause much anxiety for inexperienced cyclists, you needn't worry; passing cars are rarely the cause of car-bike collisions. Whenever it is safe to let a car pass, do so. Sometimes, though, cyclists are better off holding up cars in the interest of safety. On narrow-laned roads, for instance, squeezing right to let a car pass could send bikes off the road. Ride close to the middle of the lane when necessary; if the car wishes to pass, let it switch lanes. Avoid this, though, if the road has only one lane of traffic in each direction: causing a car to cross the center divider in order to pass can be dangerous if the car must quickly shift back over (and into you) to avoid oncoming traffic. By the same token, watch on two-way two-lane roads for approaching cars that enter your lane to pass another approaching car. In either case, be prepared to stop sharply or even ride off the road completely.

On those occasions when you need to overtake a car (or another bicycle), always pass on the left unless the other vehicle plans to turn left or the lane between the car and your bike is clear. Passing on the left, of course, means you need to leave the right side of the road for a time. That's okay. Just stay out of the car's blind spot as you pass and notify others as you approach. Then move back to the right as soon as it is safe.

## Negotiating

Switching lanes safely in traffic—a skill called *negotiating*—is among the most important riding techniques a bicyclist can learn. If you ever plan to make a left turn in traffic, you'll need to negotiate your way across the roadway to get into the proper lane. While leaving the safety and comfort of the right side to enter the main flow of traffic can be intimidating, negotiating is safe and easy when done correctly.

The first step in negotiating is to check behind to see if any vehicles are approaching and to slow down if necessary. Try to make eye contact with drivers and use standard hand signals to make your intentions known and ask to be let in. If the driver slows down and indicates a willingness to let you in, nod or wave "thanks," then move gradually left into the lane. Continue glancing behind to ensure other cars do not enter the lane. If you must negotiate across more than one lane, simply repeat the procedure. As you gradually move left, check traffic twice for each lane, once before you enter on the right side of the lane and once as you move across to the left side.

If you find yourself in the middle of heavy traffic, unable to shift into the left lane, do not stop. Continue riding forward, even if that means you miss your turn (you can always turn back later). In high-speed traffic, negotiation is much more difficult and dangerous—often impossible. If traffic is moving too quickly for you to interact with approaching drivers, simply be careful and shift lanes when you can.

## Handling Intersections

Many of the trickiest traffic situations come at intersections, where vehicles coming from various directions meet. Be careful and alert as you approach intersections because there's usually a lot going on. Don't enter an intersection while the light is yellow and try to rush through. There may be a car trying to do the same thing and not watching for you. Instead, stop and wait at the light with the rest of traffic. If a right turn is possible, move into the center of the right lane so cars will not cross in front of you as they turn.

If you reach an intersection and find a line of cars waiting—at the light or stopped in a traffic jam—you may be tempted to squeeze through to the front of the line. Unless it is specifically outlawed in your state, this is certainly your prerogative. It may annoy motorists stuck in line, but as one of the bicycle's few on-the-road advantages, it's well worth making use of. Be cautious, though, and watch for cars that may be shifting lanes in the traffic. As always, be as predictable and as controlled as possible.

If you end up in front of a group of cars at a stop light, it's best to let at least one car go through the intersection before you. This will establish the flow of traffic and avoid a situation in which a car coming from another direction does not see you and enters the intersection while you are crossing. To cross the intersection as quickly as possible, shift your bike into a low gear before you stop at a traffic light or stop sign.

To make a right turn at an intersection, simply remain in the far right lane and turn when traffic conditions permit.

When proceeding straight through an intersection, move left to avoid getting cut off by motorists turning right. If a right-turn-only lane exists, shift left to the right side of the first straight-only lane (see **Figure 7–3**). Once you cross the intersection, return to your path on the right side of the road. If the right lane offers a choice to turn right or to go straight, move to the center of the lane, cross the intersection in the normal stream of traffic, and return right once you are through. As you cross the intersection,

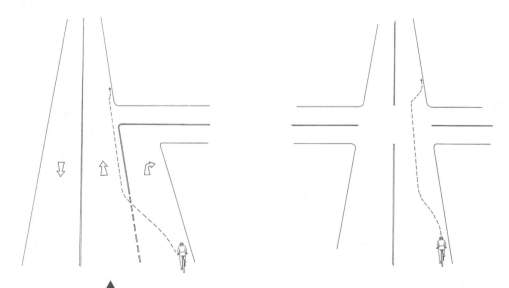

▲
*Figure 7–3* PROCEEDING STRAIGHT THROUGH AN INTERSECTION

be prepared to turn sharply right if a car from the opposite direction makes a sudden left turn into your lane without seeing you.

Left turns are more difficult and require planning long before the intersection. When in doubt, simply get into the center of the correct turn lane. While this may slow traffic, it will ensure that you are seen and not cut off. If the left lane is a left-turn-only lane, move to the right side of that lane and turn wide to the right side of the cross street. If the left lane offers a choice to turn left or to go straight, move to the center of the choice lane and turn left into the center of the cross street before returning to the right side (see **Figure 7–4**). If one left-only lane and one choice lane exist, position yourself on the left side of the choice lane to make the turn.

Be sure to look both ways down the cross street and straight ahead before attempting the left turn. If you must wait in the center of the intersection while traffic from the opposite direction passes, turn your bicycle at an angle (45 degrees or less) to make yourself more visible to approaching cars. If traffic is very heavy, consider making the left turn as a pedestrian would. Remain right as you go through the intersection, then cross left on the crosswalk.

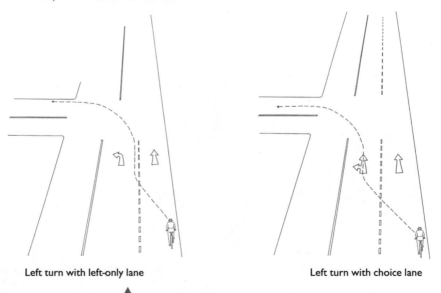

Left turn with left-only lane          Left turn with choice lane

*Figure 7–4*  TURNING LEFT AT AN INTERSECTION

At a single-lane roundabout or rotary, ride in the center of the lane until you reach your turnoff, and watch traffic behind you before making the turn. At a multiple-lane roundabout or rotary, stay in the right lane only if you plan to make the first right. Otherwise enter and ride in the left (inside) lane until turning off. Make sure the right (outside) lane is clear before making the turn.

## Expressway Driving

Though bicycles are often restricted from them, highways with clean and wide shoulders can be relatively safe for biking. Where highway riding is allowed, bikes should remain on the shoulder as far right as is safe and practical. Because expressways have limited access, bicyclists only need to worry about breaks in the right shoulder at exits and

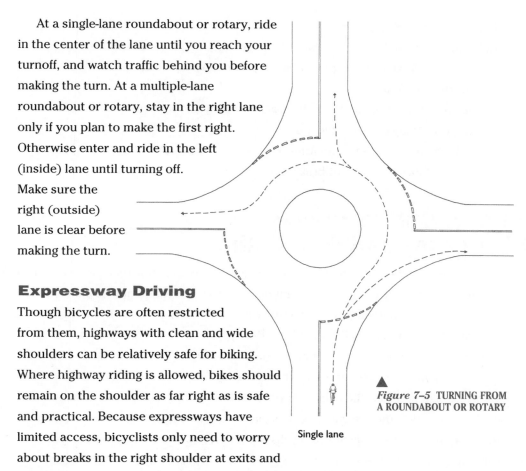

*Figure 7–5* TURNING FROM A ROUNDABOUT OR ROTARY

Single lane

feeder lanes. Where an exit lane approaches on the right, follow the shoulder into the exit until the exit completely breaks from the main road. Watch behind you for exiting cars; when the lane is clear, cut back to rejoin the highway on the right shoulder. If no traffic is approaching as you reach the exit, simply stay straight and cut across the exit. Or, if you plan to exit, follow the exit lane on the right shoulder.

Where a merging lane approaches on the right, watch for entering traffic. Shift right to the right shoulder of the merging lane as soon as possible, and avoid riding straight into the path of any entering cars. If you are entering on a merging lane, simply stay to the right as the merging lane joins the main expressway traffic.

### The Panic Stop

Riding in traffic can be unpredictable. In an emergency, sharp and sudden stops can be necessary. A safer quick-stop technique—commonly called a "panic stop"—should be performed as follows:

Shift your body weight toward the back wheel by sliding slightly off the saddle, and position your body low over the frame.

Apply the brakes evenly and firmly on the front and back wheels, then gradually increase pressure on the front brake as you stop.

## Thanks But No Thanks: Bike Lanes and Bike Paths

In what seems to be a step toward providing cyclists with better road facilities, lots of attention and money has gone in recent decades to the creation of bike paths. A bike path is typically a narrow paved lane that runs completely separate from, though often parallel to, a main road. Believing bikes would be safest off the road and in their own designated area, many state legislators enacted bike path laws that required bicyclists to use these paths instead of roads wherever they existed.

While bike paths can be beneficial when used by young and inexperienced riders, evidence suggests they cause at least as many accidents as they prevent. Though the paths are reserved specifically for cyclists, they often become dangerously crowded with joggers, dog-walkers, and in-line skaters. In addition, seasoned riders find most bike paths to be poorly designed, poorly maintained, and dangerous for high-speed riding. Some cyclists will avoid a road completely rather than be forced to use a bike path. The paths also pose particular dangers when they cross with streets and place cyclists in the path of unsuspecting motorists.

Thankfully, as it becomes apparent bike paths are not the solution to the dangers cyclists face on the road, some states have repealed the mandatory laws. Slowly, the focus of bike safety is returning to where it belongs: to making roads more hospitable to bicycles.

One attempt to integrate bicycles onto the main roadway has been the creation of special bike lanes. Unlike a bike path, a bike lane is a part of the road (to the right of the right lane) designated for bikes only. But like bike paths, lanes are full of problems that can make roads even more dangerous for bikes. Because the lanes are not used as much as other parts of the road, they accumulate gravel and other debris that can make bike riding hazardous. Because other vehicles are not allowed in the lane, traffic can become unnecessarily congested when lanes are added to existing roads. And because lanes encourage (or even require) bikes to remain on the right side of the roadway, cyclists are forced to make dangerous left turns from the right lane, or get cut off by right-turning cars.

By adapting bike laws to accommodate situations where bikes can leave the right side of the road, bike lanes become irrelevant at best. As with bike paths, special lanes do not adequately address the real hazards cyclists face. More appropriate solutions include wider roads, better shoulders, removal of on-street parking, and most importantly, driver education. As long as road planning focuses on separating bicycles from motor vehicles, though, there is little hope for reducing the real dangers to cyclists.

# What to Do if You Get into an Accident

If, despite all efforts to stay safe, you find yourself facing a collision, try to remain in control of your bike and hope for the best. If you are prepared with a helmet and proper clothing, your chances of escaping without serious injury will be much improved. If you see a collision is unavoidable, stay upright in your bicycle as long as possible to allow the car (or whatever you collide with) to pull away. The longer you remain vertical, the better your chances of avoiding being run over.

Once an accident has occurred:

- If you have been knocked to the ground, remain still until you can determine the extent of your injuries.
- Remain calm and avoid attacking—verbally or physically—others involved in the accident.

- Call for medical help or ask someone to do it for you, even if your injuries are minor.
- Call the police to report the accident, no matter how minor.
- Get the names, driver's license numbers, insurance information, and vehicle descriptions of others involved in the accident.
- Get the names, addresses, and phone numbers of witnesses to the accident.
- Ask witnesses and others involved to remain at the accident scene until proper authorities arrive.
- Cooperate with police when they arrive.
- Go to the hospital if your injuries require medical attention or documentation.

# Bike Safety Tips for Motorists

Bicyclists are not the only ones who need to respect safe biking rules. Drivers can do their part as well. If you are driving a car:

- Look out for cyclists, especially at night.
- Have good, working headlights to pick up bicycles' rear deflectors.
- Respect cyclists' rights to use the road and take up an entire lane of traffic for safety reasons.
- Never try to intimidate cyclists on the road by taking advantage of your vehicle's greater strength and size.
- Yield the right of way to bikes whenever you would normally yield to other cars.
- Do not cut off cyclists, but instead change lanes to pass on the left if necessary.
- Use caution when turning alongside bikes, and be sure to stay in your lane.
- Make eye contact with cyclists to communicate your intentions.
- Don't drive too closely behind a bicycle. Most bikes don't have brake lights, so it can be difficult to tell when they are stopping.
- Drive particularly slowly when confronted with children on bicycles.
- Don't speed closely past cyclists. Even if you don't hit them, the wind force could knock them off balance.
- Don't blast your horn at cyclists. A simple beep is sufficient to get their attention.

- Doublecheck your blind spot before turning or changing lanes.
- Look behind you before opening your car door at curbside parking, and also before pulling away from the curb.
- Be patient. Bicycles don't move as fast as cars—they'll be out of your way soon enough.

# Safety Equipment

## Lighting Systems

Just as with cars, lighting plays a key role in the safety of cyclists. Lights not only help cyclists see the road in darkness and bad weather, they also help drivers on the road see cyclists. It's a good idea to have a front headlight on your bike at all times, and essential (often mandatory), at night. Even bicyclists who don't plan to ride at night sometimes get caught after sunset, or in the rain. Be prepared for all possible situations.

Headlights are usually removable—unless used regularly—and installed onto the front fork or handlebars of the bike. The light should turn with the front wheel. Install it low enough on the frame to make small road hazards more visible. The beam of light should be strong and wide enough to illuminate an entire lane of traffic at least twenty-five feet ahead of the bike (far enough ahead to be seen by approaching vehicles around a corner). Bike lights should also be waterproof, in case of rain.

There are three categories of bike lights to choose from, each with its own advantages and disadvantages. The best type for you will depend on your lighting needs: the distances you usually ride, the light strength you require, and the convenience of use you desire. Here are the possibilities:

*Generator lights.* Dynamo, or generator, lights convert the mechanical energy of a bicycle wheel's movement into the electrical energy needed to illuminate a light. These lights involve a roller device installed onto the front wheel (usually on the side of the tire, but not always), attached to the generator, which is connected by wires to the headlight. As the wheels of the bike turn, the resulting energy provides the light. Generator lights are not as strong as other types of lights, but they require little power and run indefinitely. While they can be difficult to install and maintain, they are lightweight, inexpensive, and easy to use if operating properly. The greatest drawbacks to generator lights are as follows: they only run while the front wheel is moving (at stoplights, for instance, the light will go out), and if the bike wheel moves too fast, the bulb can blow out due to an overloaded generator. For long trips and frequent use, though, generator lights are often a favorite among cyclists.

*Rechargeable battery lights.* Batteries, such as nickel-cadmium (Ni-Cd) or lead-acid types, create a strong light and can be recharged again and again, but they don't last long before needing to be recharged. Ni-Cd batteries conveniently fit in the same appliances that fit nonrechargeable dry-cell batteries, but need to run down completely before recharging. Lead-acid batteries are not interchangeable with dry cells and fit only into specially designed lights, but are stronger than Ni-Cd batteries and can be recharged before running down. All rechargeable battery lights tend to be relatively heavy. They are also expensive to buy, though they are inexpensive to use. Rechargeable batteries are best used by commuter cyclists, who make short, regular trips and can incorporate recharging into their daily routine.

*Dry-cell battery lights.* Lights that run on disposable batteries tend to be dim and shortlasting, but are lightweight and convenient to use. They also are generally inexpensive to buy, though the cost of replacing batteries will quickly add up. These can be the best choice for cyclists who plan to use lighting only occasionally and value convenience above other considerations.

No matter which type of power system you choose, be sure the bulbs you use are appropriate for the voltage and wattage of the light, and always carry extras in case a bulb burns out. Halogen bulbs are popular because they last a long time, produce a lot of light, and don't dim with use. Be careful not to touch halogen bulbs with your fingers, though; use a clean cloth to install and remove them.

While reflectors are an adequate form of protection for the backs of bicycles, some cyclists also install rear lighting for additional protection. If you use rear lighting, be sure the light is not blocked or obscured by other equipment. Placing the light under the saddle or behind the rack is best. Strobes, LEDs, or other flashing lights are somewhat effective, although they may not provide a sufficiently wide field of vision and may also make it difficult for drivers to judge your distance.

## Reflectors

Bike reflectors should be used in addition to headlights, not instead of them. Reflectors are visible only when light shines on them. They make it easier for cyclists to be seen, but not easier for them to see. A large, flat reflector is a necessity on the back of every bicycle. Attach it to a spot where it won't be blocked by bags or racks, and where it won't become covered by dirt flying off the back wheel (just in case, clean it often). Light-colored reflectors (white or amber instead of red) tend to be brighter. Check reflectors regularly to ensure they are not cracked, and that they are properly positioned for maximum illumination.

Additional reflectors can go on wheels, on clothing, or on pedals (where circular movement makes them more noticeable), though they are not as important or as effective as rear reflectors. Side reflectors are of little use—by the time they're illuminated by an approaching car's headlights, it's too late to get out of the way!

As additional protection at night, some cyclists like to use reflective tape on their bikes and clothes. Available at bike shops or hardware stores, reflective tape is lightweight and will stick to moving parts such as wheels, pedals, or shoes. As with hard reflectors, lighter colors of tape work better.

## Horns and Bells

Cyclists should carry or attach to their bike some sort of warning device to alert other vehicles and pedestrians of their approach. Calling out can work in some cases, but won't always draw attention on crowded, noisy streets. Loud, jarring horns, such as compressed air horns, work best, while bells are good for riding on sidewalks and in quiet areas. Install noisemakers on handlebars so they can be accessed quickly. Though you should not overuse these warning devices, don't be afraid to let 'em rip when your safety is jeopardized.

## Rearview Mirrors

While rearview mirrors are mandatory on most road vehicles, they are seldom required on bicycles. Many riders would rather glance behind them in traffic than use a tiny mirror, which can be uncomfortable and ineffective. Certainly rearview mirrors should never replace a bicyclist's need to look back in traffic, but the best mirrors can nevertheless increase biking safety.

Bike mirrors can be installed on handlebars or else worn by cyclists as an attachment to their helmets or eyeglasses. Handlebar mounts are larger and easier to use, but they are also more likely to bend and break if the bike falls to the ground. Head-mounted mirrors tend to be small, and because they are not in a fixed position relative to the ground, they can make traffic difficult to judge.

## Air Pumps

On long trips, a good air pump can make the difference between being slightly inconvenienced and being helplessly stranded. Though most gas stations have air pumps, you can't count on being near one at all times. It's best to carry your own pump in case a tire becomes flat or in need of air.

While floor pumps are easy to use at home, they're difficult to take with you. For bike trips, buy a lightweight and slender pump that will clamp onto the bike's seat tube (or sometimes the top tube) for easy access and storing. The pump should fit your tire valves, and preferably will come with a built-in tire gauge (if not, get a separate gauge to measure tire pressure). Avoid pumps that have a connector hose; these trap air and make it hard to achieve a high tire pressure. They can also rip.

Compressed carbon dioxide ($CO_2$) canisters are sometimes used as an alternative to portable air pumps. These are compact and easy to use, but have a limited capacity. Where a pump can be used continuously, one $CO_2$ canister may not be enough to inflate a whole tire.

## Bike Locks

With the high occurrence of bicycle theft all over the country, a strong bike lock is necessary whenever you plan to leave your bike unguarded. Though there's no such thing as a completely unbreakable lock, some locks are clearly better than others, and the best locks can provide a reasonable surety that your bike will not be stolen.

The best lock to use on a bike is the common U-lock. U-locks are lightweight and small, yet rigid and extremely strong. Clamps can be installed on your bike frame to store the lock while you ride. Use a U-lock to secure your bike to an immovable object. The best ones are street signs (they are too tall for a bike to be lifted over them), fences, metal gates, or bike stands. Loop the U-lock through the front wheel and the frame (particularly if the front wheel is easily removable), as well as to the secure object. If possible, loop the lock through both wheels. For additional safety you can tie a thick cable or linked chain around a larger object (such as a telephone pole) and secure the chain through the bike and U-lock. Remember to take all removable accessories with you when you leave the bike.

## Tools and Repair Equipment

Though bicyclists cannot expect to carry all the bike repair tools and equipment they may need with them on the road, some are easy to bring along and can prove helpful in trouble situations. Buy good tools and equipment—even if they cost a little more— and know how to use them before you find yourself in an emergency. Carry with you as many of the following as will fit in a removable tool pouch or saddlebag:

*Tools*
    screwdriver (3/16" blade)
    adjustable and crank wrench
    small pliers
    allen keys (hex-head wrench) to fit
        the hexagon bolt on your bike
    tire lever to pry off wheel

*Equipment*
    tire patch kit, including patches,
        glue, and sandpaper
    spare tube
    spare tire (if you use tubular tires)
    spare batteries for lights
    optional parts: cable, spokes, chain
        links

*Other supplies*
    hand cleaning paste
    rags
    ID, spare key, change

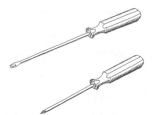

# Riding at Night

Nighttime cycling is somewhat dangerous even when you take the proper precautions. It can be extremely dangerous if you're unprepared. The two main problems are the facts that you can't see the road and that others on the road can't see you. Having a strong front headlight, a rear reflector, and wearing bright colors (white and yellow are best), will do a lot to reduce the risks of night riding, but other safety precautions can be taken as well.

Try to ride only on well-lit streets that are well paved, hazard-free, and familiar to you. Stay out of shadows on streets, and completely avoid dark off-road trails, paths, or sidewalks where pedestrians may be walking. In addition to being slippery, wet roads at night can produce a distracting glare from the streetlights that can impair your visibility.

For the most part, apply the same traffic principles to riding at night as you would during the day. Keep in mind, though, that some drivers and pedestrians may not see you or your hand signals, so be extra cautious. Be sure you have plenty of room to make a turn before attempting it.

# Child Safety and Bikes

Because they are largely unfamiliar with traffic laws—and perhaps less familiar with how to ride a bike safely—children are at high risk of having a bike accident on the road. For these reasons, it's best to keep children off the roads until they display an ability to understand traffic laws and to maneuver in traffic.

Still, it's important to expose children to bike safety from the start. If you carry kids on your bike, secure them in child safety seats. If you use a bike trailer to transport kids, make sure they are safe. As you teach your children to ride, make safety a primary concern. When they reach the age and skill level to venture out on the road, don't scare them. Encourage them to ride, as long as they can do it safely.

There are also plenty of opportunities to get your kids riding without exposing them to the dangers of the road. Off-road biking, bike tracks, and BMX riding offer more confined environments that can be safer if the proper equipment and techniques are used. Even riding on the sidewalk is a viable alternative to road riding, provided children know how to handle pedestrian traffic.

Teaching children early will help ensure that they are safe on roads; plus, many of the skills kids learn will be of use to them when they eventually learn to drive. If you don't feel able to teach safe riding yourself, enroll your child in a bike safety program such as Effective Cycling. To find out where Effective Cycling classes are offered in your area, call the League of American Bicyclists at 410-539-3399 or 800-228-BIKE.

# First Aid for Bicyclists

## First Aid Kit

In case you sustain minor injuries while cycling, it's a good idea—particularly on long rides—to carry a small first aid kit with you. This kit may include:

- adhesive bandages
- nonstick pads
- antibacterial ointment and soap
- pain relief tablets
- washcloth
- ice pack
- splints
- sling
- water

## Abrasions

Minor scrapes caused by falling on the road surface are the most common types of bike injuries. Cyclists call such scrapes "road rash." Though road rash is usually not serious, it does hurt a lot. Protective clothing such as gloves, knee pads, elbow pads, and extra layers of clothing can help reduce the risk of abrasions. Here's what to do if you come down with a nasty case of road rash:

Clean out the wounded area completely with water, a clean washcloth, and antibacterial soap or an iodine solution. Scrub thoroughly to remove all the tiny particles of dirt and gravel that may have collected in the wound. Serious cyclists often shave their body hair, which makes cleaning these abrasions easier.

Treat the wound with an antibacterial ointment or other antiseptic and cover it with a nonstick pad or "second skin" product (a few varieties can be found in drugstores). Dress the wound only if it will come into contact with clothes or other objects. Otherwise, allowing exposure to air will hasten the healing process.

Ice the area as soon as possible to reduce pain and swelling.

Scrub the wound twice a day with antibacterial soap and a washcloth to prevent infection and scabbing (scabs will harden and create more visible scars). Treat and dress the wound each time as directed above.

If a large area is lacerated, or if an infection occurs (evidenced by swelling, itching, or fever), see a doctor. You may need to take an oral antibiotic to fight the infection. Also, if you have not received a tetanus shot recently, get one from your doctor immediately.

## Bleeding

If a bike accident has caused you to bleed, apply direct pressure to the wound with a clean cloth in order to stop the bleeding. If possible, elevate the injury above your head until the blood clots. Clean the wound and dress it as described above to prevent infection. If the wound is deep or large, it may require stitches. In that case, or if bleeding continues, go immediately to the hospital emergency room.

## Sprains

Wrists, knees, and ankles are the most common recipients of sprains from bicycle falls. A sprain is caused by damage to the ligaments around joints, and can put you out of commission (at least in terms of riding a bike) for anywhere from one week to a month or more. Put ice on the sprain to help cool the area and reduce swelling. If pain and stinging continues, or if a fever develops, the injury may be something worse than a sprain—it could be a fracture. Either way, it's a good idea to see a doctor.

## Fractures

Wrists and collarbones are the most common types of bike-related fractures. If there is no visible sign of a bone break, your injury may at first seem like a sprain. The only way to tell right away if you have a fracture is to get an X-ray at the hospital. If the injury is indeed a fracture, the doctor will need to set the bone and bandage it. You may need to wear a sling or splint until the bone heals, which could take anywhere from two weeks to two months (collarbones heal quicker than wrists, though wrists can be less debilitating). Even after the doctor says it's okay to return to cycling, take it easy at first and stay off rough roads that can irritate the healing bone.

## Head Injuries

Head injuries are potentially the most serious type of injury you can sustain on a bike, and very high-impact head injuries can result in a concussion, a fractured skull, brain damage, or even death. However, they can often be prevented if the rider is wearing an effective helmet.

If you have injured your head in a bike accident, get medical attention immediately. Allow yourself plenty of rest, even for the most mild cases. A head injury can be serious if you experience headaches, dizziness, vomiting, memory loss, or collapse.

## Heat Stroke and Heat Exhaustion

Heat exhaustion, and the more serious heat stroke, result when the body becomes overheated and cannot cool itself fast enough. In cases of extreme heat and dehydration, a heat stroke can

## OUCH! DICTIONARY

Any sport with so many terms for crash has to be rough. In mountain biking and BMX, there is more than one way to skin a knee. The following terms define some of those ways:

*auger:* A headfirst crash into the ground.

*biff:* A crash or wipeout.

*cloon:* To smack into the ground, often causing a headache or dizziness.

*digger:* A headfirst crash into the ground.

*face plant:* A facefirst crash into the ground.

*involuntary dismount:* A sudden, unexpected crash that throws the rider off the bike.

*mud diving:* A crash that causes the rider to land in the mud.

*rag dolly:* A crash that propels the rider off the bike as if he or she were a rag doll.

*wash out:* To lose traction and skid while cornering.

*yard sale:* A crash that disperses a rider's equipment, such as water bottle, pump, and tool bag, all over the trail.

be fatal. To prevent becoming overheated while you ride, carry a large bottle of water (sports drinks are good as well), and drink frequently. Don't wait until you feel thirsty or dehydrated—drink at least every ten minutes in hot weather.

If you begin to develop cramps or feel weak, dizzy, or nauseous, get off your bike and lie down on cool (shaded) ground. Elevate your head, drink regularly, and remain lying down until the symptoms go away. If you feel flushed and have a headache, dry skin, and a high pulse rate, it could mean a more serious heat stroke. If possible, wet your body and have someone call for medical help.

# Bike Safety and Advocacy

The National Coalition for Bicycle Advocacy, which is run by the League of American Bicyclists, provides resources, training, government monitoring, support for new groups, and a networking database of bike advocacy organizations across the country. For more information on bike advocacy, call them at 800-288-BIKE.

## What You Can Do to Help Advocate Bike Safety

Ride as often as you can.

Know bike safety and riding techniques.

Find out about the laws and issues concerning bikes.

Contact legislators and work with government agencies to improve bike safety.

Attend meetings, organize events, and join groups that support bike safety.

Lend your financial support to advocacy groups.

Vote for legislators that support bike safety measures.

## Goals of Bicycle Advocates

Assert cyclists' rights to the roads.

Raise awareness of bike safety.

Improve bicycling facilities in all areas.

Promote safe bicycling for recreation and transportation.

Alert cyclists to discriminatory traffic laws.

Correct the misinformation and misconceptions about bike safety.

Organize a network of groups to promote bicyclists' concerns.

## Just Some of the Bicycle-related Issues That Need Advocates

Repeal mandatory sidepath laws.

Make bicycle parking available at transit stations, airports, and federal buildings.

Create bicycle accommodations on trains, buses, and other public transportation.

Enact stronger drunk driving laws and enforcement.

Improve bicycle accommodations on airplanes.

Improve bike access on all public roads, including highways.

Improve bike access to bridges and tunnels.

Address bike access concernsin the planning of new roads.

Create bike commuter facilities, such as changing rooms and showers, in government buildings.

Gain access to trails and create new trails in state and national parks.

### NICKNAMES OF FAMOUS CYCLISTS

|  |  |
| --- | --- |
| The Australian Bullet | Alf Goullet |
| The Badger | Bernard Hinault |
| Big Mig | Miguel Indurain |
| The Cannibal | Eddy Merckx |
| The Devil | Claudio Chiappucci |
| The Ebony Streak | Major Taylor |
| Le Normand (The Norman) | Jacques Anquetil |
| Pou Pou | Raymond Poulidor |
| The Professor | Laurent Fignon |
| The Rat | Joop Zoetemelk |
| Le Yankee Volant (The Flying Yankee) | Arthur August Zimmerman |
| Old Ironman | Reggie McNamara |

## References

"A Safety Handbook for Bicycle and Moped Owners." Revised 1995. Baltimore: Maryland Department of Transportation.

Chauner, David, and Michael Halstead. *Tour de France Complete Book of Cycling*. New York: Villard Books, 1990.

Drake, Geoff. "Do the Right Thing." *Bicycling Magazine*. February 1995.

Ford, Norman D. *Keep On Pedaling: The Complete Guide to Adult Bicycling*. Woodstock, Vt.: The Countryman Press, 1990.

Forester, John. *Effective Cycling*. 6th ed. Cambridge: MIT Press, 1993.

Matheny, Fred. Bicycling Magazine's *Complete Guide to Riding and Racing Techniques*. Emmaus, Penn.: Rodale Press, 1989.

Perry, David B. *Bike Cult*. New York: Four Walls Eight Windows, 1995.

Van der Plas, Rob. *The Bicycle Commuting Book*. San Francisco: Bicycle Books, 1989.

Van der Plas, Rob. *Bicycle Technology*. San Francisco: Bicycle Books, 1991.

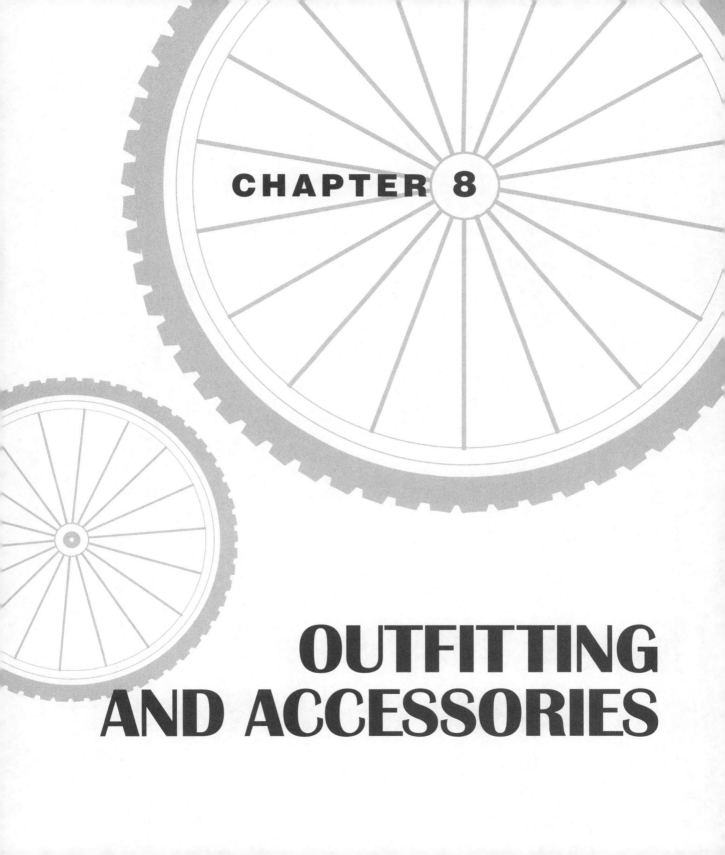

CHAPTER 8

# OUTFITTING
# AND ACCESSORIES

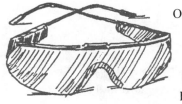

One of the best features of bicycles is that they're always ready to go. Just jump on and start pedaling. No need for gas, or oil, or even keys. But there are situations that can make riding difficult, inconvenient, or dangerous; and that's where accessories can help out. Bicycle accessories (which for our purposes include clothing in addition to equipment) help riders cycle more comfortably and safely.

Some accessories, such as special bike clothing, increase riders' comfort and potential performance. Other equipment, such as helmets and gloves, protect riders in case of accident. Still others are designed for special situations, to protect and provide comfort to riders in rain, wind, or cold weather.

How well equipped a rider will be depends largely on personal preference. Some cyclists, perhaps unwisely, use no equipment at all. Others want only the most important equipment, such as a helmet and a water bottle. Then there are those cyclists who buy enough gadgets to cover their bikes and who outfit themselves from head to toe with the latest biking fashions. Sure, it's possible to get by without most accessories. But with all the attractive, interesting, helpful equipment available to turn both bicycles and cyclists into efficient and technologically advanced creations, who can resist the temptation of a few well-chosen accessories?

Any large bike shop offers a dazzling array of bike wear and equipment to choose from. Smaller shops will have less of a selection but should sell most of the popular accessories. When you go shopping for accessories, avoid the temptation to buy too much right away. Aside from the most important equipment (helmet, water bottle), you may want to wait until you become more familiar with your bike and discover which accessories you really need and which will be a wasteof money.

In this chapter, we discuss common bicycle clothing and equipment. Remember that casual cyclists do not need as much equipment as more serious cyclists do. And some equipment is more useful to certain types of cyclists than to others. Someone who races, for instance, may not need panniers, while a mountain biker will get less use out of a windbreaker than a racer would. As you become more familiar with your biking needs, you will inevitably figure out what extra equipment would be most useful to you.

# Helmets and Caps

## Wear It!

While it's fairly uncommon for riders—particularly experienced riders—to fall off their bikes, it happens. As discussed in Chapter 7, there are hazards everywhere, and cyclists can't always depend on their riding skills to keep out of trouble. When a fall does occur, a helmet can literally make the difference between life and death. Statistics indicate that head injuries cause three-fourths of biking deaths, the vast majority of which could be avoided with a good helmet. Even a minor head injury can be devastating. That's why, in terms of safety, helmets are clearly the most important bicycle accessory you can have. They should be worn every time you get on your bike.

## Mandatory Helmet Laws

In some areas of the country, including parts of California, New York, Massachusetts, and the District of Columbia, bicycle helmets are to some degree mandatory. Unfortunately, specific laws often apply only to children or only on certain roads and trails, and these rules are substantially flawed. Often the laws aren't enforced; they discourage low-income riders who can't afford helmets; and they are not accompanied by the necessary education and awareness programs. While some cyclists strongly oppose helmet laws, any regulation aimed at saving lives is pointed in the right direction. Check with local authorities to determine whether mandatory helmet laws exist in your area or in areas where you might find yourself biking. Whether or not helmets are required by law, though, the principles of smart and safe riding require you to wear a helmet at all times.

## Materials and Standards

While helmets won't guarantee that you escape a head injury, they will certainly make serious accidents a lot less likely. Of course, it's important to buy a helmet that's strong enough to protect your head. Helmets with expanded polystyrene liners—the same material used for packaging and coolers—spread out the force of the impact and offer the best shock absorption. Another material, polypropylene, has been introduced in the last decade. Some helmets have a plastic or fiberglass shell (leather is less common) around the hard foam, while others make do with a fabric cover.

Fortunately, shoppers don't need to be physicists to determine which helmets offer adequate protection. Each helmet should have a performance standard sticker affixed to the inside of the helmet (and similar information on the box if the helmet is packaged). Three main organizations determine protective standards: ANSI, ASTM, and Snell.

*ANSI* stands for the American National Standards Institute, a well-known organization that develops standards for many products; the specific ANSI standard for bicycle helmets is known as ANSI Z90.4. Because ANSI standards were developed in 1984, they are no longer current and have been largely replaced by ASTM standards. ANSI and ASTM hope to provide a unified set of standards in the near future, but for now, because ANSI standards are well known (if a bit more lax), they remain in use.

*ASTM* is the American Society for Testing and Materials. The headgear standards committee (F-08) is made of representatives from helmet manufacturers, consumer advocates, researchers, and government personnel. The ASTM is fast becoming the more widely accepted standard. Another organization, the Safety Equipment Institute (SEI) certifies helmets that meet ASTM standards.

*Snell* is short for the Snell Memorial Foundation, a private group named for racecar driver Pete Snell, who died in a crash in the 1950s, before protective helmets had been developed. Snell's standards, which cover racecar, motorcycle, and bicycle helmets, are a bit more strict than the others. Because Snell charges the manufacturer for certification stickers, helmets with Snell approval tend to be slightly higher in price but also slightly better in quality.

A fourth standards system, devised by the government agency the Consumer Product Safety Commission (CPSC), is expected to be issued in the very near future. Most likely, these new standards will supersede the others and become the most widely accepted in the helmet industry.

All helmets on the market—certainly any you would find for sale in a reputable bike shop—should satisfy one of the accepted standards. If you happen to come across a helmet that doesn't meet safety standards, drop it immediately. Don't even consider buying it, no matter what the price. Chances are it will not provide adequate protection.

## Find a Comfortable Fit

While it's important that helmets are sufficiently strong, helmets also need to be comfortable. They should have soft padding inside in addition to the hard polystyrene protection on the outside. Try on a number of different styles and sizes until you find one that fits just right. If you can't find a comfortable helmet in one bike shop, go to others. Even if it means trying on dozens of helmets in a handful of stores, don't settle for one you're not completely sure about. Helmets that don't fit or irritate your head can become a major distraction and annoyance while riding—you may even be discouraged from wearing it.

A helmet that fits properly sits squarely and snugly, and covers the entire top of your head and upper forehead. Be sure to fasten it securely so it won't move or fall off under any circumstances. The helmet should have an adjustable chin strap made of a strong, comfortable material such as nylon with plastic buckles. Wash the straps occasionally to clean them of any dried sweat that can irritate the skin.

Never buy children's helmets in a larger size than necessary. It's just as important that helmets fit perfectly on kids. To avoid having to buy growing children a new helmet each year, buy a brand of helmet that comes with a few pads of varying thickness and use them to get the best fit as your child grows.

Fit is not the only consideration when looking for a comfortable helmet. A helmet should also be well ventilated to keep your head cool, using vents located just above the forehead to allow air to circulate. Many helmets can become almost unbearable on hot and windless days when you are climbing hills. Look for one that won't cause you to sweat excessively—some have pads that double as sweatbands—though how hot a helmet will make you can be hard to determine at first. If, while riding, you find you absolutely must take off your helmet, do so at your own risk and be sure to put it back on as soon as you cool down.

Comfortable helmets are also safe helmets. If they're too loose, they could slide around and block your vision, they may not protect you completely, or they may even fall off. If they're too tight, they could cause terrible headaches that would make riding dangerous and very unpleasant.

## Other Considerations

Beyond the major considerations of strength and comfort, some riders want helmets that won't slow them down. As helmet designs get more expensive, you'll find manufacturers pay more attention to aerodynamic design and light weight. Helmets without plastic shells will be slightly lighter, though they may not protect your head as well. Lighter helmets will also be more comfortable.

Some helmets come with visors to shield eyes from the sun. If your helmet has a visor, make sure it is shatterproof so that you don't cut your face if you have an accident.

And of course, there is some room for fashion. Helmets come in many colors and patterns. While looks shouldn't be your primary concern, you may be more likely to wear an attractive helmet. For children, attractive designs and pictures on helmets are more likely to encourage wear. In addition, bright colors and reflective surfaces are more noticeable to motorists and other cyclists.

Because helmet foam crushes on impact, helmets should be replaced each time they have been involved in an accident. A good helmet can set you back anywhere from $20 to $120. Some discount stores will sell helmets that meet minimum standards for as little as $10. But as anyone who's ever survived a bike accident will tell you, no matter what you pay it's money well spent.

For more information on helmet safety, contact the Bicycle Helmet Safety Institute (4611 7th St. South, Arlington, VA 22204; telephone: 703-486-0100; e-mail: helmets@bhsi.org; Web: www.bhsi. org).

## Caps and Masks

Cycling caps are familiar to most people through watching long distance races like the Tour de France. Racers, who are less likely to wear helmets because of their concerns about weight and aerodynamics, wear caps with cardboard or plastic brims to shield their eyes from the sun, to soak up sweat, and to protect them from sunburn. Caps are often decorated with the names of bicycle companies or races, and they can become something of a fashion statement. However, caps provide absolutely no protection in case of falls. Riders who wear caps are probably not wearing helmets—and that, of course, can be deadly.

Masks are typically used by riders in places with high levels of air pollution, such as cities or industrial areas. The masks filter out particles and contaminants such as dust, pollen, or carbon monoxide from cars. While any air-filter mask will work, you should be able to find one that is specifically designed for biking. These are lightweight, fasten securely over the mouth and nose, and stay put in the wind. Check larger bike stores—especially in big cities—for effective biking masks.

# Eyewear

Riding in the wind at high speeds, as many cyclists do, can put eyes in the path of all sorts of potentially harmful material: dirt, dust, sand, small pieces of gravel and glass, pollution, rain, mud, pollen, bugs, even the force of the wind itself. While a small particle is unlikely to cause serious damage to your eyes, it can very easily disrupt your sight, cause tearing, cause dry eyes, or otherwise distract you from the road long enough to put you in jeopardy. Though not absolutely necessary when riding at low speeds, glasses or goggles are often important to protect faster cyclists' eyes from any flying object that may cross their paths.

Continued exposure to wind in the eyes can also cause a condition called *pterygium*. Goggles that completely enclose the eyes prevent pterygium, while glasses—particularly wrap-around glasses—can help as well. Sunglasses, of course, are helpful in protecting the eyes not only from particles but also from the blinding rays of the sun, which can be just as dangerous if road visibility is lost.

Cyclists who normally wear eyeglasses can continue to wear them while riding, though they may want to get a pair of rugged sports frames. Those who normally wear contact lenses may wear goggles or opt for glasses instead. Some contact lens wearers prefer goggles because contact lenses allow better peripheral and low-light vision. Riders who don't need to wear glasses to improve their vision should get clear, nonprescription glasses simply for protection. For rough off-road riding or to be extra cautious on the road, glasses (as well as goggles) should have adjustable head straps. Tight-fitting elastic head straps keep eyewear in place, while loose straps that drape around the neck prevent the eyewear from falling onto the ground if it slips off the rider's nose.

Any eyewear you buy especially for cycling should be shatterproof and scratch resistant (and ANSI approved). It should have filtered lenses and provide proper protection from ultraviolet rays. Serious riders will look for eyewear that is lightweight and aerodynamic.

# Gloves

Gloves serve three purposes for cyclists' hands: shock absorption, protection, and warmth. Warmth being the least pressing concern, most biking gloves are fingerless, cut off just below the middle knuckles to allow hand dexterity (full gloves and mittens are available for cold weather biking). Strong materials protect hands in case of falls. A padded fabric or gel lining in the palm provides shock absorption on bumpy rides that could otherwise cause muscle cramps, chafing, or numbness. Shock absorption is especially important for mountain bikers, who endure harsh terrain, and for riders of bikes with drop handlebars, who put a lot of body weight on their hands.

Most gloves are made of a durable, synthetic fabric such as Lycra, Neoprene, or Gore-Tex, though a pair with leather palms will be most comfortable. Velcro wristbands keep gloves on securely. To keep hands cool, some gloves are meshed on top for ventilation. Gloves should fit snugly but be flexible enough to allow your hands free movement. They should hold firmly to handlebar tape or rubber, which itself should be padded to decrease the effects of riding on rough surfaces. Gloves with reflective designs are particularly useful for night riding because they allow drivers and other riders to better see your hand signals. Most adequate cycling gloves cost less than $20, though the finest brands can cost more.

# Other Protective Gear

Equipped with helmets, goggles, and gloves, most casual cyclists are reasonably well protected. However, for some cycle sports such as BMX racing, mountain biking, and freestyling, additional protection is necessary. Foam padding and leather reinforcements should cover the elbows, shoulders, knees, and hips. BMXers also must wear a mouth guard and have padding on the stem, handlebars, and top tube of their bike.

# Clothing

People ride bicycles dressed in all sorts of clothing, from business suits or dresses to full racing apparel. Any type of clothing is fine as long as the rider is comfortable and the clothes don't restrict the rider's ability to pedal, turn, and brake effectively. Clothes that are unsuitable can cause rashes, soreness, overheating, and all sorts of other discomforts. For cyclists who find it practical and affordable, special bike clothing is much better for riding than anything else they might find hanging in their closets.

What makes bike apparel so well suited for cycling? Many things: comfort, durability, performance, safety, aerodynamics. Everyday clothing tends to be loose; bike clothes, though, are more tight fitting and aerodynamic. Street clothes are heavier than bike clothes, so they weigh you down and make you hot. And while everyday clothes may not stand out in traffic, the bright, vibrant colors of most bike wear make you more visible and safer on the road.

Admittedly, bike wear is not always practical, particularly for riders who use their bike for commuting or other transportation purposes and don't have access to a changing room or shower. Such riders should compare the benefits of wearing bike clothes with the hassles and determine whether or not special outfitting is worthwhile. If their ride is short and easy, special clothing may not be necessary.

Though cotton and wool were originally the choice fabrics for cyclists, a wide array of synthetic fibers such as spandex, polypropylene, Kevlar, and CoolMax are used in biking clothes today. These fabrics wick perspiration away from the body without absorbing it. Some, such as Kevlar, are strong and provide protection from road rash, while others are designed more for comfort and easily tear if scraped on the ground. Nylon, Lycra, or a Lycra-cotton blend, are the most commonly used materials, and all are quite effective in hot weather. Materials should be comfortable and strong, suitable to the climate, and capable of protecting riders from the wind and rain. They should also be easy to wash and dry; but be careful because synthetic materials are prone to shrink a lot in a clothes dryer.

While function usually comes before fashion in cycling clothes, there's room for a little style as well. Not surprisingly, most bikewear designs have their root in racing outfits. While some bike clothes make you stand out in a crowd, others are quite tasteful, fashionable even. Like most clothes, you can choose high-priced designer brands or the more economical clothing lines. The higher price of some clothes is not necessarily indicative of higher quality, so don't feel you need to spend a fortune to be properly outfitted for cycling.

## Shorts

Because so much of your body's movement and energy on a bike comes from the legs, good biking shorts are extremely useful. They tend to be tight (but not constraining) for aerodynamics and flexible for maximum freedom of movement. They should also be soft for comfort. Causal bike shorts that resemble running shorts fit more loosely than racing shorts and are popular with mountain bikers and tourists. All shorts should have a waist high enough to cover your lower back and have legs long enough to cover your thighs to protect them from sunburn and chafing. Typically, they have an elastic waist that allows them to stay up without a belt, though some use suspenders (or have an attached bib) to avoid the constraints of tight elastic. Most bike shorts are padded with suede, chamois, synthetic fleece, foam, or gel and have a double layer of fabric in the seat (and sometimes in the hips) for extra comfort.

For practical reasons, you may want bike shorts with pockets to hold keys, identification, or money. Avoid carrying too much when riding, though, or you risk having your possessions strewn across the road. For even more practical reasons, you'll want shorts that can withstand frequent washing and quick drying. They'll need to have strong seams and be made of an appropriate fabric. Leather crotch pads, for instance, can be quite comfortable but won't dry as quickly as synthetics.

Of all bike wear, the familiar black bike shorts are the most useful and practical. Their popularity in recent years has extended way past cycling and now they're common sportswear used for a variety of purposes.

Bike shorts are typically worn directly over bare skin or over seamless underwear. Try on a number of pairs to make sure the shorts you buy are as comfortable as possible. Buy a few pairs if you plan to ride regularly because they'll probably need to be washed after each use. Expect to spend between $20 and $65 a pair.

## Shirts

Bike jerseys are made of a thin, cool, silky fabric such as Lycra or polyester, or heavier materials such as Thermax for cooler climates. They fit more tightly around the waist and are longer in back than most shirts. Bike shirts should not, though, be too tight or else they will constrict your movement—particularly if you're riding on drop handlebars. Most are short-sleeve with pockets sewn in back; long-sleeve jerseys are available for cooler weather and ventilated mesh designs are best for hot days. Many shirts also have a high, zip-up collar to protect the neck.

Some riders stick with comfortable old cotton (or cotton/polyester) T-shirts. These are thin and lightweight but can easily become heavy and clammy if you perspire, and they probably won't fit your body as well as a bike jersey. In most situations, though, T-shirts are suitable and convenient for cycling. Some cyclists wear a thin polypropylene T-shirt under their jerseys for extra protection against road rash (avoid cotton in this situation). If they fall, the two layers of clothing will rub against each other and lessen the friction on the body.

When shopping for bike jerseys, look for shirts with a strong construction in the fabric as well as in the zippers and buttons (plastic zippers and buttons are lighter and less irritating than metal ones). There should also be three back pockets to use for holding water bottles, wind jackets, snacks, or other objects you may need to reach easily without having to stop the bike. And, as always, get a jersey with bright colors—yellows and oranges may be tacky at a dinner party, but when you're sharing the road with cars and trucks, they're exactly the colors you want on your back. Depending on the brand and the quality of the jersey, each one should cost you between $25 and $75.

### Underwear

While certain bike clothes are designed to be worn without underwear, many riders prefer some sort of undergarment for added comfort, protection, warmth, or simply out of habit. Briefs or panties can be worn, though they may irritate the skin if they are cotton and have large seams. For extra support, women can wear a wireless sports bra made of Lycra or a cotton/synthetic blend. Men need not wear a jock strap, as most bike saddles provide enough support. Extra layers of underwear, including thermals, are great in cold weather.

# Shoes and Socks

Since bicycle locomotion begins with the feet, shoes can make a huge difference in a cyclist's performance. While almost any shoes (except dress shoes with completely smooth soles) will be adequate for biking, it's amazing how much more power and comfort can be attained with specially designed bike shoes. Even all-purpose athletic shoes cannot provide enough support and traction to make them truly efficient for cycling.

Stiff soles that won't bend are the key to maximizing a bike shoe's impact. They provide a strong and large base of force against the pedals and also alleviate pressure on the feet to help prevent the numb, burning sensation often felt on long rides. Thin metal or strong plastic plates stiffen the soles. The upper portion of the shoe, meanwhile, should be comfortable, lightweight, and durable. Leather, mesh, or a combination of the two works well, though a waterproof or quick-drying synthetic material such as nylon is better in case of rain.

Many bike shoes are cleated or grooved near the ball of the foot. This prevents the feet from sliding off the pedals and aligns the foot properly on the pedal to avoid knee problems. For riders using toe clips, bike shoes often have a narrow, hard toe design. There are also special shoes made to wear with clipless pedals that have clamps on the soles similar to ski bindings. These attach to a certain style of clipless pedal (the shoes and the pedals must be compatible) and offer a more comfortable, more responsive, and lighter alternative to toe clips, which some riders find restricting.

Clipless pedals and shoes are great for racers, mountain bikers, and long distance riders, but be warned—they're tricky to get used to. Make sure you practice attaching and releasing the shoes from the pedals many times before venturing out on the road. Fortunately, the latest clipless designs offer great ease of attachment, minimizing the hazards. Be aware that many bike shoes are not made for walking. If you plan to get off your bike—whether you're commuting to work or sightseeing—cleated and clipless pedal shoes are not for you (unless, of course, you don't mind bringing a pair of walking shoes along with you).

Look for shoes that fit snugly so your feet don't slide around inside, but allow enough space so you can wear thick socks in cold weather (bring appropriate socks with you when shoe shopping). Perfect fit is crucial, so try many pairs—even give them a test ride if a bicycle is available—until you find one that's just right. Keep in mind that leather stretches and molds to your feet with wear, but synthetics don't. If you want biking shoes that also allow some degree of walking comfort, get shoes with soles that are sufficiently stiff but give a little as well. Laced bindings are common, though Velcro allows quicker adjustment and fastening. Bike shoes are available in all sizes and a variety of styles, and typically cost anywhere from $35 to $120. The best place to find bike shoes is at bike shops, though large athletic shoe stores may carry some basic designs.

Socks should be made of wool or a synthetic such as nylon or Lycra to provide comfort and absorb perspiration. Riders in street clothes may want to tuck pants legs into socks to protect them from the bike chain. They should get socks that extend at least an inch above the ankle (higher socks keep the feet warmer). White socks are required of racers and recommended for all cyclists because fabric dyes can irritate or infect blisters.

# Cold Weather Wear

One of the great benefits of cycling as a sport and exercise is that the speed of the bicycle creates a natural air conditioning that helps keep the body cool in warm weather. In cold weather, however, a nice breeze blowing across your body as you ride can be positively chilling. A thirty-five degree day can feel more like ten degrees as your bike speed increases to fifteen or twenty miles per hour. In order to avoid discomfort and stiffness—or worse, hypothermia and frost bite—make sure you are appropriately dressed for riding in cold weather. Don't simply rely on the rise in your body temperature while riding to warm you. It's always best to overdress—you can remove layers later as you feel necessary.

If you plan to ride throughout the winter, it's a good idea to invest in specially made cold weather biking clothes. If you ride only occasionally off-season, you can probably get by wearing well-made ski clothing such as gloves, jackets, and goggles. Because skiers face the same weather problems (cold, downhill wind) as cyclists, a lot of the apparel is designed to accommodate either sport.

## Headwear and Eyewear

Because so much body heat escapes through the head, it's most important to keep this area well covered. However, what you wear on your head for warmth must not get in the way of your helmet or make protective gear any less stable. A thin balaclava that covers the entire head, ears, neck, and face (with necessary holes for seeing and breathing) is best. Made of a warm synthetic fabric such as polypropylene, it is inexpensive and small enough to fold into a pocket when not in use. Otherwise, use a hat that fits under your helmet, or at least a headband to cover your ears. A special winter helmet without as much ventilation is recommended as well.

Good bike goggles or sports glasses keep cold air out of the eyes, and they could be worn year-round as well. In very cold weather, a face mask may be necessary.

## Gloves

You should wear bike gloves every time you ride. As the weather gets colder, it's best to wear gloves that completely cover your hands instead of the fingerless kind. Thin polypropylene glove liners add extra warmth in lower temperatures. When it gets below freezing, gloves often aren't warm enough. Instead, wear some form of mitten or three-finger lobster glove that keeps fingers together for warmth. If you're in doubt about which kind of glove is sufficient to keep your hands warm, bring along more than one pair. That way, as your hands warm up and begin to sweat, you can switch to a lighter pair.

## Lower-body

In cold weather, the leg muscles and tendons responsible for pedaling are more susceptible to cramps and tendinitis. Long pants made out of the same tight-fitting, stretchy material as bike shorts are available. Good pants keep you warm in cold weather but do not overheat your body during a hard workout. Be sure your lower back is well insulated to avoid stiffness and soreness; either wear bib-pants or tuck your shirt and sweater into your pants. Extra material in the knees is often useful to keep your joints warm. Pants with stirrups keep them from riding up and exposing the lower legs.

In particularly low temperatures, wear tights with a fleece lining. Wool or polypropylene leg warmers, instead of or in addition to tights, will help as well. Leg warmers should have stirrups, stretch up to the thighs, and be snug enough to stay put while you ride.

## Upper-body

Because you want to be neither too cold to ride nor so hot that you sweat profusely, the key is to have many thin layers that can be added or removed as needed. The bottom layer is most crucial. A close-fitting, breathable undershirt, made of a material such as polypropylene, removes perspiration from the body without itself becoming soggy. Outer layers can include a long-sleeve jersey, a turtleneck sweater, a fleece jacket, and a waterproof windbreaker—the most you should ever need to keep you comfortable in cold weather.

Wool is great for warmth but can be itchy, while synthetics work well to insulate and block wind. All clothing should be easy to put on and take off while riding, with conveniently located zippers or Velcro fasteners. If you are going to add and remove layers, make sure you have somewhere to store everything. There's nothing more chilling (and potentially dangerous) than working up a sweat while climbing a hill only to be hit with frigid air as you begin your descent. Whenever possible, bring an extra set of clothes (at least inner layers) in case they become wet with perspiration.

### Footwear

To keep feet warm, wear thick wool or Neoprene socks under your shoes and fleece-lined booties or shoe covers over them. Booties should be made of lightweight synthetic material (such as nylon, Gore-Tex, or Neoprene—some have a fleece lining as well) that can withstand water and block wind and should fit snugly up to the ankle. Toeclip covers (also called *toe warmers*) are available as well.

If you ride a bicycle regularly, it's simply impractical to let rain keep you off the road. Cyclists who ride in the rain are bound to get wet to some degree on the outside, no matter what precautions they take. But with the proper rain clothing, it's quite easy to stay relatively dry no matter how torrential the downpour seems.

# Rainwear

Rainwear needs to be water-resistant. While your winter gear should already be water-resistant—because cold and wet tend to go together—you should also have some lightweight rain clothes to protect you from summer showers. The difficulty is in finding raingear that keeps you dry without making you overly hot. Fully waterproof materials, such as plastic laminated nylon and PVC rubber, keep wetness from getting in but also block wetness (perspiration) from getting out. Clothes made of these materials will have you sweating in no time.

However, synthetic linings, such as Gore-Tex and Ultrex, that are fused to nylon have tiny pores that allow perspiration to escape while keeping rain out. While not perfect, they're by far the most comfortable and effective water-resistant materials available. They'll also cost you a lot more than other rainwear. No matter how breathable the material, rain clothes should have some sort of extra ventilation.

Rain jackets should be tight enough so that they won't cause unnecessary wind resistance, but they should allow room in the hood to cover your helmet (be careful of large hoods that limit peripheral vision, though). Underarm vents allow your body to breathe while keeping water out. Get a jacket that can roll up small enough to fit in a jersey pocket because you'll probably want to take it on long rides even when you're not sure you'll use it.

## FABRICES FOR ALL SEASONS—THE LATEST IN HIGH-TECH MATERIALS FOR BIKE CLOTHES

 So many kinds of material are available to bicycle clothing manufacturers. Knowing the characteristics of each fabric can help you decide which clothing to buy for your riding style.

| | |
|---|---|
| *Amara* | Soft, leather-like polyester material commonly found in gloves. |
| *CoolMax* | Polyester fiber that wicks perspiration off the body without becoming damp. |
| *Fieldsensor* | Porous polyester fiber designed to move perspiration away from the body and toward the surface of the fabric for fast evaporation. |
| *Gore-Tex* | The ultimate in waterproof clothing, it lets moisture (perspiration) out, but won't allow moisture (rain) in. |
| *Intera* | Not a fabric itself, but a fabric treatment for other synthetic fibers. When applied, clothes clean easier and retain less odor. |
| *Lycra* | Stretchable spandex material commonly used in bike shorts and tights. |
| *Micromesh* | All-around good fabric for warm and wet weather. |
| *Neoprene* | Strong, stretchable synthetic fiber that provides warmth, but less breathability. |
| *Polartec Bipolar* | Fabric that absorbs perspiration. |
| *polypropylene* | Good insulating fabric that also dries quickly; can be used in cool weather. |
| *Scotchlite* | Reflective material commonly applied to other fabrics on bike clothes to improve the rider's visibility at night. |
| *Thinsulate* | Water-resistant part-polyester material with excellent insulation properties; great for winter riding. |

Source: "Defining Performance: High-Tech Fabric Guide," *Bicycle Dealers Showcase*, April 1996. p. 35.

Rain pants need to be snug and should have vents as well. They should allow enough room, though, for you to bend comfortably when riding on your drop handlebars. Capes are available also, and while these don't have ventilation problems, they don't fare well in the wind. Some capes come with spats, which lay over your legs and feet while you pedal. Gore-Tex or Neoprene shoe covers are also available to keep feet dry. Or, you could simply tie plastic bags around your shoes—they're certainly no fashion statement, but as raingear goes, they're about as inexpensive and effective as it gets.

Because visibility is lower in the rain, it's even more important that rainwear be brightly colored or have reflective surfaces. And keep in mind, when the weather is warm enough and not too windy—and you're not headed anywhere special—encountering light showers while riding is really no big deal. If you do get caught without the appropriate clothing, a little rain never hurt anybody.

# Windbreakers

Between your cold weather clothes and your raingear, you'll probably have an adequate windbreaker for any temperature. There's no sense in getting an additional nylon windbreaker when most rain jackets can serve both purposes. Recognize, though, that much of the chill you experience when riding is due more to wind than to temperature. Proper wind protection goes hand in hand with other specialty gear.

# Accessories

While some bike accessories are wholeheartedly recommended for any cyclist, not all of them are really necessary. Your need for a lot of equipment will depend on the kind of riding you do and how serious you are about it. To avoid weighing your bike down (and draining your wallet) unnecessarily, get just what you need and leave the rest on the bike store racks.

### Water Bottles

Water bottles are inexpensive, easy to find, and easy to use—and they're one of the most important pieces of equipment you carry on your bike. If you use a bike for short trips, a water bottle may not be crucial, though it certainly can't hurt. If not used for drinking, the water in a water bottle can be used to wash hands and bikes after a repair or to ward off dogs. If not used for storing water, containers can be used for holding food, pills, even a spare battery for your light. For long trips and hard workouts, though, don't start riding without a bottle filled with cold water.

Water bottles come in many designs and colors, pick whichever kind strikes your fancy. The main consideration when buying a water bottle is that it fit securely into the bottle cage on your bike (if you don't have one, get one installed). It should be made of an odorless, tasteless plastic and have an easy-to-use spout. The best spouts allow you to use the water bottle as a spray as well as for drinking.

Plastic bottles tend to crack easily, so you should buy a few at a time and replace them often. They won't cost more than a dollar or two—some shops even throw them in for free when you buy other, more expensive equipment.

## Racks, Baskets, and Bags

While long-distance tourists need large panniers (see Chapter 12) to carry all their gear, other riders can get away with, at most, a rack, a basket, or a small bag to carry what they need while cycling.

Racks are typically attached to the bike above the rear wheel, though some can be installed up front. Steel racks are strongest, though aluminum offers the best balance between strength and light weight. Make sure racks are firmly attached to the bike—either brazed on the seat stay or bolted into the wheel hub—because they may be required to support a good deal of weight. Racks must also hold loads firmly in place because shifting weight can throw a rider off balance. If a rack is not already attached to your bike, make sure you buy one that fits the design of your bike. For optimal weight distribution and handling, rear racks should carry the load as far forward as possible without blocking the seat and pedals, while front racks should be low. The load should be balanced equally on both sides (and if possible, from front to back as well), with heavier items stored lower.

## Computers

The simplest bicycle computer is basically a battery-operated electronic speedometer or odometer. Other computers do a lot more, including act as a stopwatch, regulate your workout routine, and tell you your heart rate. They generally attach to the handlebars and have sensors on the fork and front spokes for collecting data (if you use a stationary training stand, you'll need to attach the sensors to the rear wheel instead). Some computers require complex wiring, while more advanced models are wireless.

Closely follow all directions for how to install and calibrate your computer. After you install it, it's a good idea to secure any loose wires to the back of the fork and along the front brake cable with strong transparent tape so that they don't get caught on anything as you ride.

As computer quality, memory, and function increase, so do price and weight. Often, simpler is better. Decide what you need in a bike computer before buying and don't allow yourself to get carried away by a lot of functions that you don't really need. Even low-end models can be expensive to replace, so be sure you get one that's waterproof (or else cover it immediately when rain starts) and take it with you whenever you leave your bike unattended.

### References

Chauner, David, and Michael Halstead. *Tour de France Complete Book of Cycling.* New York: Villard Books, 1990.

Ford, Norman D. *Keep On Pedaling: The Complete Guide to Adult Bicycling.* Woodstock, Vt.: The Countryman Press, 1990.

LeMond, Greg, and Kent Gordis. *Greg LeMond's Complete Book of Bicycling.* New York: G. P. Putnam's Sons, 1990.

Matheny, Fred. Bicycling Magazine's *Complete Guide to Riding and Racing Techniques.* Emmaus, Penn.: Rodale Press, 1989.

Nye, Peter. *The Cyclist's Sourcebook.* New York: Perigee Books, 1991.

Perry, David B. *Bike Cult.* New York: Four Walls Eight Windows, 1995.

Van der Plas, Rob. *The Bicycle Commuting Book.* San Francisco: Bicycle Books, 1989.

Van der Plas, Rob. *Bicycle Technology.* San Francisco: Bicycle Books, 1991.

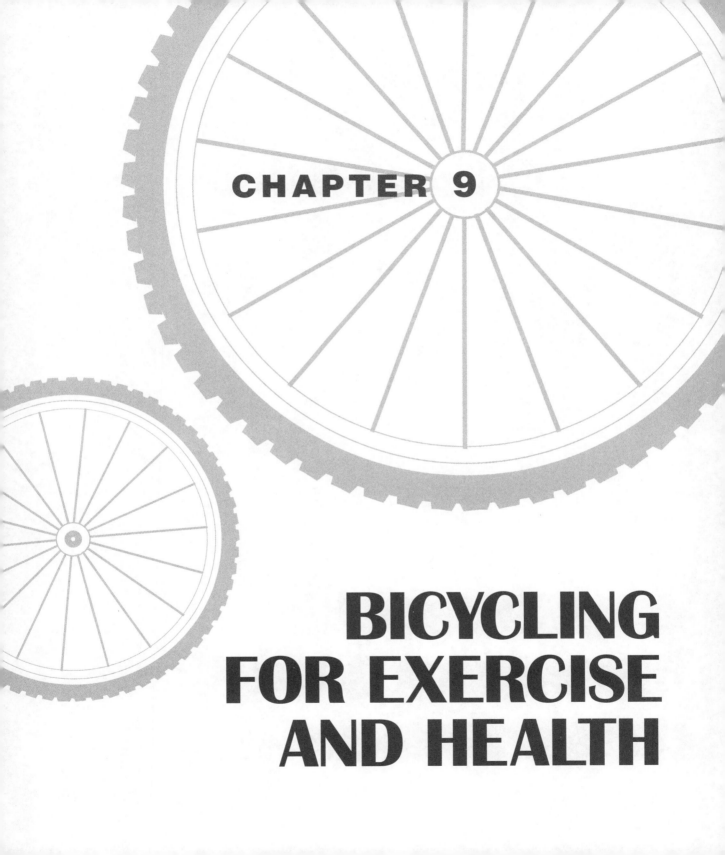

# CHAPTER 9

# BICYCLING FOR EXERCISE AND HEALTH

FOR THOSE OF US WHO THINK OF EXERCISE AS A NECESSARY EVIL IN OUR LIVES, it's amazing to find an activity that's great for the body and actually fun as well. One reason it's so easy to gain health benefits from cycling is that riding is a pleasure; there's none of that dread and boredom many people face when spending hours in the gym bobbing up and down on a stair climber or scurrying like a lab rat on a treadmill.

# Health Benefits of Biking

Like other activities that raise your heart rate and increase your body's oxygen consumption (such as jogging and calisthenics), bicycling is an aerobic exercise. Aerobic exercise serves a number of functions. It strengthens your heart and circulatory system, which pumps oxygen and other nutrients in your blood through your body. It helps you burn calories, causing you to lose weight. And when done regularly, aerobic exercise increases your energy level and lowers your blood pressure; it also makes you less tired during the day and allows you to sleep better at night. Because repeated exercise lowers your risk of heart disease, heart attack, stroke, even cancer—and keeps your body in top working order—aerobic activity such as bicycling, in effect, makes you live longer.

### All-Around Health

While any sort of aerobic exercise is good for you (if it's done safely and sensibly), cycling is particularly well suited for all-around health. When riding the right size bike with correct form, pedaling is smooth and rhythmic and is less stressful on the legs than jogging—which can damage the knees, legs, and feet. You're also less likely to pull or twist a muscle on a bike than you would in a sport that requires jumping, quick turning, or sudden stopping, such as basketball or tennis. With the exception of swimming, bicycling is the exercise that puts the least amount of stress on the joints of the body.

Biking provides a better cardiovascular workout than many other exercises and sports. It's great for burning fat (that's why stationary bikes are so popular in health clubs) and helps speed up your metabolism to make the most of the food you eat. Also, cycling keeps muscles toned and bones strong—not just in the legs, where most of the work happens, but in the arms, back, shoulders, and buttocks as well. A well-balanced muscular development will make you healthier, stronger, and probably better looking!

## Flexibility and Adaptability

Biking is adaptable to any level of fitness. If you don't think you can handle the rigorous paces and steep hill climbs of advanced riders, you can simply ride slower and on flat surfaces. As you steadily increase your fitness level you can adapt your riding routine to keep your body challenged.

Cycling for fitness doesn't take long, either. With as little as a half-hour a day yo u can get in shape. Here again, time spent is variable. You can increase or decrease the length of your rides as necessary and still get a good workout. And if the level at which you ride and your style of riding is safe, you're never too old for bicycling. Where many activities can become harmful or risky for older people, bicycling is always practicable. In fact, because of cycling's health benefits, the more you ride the more able you'll be to continue riding as you get older. With a doctor's approval, it's not unimaginable that cyclists can keep going well into their seventies and eighties. From a medical standpoint, the more you ride the younger you get!

# Mental Fitness

As an exercise, cycling is good for all parts of your body, from the bottoms of your feet all the way up to your head. Just as a good workout strengthens muscle and improves the flow of blood and oxygen, it also stimulates the most complex organ of them all, the brain. The increase of blood and oxygen to the brain helps keep the mind well nourished. The mind benefits from biking in many other ways as well.

## A Natural Drug

Bike riding, like other vigorous exercise, causes your brain to release endorphins, a natural protein produced by your body that acts as a painkiller and relaxer. Endorphins released during cycling create a feeling of well-being that is commonly referred to as a "natural high." You feel lifted up, less depressed, and less stressed.

## Boosted Self-Esteem

Getting a good workout and meeting the challenges you set for yourself give you a sense of achievement and confidence that can spread into all areas of your life. Because you feel more in control of your body, you'll feel more in control of your life, and more in tune with the world around you. With boosted self-esteem you'll feel able to take on anything that might come your way.

## An Escape

Bicycling provides a much-needed escape from the daily grind. While some exercise is best done indoors, biking gives you a great opportunity to be outside and to take in the beautiful, tranquil landscape. You get a real sense of exhilaration and freedom when you ride through the wind down a country (or even city) road. If you ride with others, cycling is a terrific way to enjoy social interaction and camaraderie. If you ride alone you have a perfect chance to get lost in thought (not too lost, though, or riding could be unsafe) or to wind down from a noisy, hectic day. Concentrating on your form or on the motion of —the pedals can serve much the same purpose as meditation: it focuses your thoughts and relaxes your mind. Riding can meet many needs; a ride can help you forget dilemmas or it can help you see things more clearly.

## A Stress Reducer

When entered into with the right attitude, a regular cycling routine can be effective in reducing stress. The key is not to let the biking itself become stressful. Don't be too obsessed with regimen—don't pressure yourself to ride a certain amount every day, especially on a day when you feel you can't handle the schedule. Also don't ride in congested, noisy areas that can make riding unpleasant. While city cyclists have much lower stress levels than motorists (because they don't get stuck in traffic), they can still suffer from the effects of noise pollution and of the aggravation of daredevil drivers.

## Mind Power in Cycling

While cycling's benefits to the mind are easy to grasp, a little understanding of how the mind and body interact can lead to increased performance for riders. Serious cyclists, particularly racers, use a variety of mental exercises to further enhance the psychological benefits of bike riding. Meditation techniques can help focus the mind on the body, and the use of repeated motivational mantras can help psyche up cyclists. Many racers practice visualization, a technique in which they sit calmly before a race and imagine the day going perfectly and without any stress. The old idea of mind over matter holds true in the world of cycling.

# Weight Loss

If you're looking to lose weight, there are few activities more suitable than bicycling. Biking—particularly sustained rides that challenge your body—burns a tremendous number of calories, which, when combined with a healthy diet, leads to weight loss. Because cyclists can adjust their workout to match their physical capabilities, a rider at any level can take advantage of biking's health benefits.

However, don't expect miracles. As for any exercise, weight loss will only come through cycling if you stick with it and properly challenge your body. Don't be discouraged if you don't shed any pounds after your first time out. If you develop new muscles, you may actually gain weight in the beginning. But if you keep up your riding, over the course of a few months, you will see effective weight loss.

## Calories Burned while Cycling

Indirectly, calories are a measure of the amount of energy foods provide. While the body needs about 2500 calories per day to operate efficiently (about 1500 for inactive people, and up to 4500 for training athletes), taking in more calories than the body needs will lead to an increase in fat stored in the body. Every 3500 or so excess calories can translate to an extra pound in body weight. To lose weight, people either need to eat less, burn more calories, or better yet—do both.

Table 9–1 gives the approximate number of calories burned per hour by a cyclist of a specified weight riding at a specified average speed. Because so many variables come into play—the weight and efficiency of the bicycle; the slope and surface quality of the ground; heat and wind resistance; the form, fitness, and metabolism of the rider—it's impossible to measure precisely calories burned while riding. There may be a huge variation in the calories burned by two riders of equal weight going at the same speed if other factors come into play. Think of the numbers given merely as a general guide.

By dividing the number of calories burned per hour in half or into thirds, it's easy to see that even a thirty- or twenty-minute bike ride can burn a good number of calories. When combined with a healthy diet, calories burned while biking can add up over time to significant weight loss.

When it comes to biking for weight loss, all the lightweight and aerodynamic bike parts so prized by some cyclists actually become a disadvantage. The heavier the bike, the greater the wind resistance and the harder it is to pedal, therefore, the more calories burned.

## Metabolism

Some new riders who hope biking will help them lose weight also worry that increased physical activity will improve their appetite so much that they'll gain back all the calories they lose biking. While it's true that people who are in shape and who exercise regularly eat more than sedentary people, there are a few reasons why eating more doesn't lead to weight gain for physically fit cyclists. First, as people burn more calories cycling, their

## TABLE 9–1:
### Calories per hour burned based on weight and cycling speed

| Weight (lbs.) | 8 mph | 10 mph | 12 mph | 14 mph | 16 mph | 18 mph | 20 mph | 25 mph |
|---|---|---|---|---|---|---|---|---|
| 100 | 175 | 215 | 255 | 305 | 370 | 445 | 535 | 845 |
| 120 | 215 | 255 | 305 | 370 | 445 | 535 | 640 | 1015 |
| 140 | 250 | 300 | 360 | 430 | 515 | 620 | 750 | 1185 |
| 160 | 285 | 340 | 410 | 490 | 590 | 710 | 855 | 1355 |
| 180 | 320 | 385 | 460 | 555 | 665 | 800 | 960 | 1525 |
| 200 | 355 | 425 | 510 | 615 | 740 | 890 | 1070 | 1695 |
| 220 | 390 | 470 | 560 | 675 | 810 | 975 | 1175 | 1865 |
| 240 | 425 | 510 | 615 | 740 | 885 | 1065 | 1285 | 2030 |

bodies require more energy and nutrients from food just to keep them operating at the same level as before. Cycling leads to an increased metabolism—their body digests food and uses nutrients quicker, plus it more efficiently burns calories. While fit people may eat more, they also tend to crave more healthy foods to satisfy their bodies' need for important vitamins and nutrients. These factors more than compensate for the increased appetite caused by exercise, thus ensuring that active people continue to burn calories and lose weight.

# Cardiovascular and Respiratory Workout

As you probably know, it's our beating heart and pumping lungs that keep us alive. Because these are the two basic organs for sustaining life, they're also the two most important factors in maintaining health. Because it is an aerobic exercise, cycling increases the amount of oxygen riders inhale and stimulates the heart, in turn, improving both the cardiovascular system (which controls the flow of blood through your body) and the respiratory system (which handles the intake, exhalation, and use of oxygen in the body).

### Good for the Heart

Cycling benefits the cardiovascular system in a few different ways. First, it conditions the heart muscles to pump a larger volume of blood more efficiently. For instance, an extremely fit person may only need half the number of heart beats per minute that an unfit person needs to pump the same amount of blood through the body. In fact, some cyclists' hearts are so efficient that they have what seems to be abnormally low heart rates.

Also, a more efficient heart ensures that nutrients more rapidly reach all parts of the body and that the maximum amount of energy is reserved for other important body functions. In addition, exercise breaks down the fatty tissue found in artery walls to increase circulation and lower blood pressure. Because very active cyclists have incredibly healthy hearts, they are able to sustain very high heart rates when at work as well as very low rates when at rest.

## Good for the Lungs

Like other muscles that benefit from exercise, the lungs expand and strengthen as a result of the greater demands put on them. As you naturally begin to breathe heavily during a workout, your lungs become more accustomed both to a greater intake of air and a larger expulsion of carbon dioxide. Soon your lungs take in more air all the time, whether or not you are exercising. More air intake means more oxygen is absorbed into the body, which leads to better health. Cyclists tend to have magnificent lung capacity, with an ability to inhale in one breath up to 25 percent more air than the average person.

## Aerobic Conditioning

There's a very clearly defined method for determining when you are getting an aerobic workout. It applies to all forms of aerobic exercise, including but not limited to bicycling. If you've ever done aerobics or put time in on a Stairmaster or rowing machine, you're probably already familiar with it. The idea is to figure out your maximum heart rate—the number of beats per minute that it is unsafe to exceed—and then exercise at a level so that your heart rate is between 70 and 80 percent of maximum for at least twenty minutes each time you workout. This target range represents the point at which the benefits of aerobic exercise are maximized while the dangers of overstressing your heart are minimized. Exercising below the target area means you're not getting the most out of your workout; exercising above the target area means you may be hurting your body.

For aerobic exercise to be truly effective, it must be done regularly. Even if you exercise only for the minimum of twenty minutes a day, you should do so at least three or four times a week (missing an occasional day here and there won't hurt you, though). You may not be able to reach your target heart rate and sustain it for twenty minutes at first. That's okay—if you push yourself too hard, exercise becomes unhealthy. If necessary, give yourself a few weeks to work up to your target area.

## Maximum and Target Heart Rates

The quickest, though not necessarily most accurate, way to determine your maximum heart rate is to subtract your age from 220. So if you are, say, forty years old your maximum heart rate would be 180 beats per minute (that is, 220 - 40 = 180). While this is by no means a scientifically accurate calculation, it is close enough to provide you with a safe measurement of your maximum heart rate while exercising.

To find your target range simply calculate 70 and 80 percent of 180. Multiplying 180 by .7 (or 70 percent) will give you 126, while 180 × .8 (or 80 percent) gives you 144. Therefore, forty-year-old cyclists should aim to keep their heart rate between 126 and 144 beats per minute for at least twenty minutes while they ride (allowing some time for warm-up, rests, and cool-down during which their heart rate will be below the target area).

For a more accurate measure of maximum heart rate, you can go to a sports medicine facility or qualified training center. Experienced doctors or trainers will put you through rigorous physical tests (preferably on a stationary bicycle) to better determine your maximum heart rate threshold. These tests will cost you and will require you to exert yourself beyond normal levels, but they're the only way to get a precise measure of what your body can handle.

## Monitoring Your Heart Rate

Once you have determined your target heart rate, you must monitor your heart while exercising to ensure the rate falls in the desired area. Do this simply by taking your pulse. Stop riding at regular intervals (unless you are on a stationary bike, where it's safe to let go of the handles while riding). Right away, put your fingers either on top of the artery on the inside of your wrist or on your jugular vein at the side of your neck and count the number of beats you feel over a period of fifteen seconds. Multiply that number by four to get your heart rate per minute. If your heart rate is not within the target area, adjust your workout until you reach the desired level.

A bicycle computer can come in handy for monitoring heart rate. Simpler computers act as a stopwatch to help you time your heart beats, while more advanced computers actually monitor your heart rate for you. Heart rate monitors use sensors that attach to your earlobe, finger, or chest; they connect to the computer either through a wire or by wireless transmission. They calculate your heart rate and let you know if you exceed the target rate. These more advanced bicycle computers, of course, cost more than simple stopwatch types. Whatever kind you use, be sure to keep an eye out for traffic while you look down at the computer.

### Breathing Techniques

Whenever possible, try to breathe through your nose while riding. Nose hairs filter and warm the air better than the mouth can. However, when a lot of air is needed for rigorous exercise, it's often necessary to take in air through your mouth. Whether breathing through your nose or mouth, be sure to inhale as much as you can and exhale fully with each breath.

The natural tendency for beginning cyclists during a workout is to huff and puff, to gasp for air with short quick breaths. A more efficient method, though, is deep breathing. Large inhalations lasting a few seconds each are easier on the muscles your body uses to breath (and are less likely to cause cramps) and get more oxygen into your system. This type of breathing may seem unnatural and difficult at first, though with practice it becomes automatic.

# Muscle Toning

Though bicycling won't make you as burly and bulky as you'd get from lifting heavy weights every day, for a nice and even muscle tone, bicycling does the job just fine. Everyone likes to have a little muscle—it's certainly a lot more attractive than the alternative, fat. But there are better reasons for developing muscle than good looks. Muscle makes your body stronger in a number of different ways. You become stronger in the sense that your arms can lift more weight and your legs can jump higher or kick harder. But you also become stronger on the inside; strong muscle tissue is less likely to be injured and recovers quicker when damaged. Also, strong muscles protect other parts of the body from harm. The more you exercise your leg muscles, for instance, the more protection they'll provide the bones, joints, and cartilage in the legs.

Because it takes energy to pedal a bicycle, muscles burn many calories during cycling. Because most of the work is done in the legs, hips, thighs, and buttocks, these areas have the most to gain from exercise cycling. However, there are literally dozens of muscles that are used in cycling, from neck and shoulder muscles, to chest and arm muscles, all the way down to muscles in the feet.

# Health Concerns

The most serious health concerns when it comes to cycling tend to be safety related. But with proper attention to traffic laws and safe riding techniques, the inherent risks of bike riding can be held to a minimum. See Chapter 7 for a discussion of safety issues.

## Know Your Limits

A different kind of health risk is posed by riders who don't know their limits. As with any physical activity, a bicycle workout can turn potentially hazardous if the participant overdoes it. While the body has clear ways of announcing when it's being pushed too far—pain and exhaustion, for instance—enthusiasts who foolishly subscribe to an exercise-as-punishment ethic sometimes ignore the messages their body is sending. All cyclists, particularly beginners, need to take into consideration any health problems they may have before they get into biking. For instance, a man who knows he has a weak heart shouldn't attempt rigorous bike sprints (though, with a doctor's recommendation, the right kind of cycling regimen may be just what he needs).

## See a Doctor

Anyone who wants to start bicycling as a means of exercise should see a doctor before beginning. In particular, people who smoke, drink, are overweight, are largely inactive, or have had prior health problems need to determine what level of stress their bodies can take. A medical checkup is an important first step in bringing your body back to health. Besides determining your fitness level, a doctor may be helpful in designing an exercise regimen that is appropriate to your abilities. Keep doctors involved as you progress; they may suggest altering your workout or change the doses of (or do away with completely) any prescription medicine you take.

## The Pollution Question

Some critics have suggested that cyclists who ride in traffic face the additional health risk of pollution. There are two sides to the argument. Because bike riders come in direct contact with outside air, cyclists who ride on roads are directly exposed to all the exhaust and fumes generated by motor vehicles. Such direct contact with pollution can be bad for health, of course. And, because a bike trip takes longer than a car ride, cyclists who use their bikes for transportation are exposed to more road pollutants per trip.

However, some evidence suggests that even in heavy traffic cyclists are actually less exposed to pollution than drivers who are sealed up in their vehicles. The main reason for this difference seems to be that cyclists' bodies work much harder, inhaling and exhaling more oxygen at a faster rate, enabling them to get rid of pollutants much faster than sedentary drivers. Also, while drivers inhale stale air in their cars, cyclists tend to ride above the level at which most exhaust fumes linger. And, cyclists come in less contact with cars than car drivers because they usually stay to the side of the road, and they usually can't keep up with cars.

## Don't Let the Risks Stop You

As in any sport or activity, bicycling can occasionally cause discomforts or injuries. These typically involve back, neck, or knee problems, or else an irritation from the seat or handlebars. If addressed properly, these problems are rarely a cause for concern. However, if they go untreated or persist despite treatment, they can become more serious. We'll deal with specific biking ailments later in this chapter.

Still, despite any health risks cyclists may face, it remains certain that almost anyone—no matter what age or condition physically—will be infinitely better off bicycling (or doing some other exercise) than not bicycling. While it's important to consider and address the dangers, they're minor when compared to the benefits.

# Women and Cycling

For the most part, bicycling's advantages do not discriminate between the sexes. Women have just as many opportunities as men to enjoy all that cycling offers. In fact, while there's something of a gender gap in all sports in that men perform slightly better than women, that gap is somewhat reduced in cycling. Many female bikers find they are able to keep up with any exercise regimen set up for a healthy man.

Women, of course, receive the same health benefits as men—though perhaps to a greater degree. For instance, because women are more likely than men to suffer from depression, cycling's therapeutic benefits can be especially helpful to women in alleviating their symptoms. The physical and emotional pain of conditions such as Premenstrual Syndrome (PMS) may also be eased through cycling.

Most cycling problems come up only if a woman trains too intensively or rides on a bicycle not well suited to her body or her riding practices. Monitoring her training schedule closely to ensure that she doesn't overtrain and riding only on a bicycle that is perfectly suited to her will do away with the vast majority of a woman's health concerns.

## Pregnancy and Cycling

While pregnancy is undoubtedly a time when women need to pay close attention to their bodies and use caution in their physical activities, it's simply a myth that pregnant women should exercise as little as possible and eat as much as possible. Safe exercise throughout pregnancy can benefit both the unborn child and the mother. Cycling, in particular, can be a healthy activity for expectant mothers, even up to the week before giving birth. A woman's physical fitness gives her stamina to withstand the strain of labor and strength to recover more quickly.

Of all the exercises a pregnant woman can choose, cycling is among the best picks because it is a smooth motion that doesn't require lifting, jumping, or sudden stops. Also, the level of exertion can be varied, making it easy for a woman to lower the intensity of her workout as her pregnancy progresses. Plus, it's easier to stay cool while cycling in the wind than while doing other exercises. All told, the only exercise more suitable for pregnant women would have to be swimming.

Because a woman's center of gravity shifts when she is pregnant, she must be extra careful about balancing on a bicycle. Some women may determine that riding slowly in a quiet park is the safest option. Others may prefer an indoor stationary bike.

Before embarking on any exercise regimen during pregnancy, it's extremely important that you consult your obstetrician or midwife. Your caregiver should be completely involved in helping you design an exercise regimen that will be to your benefit. As long as your pregnancy progresses normally and you have no prior health concerns (such as a history of problems during pregnancy), a caregiver may encourage you to stay active with moderate exercise.

The key to any exercise during pregnancy is not to overdo it. It's fine to exercise as often as you normally would, but it's best to keep the intensity level slightly lower than usual. For instance, while you may normally aim to keep your heart rate at between 70 and 80 percent of maximum while exercising, during pregnancy it's best to keep it between 60 and 70 percent. Be sure to drink lots of fluids, take frequent breaks when pedaling, and avoid overheating.

Cramps or soreness in the legs are commonly experienced by pregnant cyclists. These are usually mild and should be expected, though any severe pain should be reported to a caregiver immediately. During the first trimester, women may find they're too tired or nauseous to attempt any exercise at all. But if you can manage to get going, cycling can reduce morning sickness and keep excess weight off.

Continue to be cautious when returning to biking after giving birth. While you'll no longer be riding for two, you still need to keep your body well nourished, especially if you plan to breastfeed. Don't be in too much of a rush to lose the extra weight you may have gained over the past months—it will come off steadily if you eat properly and continue cycling.

# Planning an Exercise Workout or Training Regimen

Many cyclists want nothing more from their bicycle than to ride it every now and then for a little fun and relaxation. If that's the case with you, then just go ahead and ride. All you need is the right bike fit and a helmet on your head, and you're ready to enjoy the great outdoors. And along the way, you can even expect to get some exercise.

However, once you decide you'd really like to focus on cycling as a way to get in shape, a little more structure in your riding patterns is recommended. A well-defined exercise schedule will allow your body to develop fitness smoothly and without undue shock to your system. It will allow you to regulate your progress and measure your performance. You can maximize the health gains from exercise while minimizing the risks and discomfort that sometimes go along with it.

Some people hope only to gain fitness from their cycling regimen. Others consider it training, whether for bike competition, to get in shape for another sport, or simply to attain a personal goal. How you design your workout will depend on what you want to get out of it. Whatever your goal, the idea is to monitor and control your exercise so that you can make the most of it.

The first thing to realize is that everyone is an individual and reacts to training and exercise differently. There's no fool-proof, across-the-board method to improve performance and fitness. The only way to know what's right for you is to be in tune with your body, to know its limitations and to understand what it's trying to tell you. While everyone has an opportunity to improve their health, it's important to realize that some people, whether through genetics or upbringing, will perform at much higher levels. Some people are just born with stronger hearts, bigger lungs, better muscle definition than others. The best you can do is make the most of what you were given. If you start off slowly and gradually increase your regimen, even the least physically fit riders will be astonished at how much they can accomplish.

## Set Your Goals

In an effective exercise program, goals are the single most essential element. They come into play in the beginning, at the end, and all along the way in between. Knowing what you want to get out of cycling determines how you set up your regimen. It also keeps you focused and helps substantiate your progress once you put your program into effect. And, of course, your goals let you know when you've succeeded doing what you set out to do.

With a cycling program, both short-term and long-term goals are necessary. You should know what you want to accomplish each time you set out to ride, and you should also have a goal to work toward over the course of an entire season (or longer). Don't feel like your goals are set in stone, though. While you should make every effort to meet the challenges you set, be flexible to changing circumstances and reassessments of your routine. Also, don't feel like goals need to be monumental to be worthwhile.

Even the most modest goals are useful to give your exercise direction.

Begin by deciding what you'd like to get out of cycling. Would you like to improve your cardiovascular fitness? Do you want to lose weight? Are you training to compete in bicycling races? Are you riding to enhance your performance in another sport? If you are completely new to cycling, it may be difficult at first to translate your needs into specific goals. That's okay. Just knowing what your needs are is a good start.

Next, think about your abilities and what it takes to achieve your goal. Can you accomplish what you've set out to do? Do you have the physical ability? The time? The desire? The interest? While it's important to set goals high enough to challenge you, goals that are out of reach will only disappoint you, frustrate you, and potentially discourage you from cycling. Be optimistic, but also be realistic. And be honest with yourself: only set goals you really want to meet and truly believe you can meet.

Now plan specifically how you will attain your goals. What areas will need close attention in order to keep yourself on track? Maybe you'll need to rearrange your work schedule to make sure there's

## GOURMET GORP!

 A favorite high-carbohydrate snack for cyclists, *gorp* stands for "good ol' raisins and peanuts." At its simplest, it's just that: raisins and peanuts mixed together. Usually, though, gorp is just a little bit more involved. The following is a recipe for one nourishing variation. Just combine all the ingredients in a bowl and mix well.

*Ingredients*
1 cup peanuts
1 cup raisins
1 cup almonds
1 cup cashews
1 cup sunflower seeds
1 cup shredded coconut
1 cup banana chips
1 cup dried apricots
1 cup chocolate chips or carob chips

This gorp recipe serves three to five cyclists. All ingredients should be unsalted, with no added sugar. Mix and match ingredients, or add your own, to come up with a truly personalized gorp. Bon appetit!

time for cycling. Or maybe you'll decide to go on a diet to make weight loss easier. Perhaps you will work on your riding techniques, your form, or your hill climbing abilities, for example.

## Conditioning Techniques

The principles of maximum heart rate and target heart rate that were discussed earlier in the chapter play a large part in conditioning. If you need a refresher on what they mean or how they are determined, look back now before continuing.

*Long, steady, distance training.* The purpose of a long, steady, distance workout is to improve your cardiovascular fitness and endurance. A valuable aerobic workout is gained not by exhausting your body through all-out bursts of effort, but rather by working a bit harder than usual for extended periods. With this kind of exercise, you need not pass the point known as your *anaerobic threshold*, at which the supply of oxygen can no longer meet the demand of the muscles.

For cyclists who are not in great shape to start out, or who do not wish to overexert themselves, long, steady, distance training may be all they ever need. At the very least, it's where beginners should start. Other cyclists will want to combine it with other training techniques that are more oriented toward developing strength. However, most of the major health benefits to be gained from cycling can be attained with proper long, steady, distance training.

The aim in such training is to stay within the lower ranges of your target heart rate—say, 65 to 70 percent of the maximum. You would pedal at a moderate but steady rate, on flat land, and in a comfortable gear. A typical workout may cover five to ten miles in thirty to sixty minutes. As your endurance improves you gradually increase the number of miles you ride and your speed while remaining within the 65-to-70-percent maximum heart rate range. In cycling, increasing mileage is the key to improving endurance.

*Interval training.* Interval training is based on alternating periods of intensive pedaling, or sprinting, with slightly longer periods of recovery where pedaling is slower. Typically, an interval training session will involve anywhere from ten to thirty high-intensity intervals, each lasting from fifteen to sixty seconds, and each followed by a recovery interval lasting thirty to ninety seconds. For riders wishing to improve endurance, high-intensity intervals can be increased to two or three minutes each, with rest periods increased to five to ten minutes. However, full-tilt pedaling is difficult to sustain for long periods, so the intensity level will need to be reduced slightly.

Interval training is an anaerobic exercise, which means you are exerting your body to a point where the demand for oxygen by the muscles exceeds the supply. Because of the insufficient oxygen supply, anaerobic workouts can't be sustained for long without a rest; the body will give out. Through training, though, the length of time your body can endure such stress increases. Interval training will surely make your muscles sore and your body exhausted. However, it's also the fastest way to build strength.

In theory, interval training can involve any combination of intervals and intensities. For riders more oriented toward long, steady, distance training, interval training might involve a few minutes of medium-intensity pedaling followed by a few minutes of low-intensity cycling. The principle of alternating intensity levels to allow for both stress and recovery is the same.

At the highest intensities, though, the greatest anaerobic gain will be made. At these levels, muscles are broken down and rebuilt to be stronger. Cyclists who wish to gain strength and increase their maximum riding speeds should (with the approval of their doctor) do interval training in which high-intensity intervals push them to 85 to 90 percent of maximum heart rate (even higher for experienced riders), while the recovery periods bring them back down to 60 percent.

While interval training can be quite difficult, it is the only way to effectively increase performance. It should not be attempted by beginners, though. Intensive interval training comes only after a rider has mastered long, steady, distance training. And even then, interval workouts should not be the only conditioning technique a rider does. Two or three times a week is the most a cyclist should attempt in order to allow the body time to recover. Use the days in between to work on distance with a steady ride. Also important, to avoid strain and injury, be sure to warm up and cool down each time you do interval training.

*Periodization.* Not so much a method of training as a way to organize training, periodization refers to the practice of dividing the year-round workout regimen into several parts that vary in intensity and frequency. Periodization makes the most of the workout by focusing on different aspects of conditioning at different times—when they are most necessary. For racers, the goal may be to arrange training periods so they'll be at maximum strength precisely when the most important competition takes place.

Because most cyclists are at least somewhat affected by the weather, periodization often corresponds to the change in seasons. Winter, for example, can be a great time to focus more on developing strength in your upper body through weight training or other sports, while actual cycling time may be reduced significantly or stopped altogether. Spring is often the time to regain your form and bring your aerobic capabilities back up (if you've stayed in shape, this shouldn't be too difficult), while at the same time maintaining any other training. Summer and autumn may see an increase in the intensity of the workout and be directed more toward performance gains or to training for a specific race or event. By the end of the cycling year (late autumn), you may want to push yourself a bit further to see what you're capable of. You'll likely be in your best shape then, and any strain the added exertion may cause will have plenty of time to heal once winter arrives again.

*Supplemental training.* While an effective bicycle training program will take you most of the way toward achieving your fitness goals, incorporating your bike riding with other exercise can make your fitness program even more well rounded. Other exercises will not only fill in the gaps in areas cycling doesn't cover but also can improve your cycling ability, strength, and endurance, and lessen the chance of injury (conversely, cycling will improve your ability to do other exercises as well).

Many cyclists supplement their bike conditioning with a program of weight training and other resistance exercises such as sit-ups and push-ups. Because cyclists typically develop muscles and fitness faster in the lower body than elsewhere, many supplemental exercises focus on the upper body. Strength in the back, neck, shoulders, arms, and abdomen can be developed with only a small set of free weights, such as dumbbells or barbells.

In the winter off-season, some riders replace cycling for a short time with indoor swimming, skiing, aerobic dancing, or skating. These offer similar aerobic workouts to bicycling and allow cyclists to stay in shape during the months when it becomes more difficult to ride.

## Monitor Your Progress

Once you begin training, you'll be able to feel increases in fitness and strength. Pay close attention to your body and the changes it goes through. No matter how tuned in to your body you are, though, it's difficult to know for sure—particularly on a day-to-day basis—how well you are progressing. The most effective way to monitor your progress is to actually write out your cycling routine and to record your activity each day in a training log. It will enable you to see exactly how you are developing and will help you stay on track.

The log need not be complicated; all that's necessary is a place to write the kind of training you do, the number of miles you ride, and the time you spend cycling. If you want to get more involved—and you have a good bike computer to keep track of such information—you can include the average hill incline of your ride, your average r.p.m., your average speed, your heart rate (before, during, and after riding), the amount of calories you burn, and your current body weight. Allow space, as well, for comments that don't fit into any particular category, such as notes on any discomfort you feel, on any new equipment or techniques you use, or on good routes to take while riding. These extra notes can be quite helpful as well.

Look back at your training log regularly to see if you can find any patterns, peaks, or slumps. Whenever possible, apply this information to improve your performance. Determine what it was you were doing right at times of peak performance and what you were doing wrong during slumps. You'll be amazed how much you learn about yourself when it's all there on paper in front of you.

## Rest and Recovery

So much attention is paid to performance and development in bike training, one crucial factor is too often overlooked. Just as important as when and how you ride is when and how you *don't* ride. Without the right amount—and the right kinds—of rest and recovery, any gains you've made in fitness can just as easily be lost.

No matter how enthusiastic you get about bike training, you must never view rest days as something only for wimps. Think of them, instead, as what they are: an integral part of your workout program. That's not to say that the more time you spend loafing around the house the better off you'll be. In fact, too much rest will only lead to a loss in your fitness and performance levels. There is a delicate balance between too much rest and not enough. Doing nothing, it seems, was never so complicated!

For serious cyclists, the goal in recovery is to make the process as quick and complete as possible and to allow the most time for active training. Younger and more physically fit people will tend to recover quicker, but recovery time for anyone can be minimized through appropriate training. That includes stretching, making sure your body is adequately nourished and hydrated beforehand, and not overexerting yourself during the ride. Afterward, allow time for a cool-down and stretch, then be sure to replenish carbohydrates and proteins as soon as possible. Get plenty of sleep at night, when a lot of the most important restoration takes place. And treat your body to some pampering; a massage, sauna, or hot bath will do wonders for your recovery.

It's not hard to tell when the recovery process is complete. You'll know, simply, when your body feels rejuvenated. If you feel ready to ride hard again, and indicators such as your heart rate have stabilized, you probably are ready.

## Overtraining

For the most part, your body will adapt to the added stress of a cycling workout. But if the stress is simply too great to handle, the reverse will happen—your body will reject the exercise. Training too hard, not allowing enough time for your body to recover, and not maintaining appropriate calorie intake can lead to a condition called *overtraining*. With overtraining, your body just seems to give up. You feel fatigued but unable to sleep soundly. Your heart rate is higher than normal; you feel irritable, unmotivated, even depressed. Your performance decreases significantly.

Because your body has worked so hard at pedaling, other body functions may be affected. Your muscles may become sore, abrasions may heal more slowly, and you may become sick with a cold or flu. If you've worked hard to increase your stamina and fitness, overtraining can make you feel like all your effort has been wasted.

But if dealt with immediately, overtraining will most likely cause no long-term harm. You can overcome it simply by lowering the intensity of your workout and by allowing your body enough rest between rides. Take a break from riding for a week or more until the symptoms start to disappear. To be sure the symptoms of overtraining aren't actually pointing to some other condition, though, it's best to see a doctor. As with health concerns, preventing overtraining beforehand is preferable to treating it after the fact. Keep workouts well monitored and manageable, and you should never need to worry about overtraining.

## Training on a Tight Schedule

Unless you plan to quit your job, abandon your family, and join the professional racing circuit, chances are good you don't have all day to dedicate to riding. Most likely, it's difficult to find even an hour in your busy day to devote to cycling. But if fitness is important to you—and it should be—you'll find ways to make time for bicycling.

The good news is, if you can fit it in, the minimum workout of thirty minutes at least three times a week (four times a week is even better) should be enough to improve or maintain fitness. Most people can squeeze a half hour of cycling somewhere in the day, whether it's first thing in the morning, during a lunch break, or right after work. Cut out any unnecessary activities during the day, or shave time off by doing everyday things like cleaning or showering a little bit faster. If it's practical, commuting to work or running errands on bike is a great way to get in a workout while doing something you'd need to do anyway.

Once you find that half hour, it's important to make the most of it—there's no time to lose. Expect to do a higher intensity workout than you normally would, but don't sacrifice your warm-up and cool-down.

# Stretching Before Riding

No matter whether you ride for fun or for conditioning, a ten- to fifteen-minute stretch beforehand is not only recommended, it's required. Stretching prevents injuries such as muscle tears and overextensions by loosening muscles and increasing flexibility. It also helps your body prepare for a workout by getting an increased amount of blood flowing to your muscles in advance of when you'll actually need it. A second period of stretching should come after your ride to reinforce flexibility and help prevent muscles from tightening up and becoming sore.

Stretches that prepare you for a bike ride concentrate on the neck, upper and lower back, hips, upper legs (quadriceps and hamstrings), and lower legs (calves and ankles). Perform all stretches slowly and smoothly, without bouncy or jerky motions. Stretch to a point where the muscle begins to hurt and hold each stretch until your muscle becomes accustomed to the extension. Breathe deeply and evenly as you begin a stretch, then exhale as you release.

## Head Rolls

Slowly and smoothly rotate your head, from one shoulder (head is sideways), to your back (head faces up), to the other shoulder, to the front (head faces down). Hold each position for ten seconds. You should feel your neck muscles stretching.

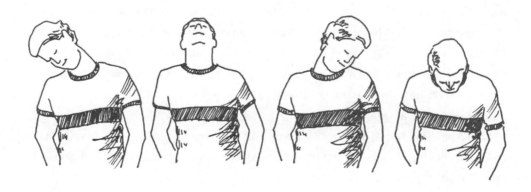

## Side Stretch

Stand with legs straight and slightly apart. Keeping your left arm at your side, raise your right arm straight up over your head. Bend sideways at your waist while your extended right arm hangs over your head and points left. You should feel a stretch in your side. Repeat the exercise with the opposite arm to stretch the other side.

## Hip and Lower Back Stretch

Lie flat on your back. Bring your legs up so they're bent and your knees touch your chest. Wrap your arms around your legs and hold them close to your upper body for fifteen seconds. You should feel a stretch in your lower back and hips.

## Quadricep Stretch

Stand facing a wall in case you need extra support. Lift your lower left leg behind you, then reach back with your left hand and grab your ankle. Pull your left foot forward until your heel touches your butt, or until you feel a stretch in the quadriceps, the muscle in your upper leg above the knee. Hold for ten seconds. Repeat the stretch using your right leg and hand.

## Groin and Inner Thigh Stretch

Sit on the floor with your back to the wall for support. Fold your legs so the soles of your feet are together and your knees are pointed out to the sides. Pull your feet in toward the groin as far as is comfortable and gently press your thighs down so your knees approach the floor. If you can, bend forward at the waist slightly, making sure to keep your back completely straight. Hold the position for fifteen seconds. You should feel the stretch in your groin and inner thigh area.

### Hamstring and Lower Back Stretch

Sit on the floor and extend your legs in front. Bend one leg so the sole of the foot butts up against the inner thigh of the other leg. Bend at the hip, over the extended leg, and reach out toward your foot. Hold for a few seconds. You should feel a stretch in your hamstring, at the back of your extended leg. Switch the positions of your legs and repeat the stretch for the other leg.

### Toe Touches

Stand straight with your feet close together. Bend forward from the hips and extend your arms down to try to touch your toes. If you cannot reach your toes, simply stretch as far as you can so that you feel a stretch but no unusual pain. Do not jerk down to try to get closer to your toes. Bend the knees slightly if you need to to take pressure off the back. Hold the position for about twenty seconds. You should feel a stretch through your back, hamstrings, and the backs of your knees.

### Calf Stretch

Stand a few feet away, facing a wall, and lean forward to place your hands on the wall. With one leg step forward so your foot is flat on the ground and your knee is bent. The other leg should be fully extended and stretching back, also with the foot flat. You should feel a stretch in the calf as well as in the ankle of your back leg. Hold for fifteen seconds, then switch leg positions to stretch the other calf and ankle.

## Stationary Bikes

The simple truth about stationary bicycles is that, when used properly, they can give riders exactly the same health advantages gained by riding outdoors. That said, the most common complaint among cyclists who thrive on the outdoors—the fresh air, the scenery, the challenging hills, the people they meet—is that stationary bicycles are dreadfully boring. They're forced to sit, surrounded by four walls, and pedal endlessly without moving an inch. It's guaranteed to drive any bike enthusiast absolutely nuts!

Of course, indoor cycling continues to thrive, from the bedrooms of suburbia to the gyms of the cities. And for good reason, too. Despite the monotony of stationary bikes, they have many advantages over real bikes. In fact, for the purposes of exercise and conditioning, some bike heretics might go so far as to claim that indoor cycling is even more efficient than riding outdoors.

The most obvious benefit of stationary bikes is that they can be used at any time, no matter how cold or rainy or dark it is outside. Though there are folks who swear by winter riding, the frigid winds of February are certainly not for everyone. While it's certainly possible to ride safely and comfortably in a wide variety of temperatures and at any time of day, some people just don't want to ride in less-than-ideal conditions.

For people who need to juggle work and family with their workouts, indoor bikes make it easier for them to get in exercise over the course of a day. People with children to watch can ride without ever having to take their eyes off the kids. Working people can ride safely at night, or they can save time in the morning by pedaling while they watch the news or read the paper (don't try that while cycling in traffic!).

Another way stationary bikes save time is by doing away with time spent getting to the place where you normally ride. If you train on a track or ride a favorite bike trail, it may take you twenty minutes just to get there before you ride. That's time many people can't afford. With indoor bikes, you just walk into the room, stretch, and start pedaling.

Stationary bikes can also make for a more focused workout. Riding on the streets, there's usually traffic and other road hazards to contend with. Stopping at red lights and dodging potholes can take away from your ability to get the best workout possible. And unless you've found the perfect training course—completely flat or with uphills and downhills ideally placed for maximum conditioning—you'll do better on a bike where you can regulate the pedal resistance. Use the stationary bike to arrange the ideal workout for you. The added control can pay off in increased fitness.

Stationary bikes also allow the rider to listen to music—either on the stereo or through a headset—a luxury most road cyclists are prohibited from doing. The right music can be a great motivational force. On the other hand, the wrong kind of music can be a distraction.

When buying a stationary bicycle, look for a strong, sturdy metal frame, just as you would for a regular bike. Because you are not going anywhere, weight is less of an issue. The bike should have all the features you need, including a resistance mechanism, a speedometer, and an odometer.

If you have a bicycle and enjoy riding outdoors, but would like to supplement your riding with an indoor workout, it is not always necessary to buy a stationary bike. There are many types of training stands and rollers that allow you to use your own bicycle at home. Though they can be expensive in themselves, they may save you money if you find one that is cheaper than a stationary bike. Besides, if you are a frequent outdoor rider, you are probably very comfortable with the fit and feel of your bike. You may welcome the chance to use your own bike all year around, indoors as well as outdoors.

# The Biker's Diet

Diet goes hand in hand with any kind of exercise. Without proper nutrients, cyclists will not perform as well as possible. And without physical activity, nutrients are not well utilized. What makes up a good diet for cyclists is essentially the same as what's good for anyone, though an active cyclist may need more of certain nutrients than the average person.

Building a proper diet is a matter of figuring out what the body needs and supplying the right amount of it. There's no magical guide to perfect food intake—each person has different needs. In fact, because there are so many levels of cycling performance, the variation in bikers' diets is especially great. There are, though, a number of dietary needs that each person must satisfy. And there are many suggestions that will help each individual define a suitable diet.

## What Your Body Needs

Our bodies get three things from the food and drink we take in: energy, water, and nutrients. Energy, in the form of calories, we've already discussed earlier in the chapter. Water and nutrients relate to energy in that they enable the body to function: to build cells, to perform physical actions and processes, and to replace needed materials.

*Water.* When you consider that a person's body is made up of more than 90 percent water, it's not hard to imagine what can happen to us when we are not properly hydrated. Just a minor deficiency can result in heat exhaustion or heat stroke. Though it provides no nutrients or energy, water is the single most important component in our diet—particularly crucial for physically active people. It not only keeps the body cool through perspiration, it also cleanses the body, enables metabolism, and ensures that the body stays chemically balanced. Without water, your body could not process nutrients into energy. For heavy exercise, in which the muscles build up lactic acid, water helps flush out the acid that can cause sore muscles.

Other liquids, including juices and special sports drinks such as Gatorade, provide minerals lost through perspiration and replenish glycogen levels. Most are somewhat helpful for cyclists, but they can be unnecessarily high in calories. While they may improve performance in serious training, they may not be needed for regular fitness workouts. Drinks with caffeine, such as coffee, tea, or colas, will give you a lift but will also cause you to lose liquid through urination. For pure hydration purposes you can't go wrong with water. Water is calorie-free, so you can drink as much as you want.

Drinking too much water before a ride can lead to stomach cramps, but a moderate amount about a half hour before your workout helps prepare your body. If you go on a long or particularly strenuous ride, bring along a bottle (or two) of cool water and drink regularly—at least every fifteen minutes. Don't wait until your body feels weak and dehydration sets in—by then it is too late. Drink slowly; gulping down large amounts only causes stomach problems. And make sure you drink plenty of water after a ride to replenish any liquid you've lost through perspiration.

*Carbohydrates.* Carbohydrates are the body's main source of energy. Because they are absorbed into the body faster than proteins or fats, carbohydrates are a great source of nutrition for active people. To keep the energy supply at a level suitable for physically active people, a diet should consist of about 65 percent carbohydrates. Without enough carbohydrate intake, blood sugar drops, causing muscles to tire and fail; in extreme cases, low blood sugar can cause dizziness, nausea, even collapse.

There are two types of carbohydrates (carbs): simple and complex. Simple carbs (monosaccharides and disaccharides) are sugars such as glucose, lactose (milk sugar), and sucrose (found in table sugar and honey). They are absorbed directly and are therefore good for quick and easy energy in training or as a snack during long rides. However, they are burned quickly and don't provide long-term energy. And unless you use the energy provided by simple carbohydrates for exercise, too much can make you fat.

## CARBO BARS!

 The following recipe makes a perfect snack to take along with you on a grueling long-distance bike ride. Keep one or two carbo bars in your pocket, to eat whenever you need an energy boost. Modify the recipe to fit your own tastes.

*Ingredients*

| | |
|---|---|
| 1 cup raisins | 1 cup oats |
| 1 cup dried apricots | $1/2$ cup shredded coconut |
| 1 cup almond slices | 1 egg |
| $1/2$ cup sugar | $1/2$ cup molasses |
| $1/4$ cup toasted wheat germ | $1/3$ cup margarine |
| $1^1/2$ cups whole wheat flour | $1/2$ cup nonfat dry milk |
| $3/4$ cup nonfat milk | $1/2$ teaspoon salt |
| $1^1/2$ teaspoons baking powder | $1/2$ teaspoon baking soda |
| $1/2$ teaspoon ground ginger | |

*Directions.* Whip together the egg, margarine, molasses, and sugar. In a separate bowl, mix the dry milk, flour, baking powder, baking soda, salt, ginger, and wheat germ. Stir in the liquid milk. Add the egg mixture to the milk mixture and blend together. Chop the apricots, raisins, almonds (if desired). Stir the raisins, apricots, coconut, almonds, and oats into the mixture. Pour the mixture into a lightly greased shallow cooking pan. Bake at 350 degrees for 30 minutes. Let cool, and cut into individual bars. Makes about 30 bars.

Complex carbs (polysaccharides), including starches and pectins, are made up of chains of glucose. They are found in foods such as pasta, potatoes, bread, cereal, fruits, and vegetables, though in smaller concentrations than in simple sugars. Because these take longer to break down, they provide long-term energy and are better suited for regular daily meals between workouts. And because the foods that have complex carbs also contain other nutrients, they help provide a more balanced diet.

Four servings of fruits and vegetables and three servings of breads and cereals per day provide enough carbohydrates for most people. The more energy cyclists need, though, the more carbohydrates they should consume. While a steady diet is most beneficial, racers often load up on carbohydrates a few days before a race to maximize their energy. If you increase the amount of carbohydrates you eat, be careful not to overeat. Overeating can cause a loss of blood to the muscles (because more blood is needed in digestion) and, of course, an unhealthy gain in body fat.

*Protein.* While proteins are a necessary part of every person's diet, cyclists do not need much more of them than anyone else. Protein in food helps the body form muscles, bones, skin, red blood cells, and the many biochemical proteins (enzymes, hormones) that make up our body. However, they are not a particularly good source of energy.

Proteins are commonly found in foods such as meat, poultry, fish, eggs, cheese, and other milk products. For people who don't eat meat, a mixture of foods like rice, beans, tofu (and other soy bean derivatives), whole wheat, and nuts can fill the body's protein requirements. Only 10 to 15 percent of our diet should be made up of proteins, so it's best to limit high-protein food intake to two servings a day.

Getting enough protein is not usually something we need to worry about, for two reasons. First, the body doesn't need a large amount, and second, Americans tend to eat much more protein than necessary. However, because the body cannot store excess protein, a constant (though moderate) supply is necessary. Excess protein is either discarded or converted into glucose (for energy) and fat. And because high-protein foods also tend to be high in fat, getting too much protein also means you're getting too much fat.

*Fat.* Unlike proteins, fats are a good source of energy because they are dense in calories (higher in calories even than carbohydrates). Fats, though, are not as easily retrieved for energy as carbohydrates, so they are used as a secondary source of energy after the glycogen from carbs has been depleted.

Of the two types of fats—saturated and unsaturated—unsaturated fats are healthier. These are found in grains, corn, soybean, nuts, and some oils (such as olive, sunflower, and corn). Saturated fats come from meats, poultry, fish, dairy products, egg yolks, and some vegetable oils. Because they are high in cholesterol, eating too much of them can lead to heart disease. However, fats are a necessary part of the diet—they supply fat-soluble vitamins (A, D, E, and K), though not many other nutrients. They should make up about 15 to 20 percent of your total calorie intake, with three-fourths of it from unsaturated fats. Like proteins, though, most people eat plenty of fat. It's usually not a matter of trying to get enough fat, but rather trying to limit it. Most Americans are lucky if their fat intake totals less than 30 percent of their daily intake.

Some amount of body fat is healthy; it helps insulate the body from cold and protect it from viruses. Plus, it's the fat in foods that tends to taste good. Too much fat, though, limits the amount of blood that reaches the muscles, sometimes leads to heart disease, and of course, makes you fat.

Because fats can take a long time to digest, any fat intake should come long before—at least three hours prior to—your workout. Otherwise, it takes energy away from your muscles and could hurt your stomach. The good news for cyclists is that, because they burn so many calories, they can take in a little more fat without gaining weight.

*Vitamins and Minerals.* Vitamins and minerals found in all foods are necessary in the diet. While they are not nutrients, they enable the body to break down nutrients. A well-balanced diet generally supplies all of your vitamin and mineral needs. However, a good way to make sure you get everything you need is to read the chart of recommended daily values on the side of food packages.

Our bodies use vitamins to control enzymes during metabolism and to form bones and muscle. Water-soluble vitamins—B-complex, bioflavinoids, and C—are not stored in the body, so they must be ingested daily. B-complex vitamins, used to convert carbs, proteins, and fats into energy (therefore very important to cyclists), are found in meat, fish, vegetables, milk products, and eggs. Vitamin C—which fights sickness and builds tissue, among other things—can be found in citrus fruits and green vegetables. Bioflavinoids, which assist vitamin C, are found in fruits.

Fat-soluble vitamins (A, D, E, and K) are stored in body fat and can be dangerous if held in large amounts. Vitamin A, which helps grow body tissue, is found in vegetables and meats. Vitamin D, found in dairy products, fish, egg yolks, and green vegetables, strengthens bones and teeth. Vitamin E, which helps cells remain strong, is in wheat germ, nuts, grains, and some vegetables. Vitamin K helps bones develop and clots blood; it is developed naturally in the body, but is also found in dairy products and egg yolks.

Minerals also play an important part in metabolism. They activate chemical reactions in the body that enable the breakdown of nutrients and also regulate muscle contractions. In addition, minerals are used in forming bone and muscle. The major minerals found in the body include calcium, iron, magnesium, phosphorus, potassium, and sodium (the most abundant). Small amounts of minerals such as aluminum, boron, copper, fluorine, iodine, manganese, nickel, and zinc can be found in the body as well.

Calcium, which forms bones and teeth, can be found in vegetables and milk products. Iron, which helps form hemoglobin (which carries oxygen in blood), is in meats, eggs, and many vegetables. Nuts, spinach, soy, and wheat germ are good sources of magnesium, which plays a role in many body functions. Peas, corn, and sprouts are high in phosphorus, needed in body metabolism. Bananas, citrus fruits, and vegetables provide potassium, which helps nerves and muscles function. And sodium, which serves many functions, is found in many fruits, vegetables, and grains.

A group of minerals called electrolytes (chlorine, sodium, and potassium) are particularly important to cyclists. A lack of electrolytes will hurt physical performance and may lead to heat exhaustion or stroke. Sodium, potassium, and iron are lost through perspiration and need to be replenished by eating foods high in those minerals or by drinking special electrolyte replacement drinks and taking iron supplement pills.

Though cyclists need more vitamins and minerals to replace those that are lost through physical activity and perspiration, an excess of them does not increase health or fitness. Too much of them, in fact, can be unhealthy, or at least counterproductive to fitness.

## Diet Guidelines

A healthy diet includes food from all the nutritional categories. Ask dedicated cyclists, however, and they'll undoubtedly emphasize one category in particular: carbohydrates. While fats and proteins can be reduced in your diet, carbohydrates should be increased to at least 65 percent of total intake, or as much as 75 percent for those in intensive training. Proteins and fats should make up from 10 to 20 percent each.

For cyclists in intensive training, the body may require a higher food intake. A practice known as *carbo loading*, in which cyclists overload on carbohydrates a few days before a race, has been somewhat in vogue since the 1980s. While it's been shown to increase performance in long competitions, there's no need to carbo load unless you are a professional racer (even then it may not be a good idea).

Whatever you eat, allow about three hours before a heavy workout to digest a large meal. And be sure to eat another large meal within two hours of completing a heavy workout. Never try to deprive your body of needed nutrients in the interest of losing weight. If you plan to remain physically active, fasting will make workouts extremely difficult and possibly dangerous.

As important as what and when you eat is what and when you drink. In cycling, it's often said, "Drink before you get thirsty." A continuous, moderate intake of water, though, is much better than drinking large amounts at one time.

| The Best Foods for Cyclists | Foods to Avoid |
| --- | --- |
| Fresh fruits and vegetables | Fatty meats and poultry |
| Pasta and noodles | Fried foods |
| Whole grain breads | Whole milk products |
| Cereals | Egg yolks |
| Low-fat meat, chicken, and fish | Saturated oils and shortening |
| Peanut butter sandwiches | Sugary foods and snacks |
| Potatoes | |
| Nuts and legumes | |

# Common Biking Ailments and Treatments

The more you ride the better chance you have of suffering discomfort from time to time. Though not usually serious, any discomfort may make riding painful or develop into a worse problem if it is ignored. Sometimes the ailment stems from a problem with your form or with the fit of your bike. Other times it's just a matter of wear and tear on your body. In either case, there are usually remedies—either behavioral changes or treatments—that can cure your discomfort, or at least minimize it. Whenever an ailment continues or worsens over time, though, professional medical help should be sought.

## Back and Neck

Back problems are very common in society in general, and particularly prevalent in cyclists. Most often, the problem is a matter of poor posture—not only while riding but also when sitting and standing. People often roll their backs, which puts undo stress on the spine and lower back muscles, rather than keep backs straight or arched.

Posture problems are remedied, simply, with better posture. While riding, your back should be completely straight. Practice pushing your belly out and toward the top tube in order to achieve a flat back. Off the bike, provide support for your lower back by using cushions and pillows and by remembering to sit up straight.

Sometimes, backaches afflict new riders because they are using unfamiliar muscles. Riders with excessive fat around the waist may put extra strain on their backs while cycling. On long rides, even trained riders can feel back discomfort from many hours of leaning forward. These pains should go away as lower back muscles are developed. Stretching and exercising both back and abdominal muscles will help speed the process; so will making sure your back stays warm while riding.

Often, improper positioning or bike fit can strain your back. Consider temporarily raising your handlebars to make it easier to straighten your back. For chronic back pain, consider switching to a recumbent bike.

Neck problems can also result from improper body position or a bike fit that makes you cramped. It can often be prevented by alternating your position regularly between upright, drop position, and out-of-the-saddle riding. If your bike has been properly fitted to your body, the most adjusting your bike should need is to slide the saddle back, raise the handlebars, or get a longer stem. Proper stretching and exercises will help strengthen neck muscles as well.

Ice packs, heat treatments, and light massage can help reduce pain and inflammation in the back and neck. Medications such as pain killers, muscle relaxants, and anti-inflammatory drugs can help as well. You may need a doctor's prescription for more powerful medications.

## Knees

The knee is a large, complex—and not particularly strong—joint, giving the dedicated cyclist plenty of opportunities for injury. Four bones, three muscle groups, cartilage (for cushion), fluid (for lubrication), and ligaments (to hold everything together) all meet at the knee in an arrangement that is not fully prepared to accommodate the stress of heavy pedaling.

Knee trouble can arise for a number of reasons. Improper saddle height or seat positioning can damage knees. When the seat is too low, knees cannot extend properly and may become cramped or strained; if the seat is too high the kneecap becomes overextended. Improper foot position can also make your knees vulnerable; and problems with the bike itself—particularly in the pedals or cranks—could throw off your form. Ideal seat height will allow your knee to be almost fully extended at the bottom of the stroke, though not extended far enough to lock into place (for more specifics on bike fit and adjustments, see Chapter 4).

But even on properly sized bikes, cyclists necessarily put a lot of pressure on their knees. Pedaling is a repetitive motion that requires continuous bending of the knee joints and flexing of the surrounding muscles. Knees bend and straighten thousands of times over the course of a few miles; in time even mildly stressful pedaling will take its toll. Riding too much, too hard, or in too high a gear before your leg muscles are properly developed can strain knees and make them sore. Also, the limited range of knee extension puts more stress on certain muscles than others, causing an imbalanced muscle development and excessive friction between muscles, bones, cartilage, and ligaments.

The treatment is simply to take it easy. Realize your body's limits and respect them. If you experience pain, allow your knee to rest for a few days. Don't put any unnecessary pressure on it; ice packs can help, and pain relievers will ease the discomfort. Once the pain has dissipated, start riding again, but with less intensity. To prevent stiffness, be sure to keep the knees warm. Also, stretching the muscles around the knees—the hamstrings, quadriceps, and calves—will reduce the likelihood of knee pain.

If knee pain is not addressed at the earliest signs, more serious conditions such as tendinitis, bursitis, and chondromalacia can develop. Tendinitis is an inflammation of the tendons surrounding the knee, either below the kneecap or on the side of the knee. Bursitis is an inflammation in the knee that results when the fluid sacs that lubricate the joint (bursa) become irritated. Chondromalacia occurs when the inside surface of the kneecap and surrounding cartilage become worn down through excessive friction, resulting in pain and a grating feeling in the knee.

Again, the best treatment for mild cases of any of these conditions is rest, proper knee exercises, ice treatment, and anti-inflammatory drugs. Appropriate adjustments to seat height and pedaling form should be made as well. For advanced cases, an orthopedic doctor or physical therapist should be consulted. More involved treatment, perhaps even surgery, could be necessary. Chondromalacia, for one, is difficult to treat once it reaches an advanced stage. Through inflammation and pain, your body will alert you to any problems; just be sure you're paying attention.

The good news, though, is that under proper conditions, cycling puts much less strain on the knees than other sports that require running. The chances of seriously hurting the knee are significantly reduced when feet are on pedals instead of on the ground.

## Seat Discomfort

A comfortable bike seat will help reduce saddle discomfort. Seats should be well padded, smooth, and wide enough for your body (too wide, though, can make matters worse). Women's and men's seats are designed differently to better support different bone structures. Take some time to find a seat that fits your body and will keep its shape over long rides. Leather seats will take longer to break in than gel seats, but they may provide more comfort in the long run. To reduce friction on the seat, use a synthetic seat cover or apply a leather wax. While a seat that is too slippery can be dangerous (if you slide off), one that is not slippery enough will cause irritation. Look for a happy medium.

## Feet and Hands

Many miles of riding in the same position can cause numbness in the feet and hands. The most obvious solution is to change positions by shifting your weight, moving your hands, or riding out of the seat for a while.

Shoes that are too small, narrow, or tight can also cause numbness or even calluses and blisters. While some shoes need to be broken in, shoes that continue to cause discomfort after weeks of heavy use are simply not the right shoes for you (toe straps can irritate as well). In addition, riding with soft-soled shoes can cause a burning sensation in the bottom of the feet; hard soles distribute the pressure of pedaling throughout the feet to provide more comfort.

Numbness of the hands is caused by handlebar pressure on the palms that cuts off circulation to the fingers. Numbness can usually be prevented by easing up on your grip and switching handlebar positions as much as possible. Bikes with drop handlebars provide at least three completely different hand positions, while straight handlebar bikes (mountain bikes) give the rider less choice. Continued discomfort may require you to wear riding gloves or (if you already wear gloves) gloves with more padding. Padding on handlebars also reduces the road friction that causes hand pain and numbness.

The shocks of the road can take their toll on the wrists as well as the hands. Carpal tunnel syndrome, a nerve condition in the wrists that commonly affects typists, can also plague cyclists. Rest, better shock absorption, and a modified grip will lessen the stress on wrists.

## Sunburn

Hardly a problem faced by cyclists alone, sunburn must be dealt with by anyone who spends a lot of time outdoors. But because the wind cools cyclists as they ride, they often don't feel the sun burning down on them. That's why it's even more important for bike riders to prepare for the sun before they even venture outside.

The best way to prevent sunburn is to put on sunscreen. Depending on your skin tone, it's best to start with a lotion having a sun protection factor of at least 15 or as high as 30 for particularly fair-skinned cyclists. Lotion should be waterproof and sweatproof. Apply it everywhere skin is exposed: face (including neck and ears), arms, and legs.

If a sunburn has already occurred, apply cream or lotion to moisturize and cool the skin. Pain relievers can ease the burn as well. Other than that, you just need to wait it out; most sunburns will subside within a few days.

## References

*Adventure Cyclist.* July 1996.

*Bicycling Magazine.* Jan. 1995–July 1996.

Chauner, David, and Michael Halstead. *Tour de France Complete Book of Cycling.* New York: Villard Books, 1990.

Ford, Norman D. *Keep On Pedaling: The Complete Guide to Adult Bicycling.* Woodstock, Vt.: The Countryman Press, 1990.

Honig, Daniel. *How to Bike Better.* New York: Ballantine Books, 1985.

LeMond, Greg, and Kent Gordis. *Greg LeMond's Complete Book of Bicycling.* New York: G. P. Putnam's Sons, 1990.

Matheny, Fred. Bicycling Magazine's *Complete Guide to Riding and Racing Techniques.* Emmaus, Penn.: Rodale Press, 1989.

Perry, David B. *Bike Cult.* New York: Four Walls Eight Windows, 1995.

Van der Plas, Rob. *The Bicycle Commuting Book.* San Francisco: Bicycle Books, 1989.

Weaver, Susan. *A Woman's Guide to Cycling.* Berkeley, Cal.: Ten Speed Press, 1991.

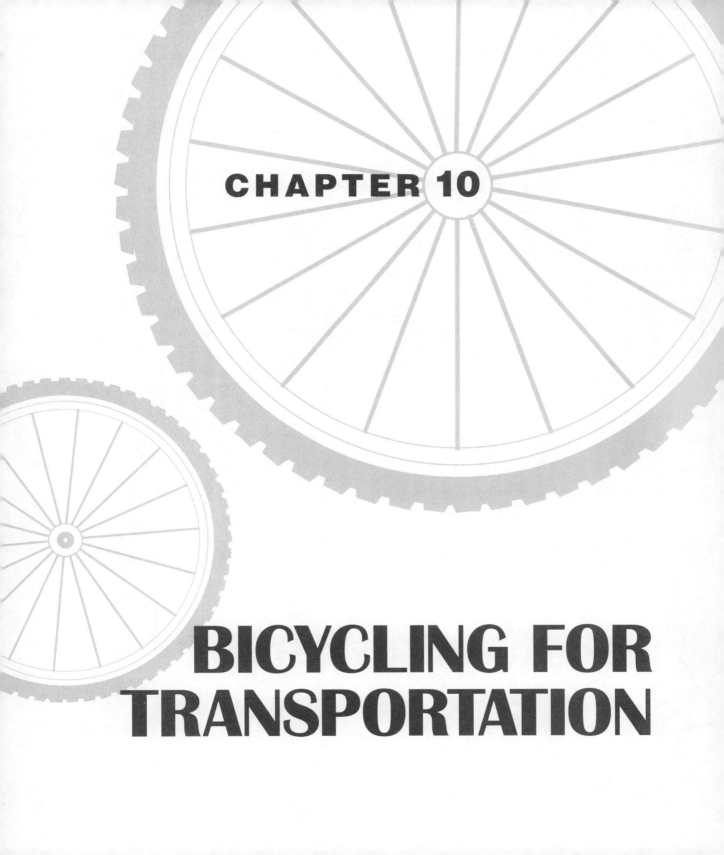

# CHAPTER 10

# BICYCLING FOR TRANSPORTATION

# Why Use Bicycles for Transportation?

You may ask, "Why use bicycles for transportation?" But, as you'll discover as you read this section, the better question is, "Why *not* use bicycles for transportation?"

## Environmental Benefits

In recent decades concern for the environment has grown tremendously. As natural resources dwindle, the ozone layer depletes, and pollution becomes a health threat, more and more attention has been given to promoting practices that will help preserve the earth and keep it a safe place to live. The energy crisis of the 1970s is in large part responsible for the bike boom of that decade. Besides walking, no other form of transportation is as environmentally sound as cycling. And no other means of transportation—including walking—is as healthy, practical, and energy efficient.

*Bikes create little or no pollution.* Motor vehicles burn fuel in a process that releases harmful chemicals such as carbon monoxide into the air. These pollutants adversely affect the air we breathe, the rain that falls, and the ozone layer that protects us from the sun's damaging rays. Pollution from motor vehicles is at least partly responsible for tens of thousands of deaths each year. And ironically, short car trips (trips that could be made by bikes instead) cause the most pollution per mile.

Riding a bicycle releases no pollutants into the air. The amount of oil that enters the environment via a bike chain is negligible compared to that used by motor vehicles. Even the process of making a bicycle, which is an industrial process that involves a good deal of hazardous waste and pollution, creates nowhere near the environmental assault that car manufacturing does.

Another environmental concern is noise pollution. Again, bicycles beat every other form of transportation. The majority of the world's noise pollution can be attributed to motor vehicles—roaring engines, screeching tires, blaring horns, whining security alarms, screaming sirens. The effect of noise pollution is difficult to quantify, though it clearly increases stress levels and causes sleep loss. Everyone at some point—some of us daily—has been disturbed by the harsh noise of a vehicle. But when was the last time you were severely shaken by the sound of a bicycle? Bikes have no engine noise, no loud horns, and no alarm systems. Unlike motorists in their sound-proof cars, though, cyclists, who are least responsible for noise pollution, are unfortunately the people who suffer most from it.

*Bikes use up fewer natural resources.* Much of the same raw materials go into making cars and bikes: metal, rubber, some plastic, perhaps a little leather. And there's even some similarity in the methods of production; most bikes, like cars, are made in factories that use the latest industrial processes. Bikes are smaller, though, and have many fewer parts than cars. Therefore, dozens of bikes can be made using the resources and energy needed to construct one car.

*Bikes make better use of land.* Typically, about half the land in a large American city is taken up by roads. And judging by the constant traffic jams, there still doesn't seem to be enough room for all the cars and trucks. We're constantly building newer, wider roads to ease congestion, yet we haven't even begun to solve the traffic problems in our cities. The solution? Bicycles, of course.

Bikes take up only a fraction of the road room that cars require. While one car can carry more people than one bike, over the same period of time a road full of bikes could transport a lot more people than a road full of cars. If more people used bikes—even just for short rides—there would be no traffic jams and no need to use up more precious space on expanding roads. We probably would even be able to make roads thinner!

## Economic Benefits

You do the math. A new car can cost anywhere from $10,000 to $20,000, or more. As we learned in Chapter 4, a respectable new bicycle will run from around $300 to $600. Where a car could easily cost a buyer half a year's salary, a bike may not even add up to a week's pay.

Then there's the cost of maintaining a vehicle. Gas alone costs five to ten cents per mile, which adds up quickly when you're driving 10,000 miles a year. And don't forget about the price of oil changes, tune-ups, parts replacement, repairs, and of course, insurance. Bikes, on the other hand, have absolutely no fuel costs, very low maintenance costs, and no special insurance charges.

Of course, you don't need to do away with your car completely. When it comes to long-distance traveling and load-carrying, bikes simply cannot compete with a car or truck. But if everyone who traveled alone in a car on a trip of less than four miles took a bicycle instead, even that would save society billions of dollars a year in gasoline and other expenses.

People who use public transportation could save money as well. The cost of taking buses, trains, and cabs every day adds up, while using a bike on a daily basis is virtually free. And by biking, it's not only you that saves money, but potentially the whole country. More cyclists on the road means less money paid in taxes for road maintenance and construction, pollution control, parking facilities, and auto industry and gasoline subsidies.

## Efficiency

Most people assume cars will get them to their destination a lot faster than bikes. It's an understandable conclusion—after all, a speeding car can move four or five times faster than a speeding bike. For city riding, though, speed limits, traffic, stop lights, and a lack of parking slow motorists down considerably. In fact, bicycles typically outrun cars on a trip through town. Most of the time, cyclists even beat buses and subway trains, which usually can't take you exactly where you want to go anyway.

## Health Benefits

For people with hectic schedules, there's no better way to fit in a workout than by using your bike as transportation. Almost everyone needs to spend some part of the day traveling—whether to work, to the store, or to school. Instead of sitting passively in a car for that period of time, why not use your travel time to increase your fitness and decrease your stress? You'll feel a lot better when you get wherever you're going.

For a more detailed discussion of the many important exercise and health benefits (and health concerns) of cycling, refer back to Chapter 9.

# Bike-Friendly Communities

While bicycles are versatile enough to use in just about any environment, using them as a legitimate form of transportation is a lot easier when your city, town, or neighborhood is receptive to cyclists and cycling. Your decision whether or not to commute to work on a bike, or even to cycle to the store, will no doubt be based in part on how dangerous and difficult riding is in your area. Some cities are well known to be bike-friendly, while other cities can be downright hostile. Most places fall somewhere in between.

Before you start riding seriously around your hometown, you may want to determine whether the area is bike-friendly. The more of the following criteria in your area, the happier you'll be riding around:

*Plenty of cyclists on the streets.* Lots of bicycles probably means people enjoy riding around town. That's a good sign. It should make you feel more comfortable to use the roads as well. Besides, the existence of cyclists can make a town seem more welcoming, and the roads less impersonal.

*Clean air and well-kept streets.* No one wants to ride in a city where the smog levels are dangerously high. Cyclists can be even more affected by pollution than other road users because they are directly exposed to the exhaust of motor vehicles. Streets that are filled with litter and poorly maintained are also hazardous for cyclists.

*Government support of cycling.* If a city is bike-friendly, it means that either the government actively encourages bikes or else private bike organizations have been very successful in influencing government to act. Ideally, there will be a combination of both. One way to determine how much interest local government takes in bikes is to check if the city has a city-supported office or committee dedicated to bicycling advocacy. These agencies may reward government employees who commute to work on bike, recognize businesses that encourage bicycle commuting, or require the creation of bike facilities in office buildings. Another indicator of bike-friendliness is a police force that uses bicycles on patrol. Of course, one of the most important factors is how much funding a city gives to bike projects. All the good intentions in the world don't mean a thing unless the city is willing to pay for improvements. One of the simplest and most helpful is conveniently located bike parking facilities.

There should be plenty of parking in the downtown business areas as well as near government buildings, parks, and in train and subway stations. Cities can take this one step further by offering fully equipped bike parking facilities that include lockers, changing areas, and showers for commuters, plus repair services and parts.

*Locally active bike groups.* There should be a wide range of groups that encourage riding and represent the interests of riders. These range from advocacy groups to bike clubs to special-interest singles clubs for cyclists. In addition, these groups should be active and vocal in city life and politics. The more groups the better.

*Good bike shops.* Lots of bike-related businesses means lots of riders. The best bike shops tend to be located in areas where there are large concentrations of serious, active riders.

*A variety of programs to encourage cycling.* These may include bike-related charity events, swap meets, organized mass rides, educational programs, amateur and professional races, and bike shows and conferences.

*Plenty of road access for bikes.* Though the effectiveness of bike paths and bike lanes is dubious at best, their existence indicates that local officials are aware of bike traffic and wish to encourage it. Bike lanes may also encourage bike riders who feel safer and more welcome riding on city streets in specially designated areas. Before you use a bike path or lane, though, be sure to read the section in Chapter 7 explaining the dangers these bikeways pose. Cities can also provide off-road bike access by creating trails, bike bridges, and road underpasses that may be safer and quicker than streets.

*Bike access on mass transit.* Bikes should be allowed on all buses, subways, and commuter rails. There should be parking and lockers available in subway, rail, and major bus stations.

*Recreational areas designed for bikes.* Parks should have paths and trails—preferably some for bikes only—and possibly even a bike track for exercise and training. Tourist sights should have nearby bike parking as well. A city may also have designated areas that, either permanently or on certain days, are off-limits to motor traffic.

*Favorable weather and topography.* Unless they're in training, most people don't want to have to climb huge hills on a regular ride through town. Flat land makes biking more inviting in a city, while proximity to parks and trails offers convenient opportunities for more adventurous riding. A more compact and well-designed metropolitan area, in which most of the places you want to go are within a few miles of your home and easy to find, makes riding for transportation purposes more practical and efficient. Warm, dry weather is also a plus because it makes year-round riding more convenient. Weather conditions, though, are easily overcome in cities that encourage riding. Ironically, many of the most bike-friendly cities are located in cooler and wetter climates such as the Pacific Northwest and Canada.

## What You Can Do to Make Your City More Bike-Friendly

Ride safely, ride correctly, and ride often.

Encourage others to ride.

Get involved with a local bike advocacy group.

Start your own bike club or advocacy group.

Form networks with other bike groups, local or otherwise—there's strength in numbers!

Work with government offices on specific measures to improve conditions for cyclists.

Attempt to create an atmosphere in town in which bicycles are a familiar and accepted part of everyday life.

# Business Uses of Bicycles

Bicycles don't get enough credit for their use as beasts of burden. Sure, they're not as strong as motor vehicles when it comes to load carrying capability and speed, but they're a lot cheaper and healthier to use. Measured against work done on foot, however, bikes prove to be far more efficient in all ways. Given an appropriate task, bikes can be the most economical and efficient all-around vehicle for the job.

In the past, bicycles were used for many business purposes. They transported goods, moved people, acted as mobile storefronts, and were used in farming and harvesting. Bikes have even been used as ambulances and in fire fighting. While bikes in the United States have been largely replaced by motorized vehicles in business and public service, they still play a large role in foreign countries, especially non-Western nations.

In the United States, however, a good number of utility bicycles and tricycles are still made by companies like Worksman. Some have large platforms and are used to move loads around factories, warehouses, hotels, or airports. Others are designed to carry produce, ice cream, or hot dogs, or anything else street vendors might sell.

Bicycles are perhaps best used by companies that make deliveries. In cities, it's quite common for pizzerias, Chinese food restaurants, grocery stores, or other food establishments to make deliveries on specially equipped bikes. Bike messenger services advertise their ability to get packages across town, between businesses, in less time than any other mail service. And who could forget the newspaper carriers who rely on their bikes? For many young people, bicycles provide their earliest chance to have a job and make some money.

## Pedicabs

One of the most popular business applications of the bicycle has been pedicabs. Sometimes known as rickshaws, these pedal-powered taxis can be found all over the world—most commonly in East Asia, where they're used instead of taxicabs. Pedicabs typically have three wheels and carry two passengers along with the driver at speeds of up to ten miles per hour. In the United States, pedicabs are often found in tourist areas. Their slower speeds and open cabs make them well suited for sightseeing.

## Police Use of Bikes

A recent trend in police departments across the country is the creation of bike patrols. While police officers commonly used bicycles in the days before motor vehicles, it's only been in the last decade—since the rise of mountain bikes—that the bicycle has been reintroduced into law enforcement.

Mountain bikes have proven to be an effective tool in policing. They are quieter than motorcycles, allowing police to sneak up on criminals. They can go into narrow alleys, on sidewalks, down stairs, and on grass and trails where squad cars cannot go. They are a lot quicker than foot patrols and often even faster than cars in heavy traffic.

And of course, they're a lot less expensive than motor vehicles. An estimated twenty officers can be provided a bicycle and necessary equipment for the cost of one squad car.

Bike police are more approachable and more aware of their surroundings, making them perfectly suited for another trend in law enforcement—community policing. Because bikes are more low-key, they are quite good for undercover policing as well. And the extra exercise helps keep police in optimum shape. Because bike police are required to ride in many different situations, often under pressure, they also need to be particularly skilled cyclists. They should be well trained in safe riding and in the special demands of bike policing.

Police biking has become so widely accepted that there is an organization, the International Police Mountain Bike Association (IPMBA), that provides training, resources, and networking for bike police across the United States and Canada. The IPMBA is a division of the League of American Bicyclists, and can be reached at 410-539-3399.

# Using Bicycles with Other Transportation

While bicycles can take a person almost anywhere, they can be even more useful when used in conjunction with other forms of transportation. For instance, riders who wish to commute by bike but live too far from work can drive or take a train part of the way and bike the rest; or they can bike to the train station and then get on a train. Tourists and campers who don't have the time or capability to travel solely on bike can transport their bicycles on a plane or by car and then ride locally at their destination.

## Trains and Buses

The problem with combining bikes with other modes of transportation—called *intermodal transportation*—is often access. Many train systems, including city subways, either restrict bicycles during certain hours, charge extra to bring bicycles aboard, or else do not allow them at all. Buses are often not equipped to handle bikes, though bike racks have become more common on buses in recent years.

For commuters determined to combine public transportation and bike use, there are a few solutions. The first, which may or may not be practical, is to live in a more bike-friendly city that allows bikes on mass transit. If moving is not practical, folding bikes may solve the problem. These bikes are more widely welcomed on other forms of transportation, particularly when they are carried in a case and treated as luggage. Another solution, if there are suitable parking facilities, is to use two bikes, one that you take from home to the train or bus station and a second one that you take to work when you get off the train or bus.

## Planes

When it comes to airports and airplane travel, bikes are less accepted than they are on mass transit. In general, airlines only allow you to transport a bicycle if it is packed in a box or bag, often for an added fee of up to $50. That makes it nearly impossible to use the bike as transportation to and from the airport (plus, most airports are not easily accessible to bikes).

Some airlines are more hospitable than others. A few offer special arrangements for members of racing or touring organizations. If you plan to fly a lot with your bike, you'll probably want to invest in a bike bag, a piece of luggage specially designed for transporting a bicycle. These bags are large, often padded, and roll on casters to make them easier to move. Some can be collapsed to a size small enough to fit in a pannier—or at least in an airport locker.

## Cars

Unlike public transportation, you can decide for yourself how you'd like to transport a bike with your car. There are a few possibilities: on a rear hook rack, on a roof rack, in the trunk, or in the back seat. For the most convenience, use an outside rack. If you want to keep the bike out of the rain or protected from theft, keep it inside the car. Most bikes will only fit in the trunk or back seat if the front wheel is removed. If you put a bike in the back seat, be careful that neither the chain, the pedals, nor the fork rip or stain the car's seats. If possible, cover the bike with durable plastic, such as a heavy duty garbage bag.

# Finding the Best Routes

When it comes to biking around town or through a city, the rule that the shortest distance between two points is a straight line is not necessarily true. Plenty of other factors come into play when determining the best routes to take, including the traffic situation, street conditions, bike accessibility, the existence of hills, and the possibility of off-road shortcuts. When venturing out on a ride, don't simply follow the path you'd take if you were driving a car—that may be neither the safest nor the quickest route for a bike.

To determine the best course to take on a bike, start with a detailed street map of the area. Try to find a map that also contains topographical information so you can determine which streets have large hills. If you can't find a map that has both streets and topography, buy two different maps. Use the map (or maps) to chart rides—such as a commute to work—you plan to take regularly. For leisurely rides that you don't plan to repeat, such involved planning may not be worthwhile.

To minimize your riding time, consider routes that are free of road obstructions such as new construction. Temporary blockages will not show up on a map and may not last long, so keep an eye out for changing road conditions. Also pick roads on which traffic moves steadily and on which stop signs and lights are infrequent. Consider as well the time of day. On some roads, traffic passes freely during off-hours but jams severely during rush hour.

Unless you desire the extra workout (or don't mind arriving at your destination drenched in sweat), avoid routes that require you to climb large hills. If hills can't be avoided then consider whether you'd like to tackle them early or late in the ride. Also factor in wind resistance because strong head winds can slow a cyclist down considerably.

For safety reasons, use streets that are hospitable to bikes; roads that are rough, have no shoulders, cross bridges, or go through tunnels should be avoided. Small roads with light traffic are not necessarily less dangerous than large roads, so be careful no matter where you ride. One definite advantage to roads with light traffic is that: you'll breathe in less exhaust from motor vehicles. Obey the traffic rules on all roads, large or small. If you must ride at night, choose roads that are well lit, even if it means making your trip a little longer. For more specific information on safe road cycling, see Chapter 7.

Most of all, when choosing a route don't settle for the first one you find. Though it may seem to be the shortest and fastest path, you may discover better roads to ride. Try several different routes to determine which is best. And even once you have determined, beyond a doubt, the shortest path between two points, continue to alter your path every now and again just to get a change of scenery. After all, a little variety is the spice of life.

## RAILBIKERS

Did you know there are over 80,000 miles of abandoned railroad track in the United States? One small cycling subculture knows this fact very well. They take abandoned train rails and turn them into "bike rails," which they ride using specially designed railbikes.

Though there are probably fewer than 500 railbikers in the entire United States, they are a dedicated and active group. Because railbikes are not sold commercially, railbikers must build their own (therefore the bikes are only as safe as the designer makes them). Any fat-tire bike can be turned into a railbike; all that's needed are a few attachments that enable the bike to stay on the tracks. Railbikes have a small flanged guide wheel that runs in front of the front wheel along one rail. They also have steel outrigger bars on the frame that connect with and run along the other, parallel rail to help balance the bike.

Railbiking is a fun way to tour through miles of countryside without worrying about traffic, steep hills, or rough terrain. It's also a good way for blind and disabled people to ride safely. But for railbiking to be safe and legal, cyclists must only ride on *completely* abandoned rails and get the permission of the railroad's owners beforehand.

An organization called the Rails-to-Trails Conservancy is working to convert more of these abandoned railways into paths for biking or other uses. The group publishes *700 Great Rail-Trails* (1400 16th St. NW, Washington, DC 20036, 202-797-5400). In addition, a group called Rail Riders (P.O. Box 1480, Hillsboro, NH 03244, 603-927-4690) allows railbikers to network and share their enthusiasm for riding the tracks.

# Parking

Horrific as it may seem for the most paranoid of riders, there comes a time when all cyclists must leave their bikes unattended. It's called *bike parking*, and it causes some city bikers plenty of anxiety. Bike theft being as common as it is, most cyclists can rattle off a woeful list of all the times they or their friends had bikes or parts stolen.

Good bike parking not only prevents your bike from being stolen, it also should protect your bike from being damaged by another vehicle or even vandalized. And for cyclists who have accessories that are not waterproof, even a little rain can be a major inconvenience. While it's not practical to expect bike parking to shield your bicycle from all harm, it's important that your bike is safe enough that you feel comfortable leaving it.

Consider safety first when choosing a spot to lock up your bike. There are many degrees of acceptable places, from the impromptu locations, such as strong metal gates, tall poles, or trees, to the familiar wheel-mounted bike racks found outside of schools, parks, and libraries, to the fully protected indoor bike parking facilities. While regular commuters may want something that provides a bit more security (if it's available), most cyclists depend on what's available in the immediate vicinity. Wherever you decide to lock your bike, make sure it's safe for the bike and safe for everyone else as well. For example, don't chain your bike in a place where it will block people's paths. Besides being obnoxious, it may also be illegal.

Whenever possible, it's a good idea to park your bike in an area that's easily visible to people walking by. Hiding your bike may seem like a good strategy at first, but it only makes theft easier for thieves who prefer to work out of the public eye. Fully protected indoor parking facilities such as bike garages and lockers provide the best protection. These cost more than outdoor parking racks (which are generally free), but they also give you the most peace of mind if you leave your bike for long periods. Unfortunately, these more secure parking facilities are quite rare.

If you're lucky enough to find a conveniently located bike parking rack, use it. They are effective and they send a positive message to city officials about the necessity of bike facilities. Unless you leave your bike at a safe, supervised parking lot, always use a strong bike lock, preferably some sort of U-lock (see Chapter 7). And don't forget to take any accessories or easily removable parts with you when you leave the bike.

In towns where cycling is a popular form of transportation, the issue of bike parking has become a challenge for city planners. But no matter how many bikes are fighting for the same precious spaces, bicycles will never create the parking problems that cars routinely cause. At least a dozen bikes can fit into the space taken up by a single car.

# Protecting Your Bike from Theft

It's the thing every cyclist who cherishes his or her bicycle fears most: theft. Unfortunately, it's also one of the most common crimes perpetrated in the United States. Exact figures are unavailable because bike theft so often goes unreported, but it's no stretch to say that millions of bikes are stolen each year in this country alone. If you are lucky (or perhaps smart) enough never to have had a bicycle stolen from you, talk to other cyclists around you. Don't be surprised if every other rider has a sob story to tell. In the paragraphs that follow are a number of ways to avoid bike theft.

*Make bikes as undesirable as possible when parking them.* Some cyclists remove brand name decals or repaint the bike to disguise a top-of-the-line model as a piece of junk. Many cyclists remove wheels and saddles to make it impossible for thieves to ride away on a bike. Even thieves who load bikes onto trucks may avoid those with missing parts; they don't want the hassle of finding spare parts when they can simply steal another bike without missing pieces. An easily removable accessory such as a water bottle, headlight, saddle bag, or computer can be stolen individually and should also be removed each time you leave the bike unattended.

*Register your bike with the local police or other service.* Many police departments offer a bike registration service that can help in retrieving your bike if it has been stolen. Each bike frame has a unique serial number (usually found at the bottom bracket) that the police keep on file. If your bike is found, this number enables police to identify the bike as yours. Even if you can't register the bike, marking your name permanently on the bike can serve the same purpose. Or, you may want to pay a security company such as the National Bike Registry to keep a permanent record of your bike.

*Report stolen bikes.* Most times, police can't do anything to help you find a stolen bike, especially when it is unregistered. It may be either impossible to find the thief or too time consuming at a busy precinct. However, a large number of stolen bikes are eventually recovered, so it's worthwhile to report a theft just in case.

*Park your bike only at the most reliable parking facilities.* Easier said than done, particularly in towns that aren't especially bike friendly. In general, supervised parking is safest, while racks designed for bicycles are also good. Chaining bikes to any stand that's not made of thick metal can be dangerous, as can leaving bikes in places not designated as parking spots.

*Use an effective bicycle lock.* Rigid U-locks are better than cables, no matter how thick. Or better yet, use two locks, one cable and one U-lock. Many thieves are not prepared to break both types of locks. If you commute or ride to the same place every day, leave the heavy U-lock chained to your parking space and use the lightweight cable lock for other, shorter trips. See Chapter 7 for more information on locks and how to use them.

*Ride defensively to avoid bike-jacking.* Though relatively uncommon, a bike with an excellent lock can be stolen anyway while the owner is riding it. Worse than a typical bike theft, a bike-jacking puts the rider in a great deal of personal danger. Avoid it by riding safely on well-lit streets and by staying out of crime-ridden neighborhoods.

*Avoid parking your bike in places where bike thieves are known to operate.* Talk to other area cyclists. If they haven't experienced theft, they may know someone who has. Find out where thefts often take place, and park your bike somewhere else.

*Never buy a stolen bike.* Without a thriving market for stolen bikes, the huge problem of bike theft would not exist. Besides, you may be held partly responsible for a theft if you buy a stolen bike. To avoid stolen bikes, only buy from reputable bike shops. If someone offers you a great deal on a used bike, ask to see a receipt or registration. Without either of these, it's impossible to be sure the bike was not stolen at some point.

# Commuting Basics

If you would like to ride more often but can't seem to find the time, consider commuting to work by bike. It offers the perfect opportunity to get some exercise while doing something you have to do anyway. Depending on what kind of shape you're in to start, you may need to work up to an appropriate level of fitness before attempting the commute. With very little preparation, though, most people are able to start bike commuting right away.

## Too Far to Commute?

Before you begin commuting to work, you'll need to address a few practical concerns. First, consider the distance you live from your job. Commutes of less than five miles are no problem on a bike—they may even be quicker than commuting by car. Rides of ten miles or less are also easily manageable, though they may take a little longer than a car commute. That means you may have to get up a little earlier—a dreadful thought to some, but a small price to pay for all the health, economic, and environmental benefits. Longer commutes are possible but can be more time-consuming and difficult, especially for beginners. If you live too far away from work to make an entire bike commute practical, consider cycling part of the way and driving or using public transportation for the rest.

## Is Your Bike a Commuting Bike?

You also need to think about whether or not your bike is prepared for commuting. Most bikes, particularly touring bikes and city bikes, are well suited for commuting. As long as your bike is safe, reliable, in good shape, and meets the challenges of the roads (tires are thick enough, gears are suitable for hills), just about any bike will do. In fact, many commuters prefer to ride less expensive bikes in order to discourage theft.

If you need to carry materials such as clothing or a briefcase to work, your bike should be equipped with panniers or a rack. These are easy enough to install if your bike doesn't already have them. Commuters can also choose to wear a knapsack, though it will increase wind resistance and raise your center of gravity (making handling more difficult). Avoid carrying too much weight on your bike if at all possible.

If you're buying a new bicycle, touring bikes are generally well suited for a commuter's needs. And if you ever plan to commute on wet roads, by all means install fenders.

## Parking Facilities

While die-hard commuters will insist that anyone who wants to bike commute can and should do it, some cities or jobs make commuting a lot easier than others. First, consider the special facilities you will need—mainly, a place to park and a place to wash up. In bike-friendly cities, public bike parking and locker rooms are provided for bike commuters in the business district. Some employers offer these services.

If there is no safe outside parking close to work, you may be able to bring your bike into work with you. Perhaps there's a safe, empty closet where the boss will let you store your bike. Maybe you have room in your office or work area for the bike. As a last resort, there is undoubtedly some gate or tree near your place of employment where you can chain the bike. Remember, though, this will put your bike at a greater risk to theft.

## Washrooms

Because most cyclists work up a sweat when riding a number of miles at a brisk pace, it's important for commuters to have access to a place where they can wash and change clothes. Even on short rides where commuters don't even break a sweat, most riders still won't want to ride in their work clothes. They will need an area to change out of bike clothes and into proper work attire.

The most convenient situation is to have showers at work. Many large companies, particularly those that encourage bike commuting, have a locker room and showers on the premises. If not, perhaps there is a gym or health club nearby where you can shower and change before walking to work. Some commuters can make do without a shower (though their coworkers may beg to differ). They may wash up in the bathroom, using some soap, a washcloth, a towel, and deodorant.

If your employer does not offer suitable facilities, the best thing you can do is encourage others to start riding to work as well. You'll be setting a good example simply by commuting yourself. The more people who bike commute in your company, the more likely the boss will spring for better facilities.

## Wardrobe Planning

If you've ever witnessed a man dressed in a suit and tie pedal down the street on a mountain bike, you know that some cyclists think nothing of simply wearing their work clothes while they commute. Perhaps they tuck in their pant legs, but otherwise they dress no differently than if they were driving a car to work. If you feel comfortable biking in work clothes—then wearing them throughout the day—that's fine; it's the fastest and most convenient way to commute.

Most commuters, though, want to ride in clothes better suited for biking and then change into clean work clothes. To do this they need changing facilities (easy enough—any restroom or private office will do). They also need to pick out what to wear beforehand. Some commuters ride to work each day with their work clothes rolled up neatly and carefully in a knapsack or pannier. Others drive to work once a week and bring clothes for the entire week. Some never bring their work clothes home at all; they take them from work to a nearby dry cleaners and back again.

Once more, the type of job you have and your company's culture can make commuting easier. Commuters with jobs that require them to wear a business suit every day have to work a little harder to transport clothes and to keep them clean and uncreased. Jobs where T-shirts and jeans are acceptable make wardrobe planning a lot easier. And no matter what your company's dress code, if it frowns on bike commuting as unprofessional or unbusinesslike, commuting can be unpleasant. For people who commute to work daily, though, the extra planning is worth it.

## Bad Weather

A little rain or cold weather doesn't have to prevent you from biking. It could, though, make commuting more complicated. Some commuters simply abandon their bikes and drive their cars. Others just dress accordingly and stay on their bikes. While many commuters decide riding in bad weather is not worth the trouble, it is certainly possible to bike commute all year round if you want. See Chapter 8 for details on how to dress on cold or rainy days.

## Do You Need Your Car at Work?

Of course, people who need to use their cars for work will not be able to bike commute (unless they leave their cars at work overnight). Parents who need to pick up children from school or run errands after work will also have difficulty bike commuting. While most people could make arrangements to enable them to continue bike commuting, it's clearly not for everyone. Consider all factors before getting yourself into something that doesn't fit your lifestyle. Or, you may simply want to give it a try and see how it goes. If bike commuting doesn't work out, your car is always waiting for you in your driveway.

## References

Ballantine, Richard, and Richard Grant. *Richard's Ultimate Bicycle Book.* New York: Dorling Kindersley, 1992.

*Bicycling Magazine.* November 1995.

Forester, John. *Effective Cycling.* 6th ed. Cambridge: MIT Press, 1993.

LeMond, Greg, and Kent Gordis. *Greg LeMond's Complete Book of Bicycling.* New York: G. P. Putnam's Sons, 1990.

Matheny, Fred. Bicycling Magazine's *Complete Guide to Riding and Racing Techniques.* Emmaus, Penn.: Rodale Press, 1989.

Perry, David B. *Bike Cult.* New York: Four Walls Eight Windows, 1995.

Van der Plas, Rob. *The Bicycle Commuting Book.* San Francisco: Bicycle Books, 1989.

# CHAPTER 11

# BICYCLING FOR SPORT

# A History of Cycling Sports

## The Early Years

Ever since people started riding bicycles, they've also been racing them. A hundred years ago, before most professional sports even existed, cycling was the most popular sport in America.

Even before the modern bicycle had been invented, bike racing was a thriving sport. Back in 1868, only a few years after Pierre Michaux got the idea to put pedals onto a swift-walker, his Paris-based company organized a bicycle race, the first on record. Bringing together the ten top riders in Paris for a 1,200-meter race in the Parc de Saint-Cloud, the come-from-behind winner was James Moore, an Englishman who was friends with Michaux. He won 600 francs for his efforts.

Soon bicycle racing became a familiar sport in France as well as in Italy. The best racers were making pretty good money, both from race winnings and through the sponsorships of bicycle companies. As the bicycle industry began to move to Wolverhampton (outside of London, England) in the 1870s, it was the British who produced the top racers—at least until the 1890s when road racing was outlawed in England as a safety hazard.

It was also during the 1870s, in the era of the high-wheel bikes, that racing made its way across the Atlantic Ocean to the shores of the United States. Though baseball was already established as the top professional sport in the country, cycling soon made its mark. The cycling event of choice for Americans became the century, a one-hundred-mile road race that was a great accomplishment just to complete.

While early two-wheelers were quickly transforming into the modern bicycle, racing during the 1880s and 1890s lagged behind the latest technologies. Racers were less than enthusiastic about the invention of the chain-drive bicycle, which brought riders down off the dangerous high wheels of the ordinary bikes. The dare-devil image of the riders who were brave enough to pedal fast on high-wheelers was in jeopardy. Then with the invention of air-filled pneumatic tires, bicycles suddenly became more comfortable. Again, the rugged image of cyclists was threatened by the notion that bicycle riding could actually be pleasant. Within a few years, though, as it became clear that the new inventions not only made cycling safer and more comfortable but also faster and more efficient, racers embraced the pneumatic-tire safety bike.

## The Six-Day Races

As racing continued to catch on in the United States, bike races became longer and more of an entertainment spectacle. The most spectacular race event of them all was the six-day race, which caught on in America around 1890. Held in small racing arenas, cyclists would ride around for six days. While early races required cyclists to ride for a grueling eighteen hours a day, the circus-like competition soon degenerated into a nonstop 144-hour fiasco. Cyclists were pushed well beyond the point of exhaustion, while bands played in the infield, gambling ran wild, and gawkers filled the grandstands hoping for the chance (and often getting it) to see one of the racers collapse and crash to the ground.

By 1898, New York City—home to Madison Square Garden, the best-known site for early six-day races—mercifully passed a law that banned nonstop racing and forced the event to evolve into a two-person team contest. The new Madison racing style caught on across the country and gave six-day racing an air of legitimacy. The sport continued to thrive well into the twentieth century, and a tamer version still exists today in Europe.

## Early American Cycling Champions

The first great American cycling champion was a New Jersey racer known as Arthur August Zimmerman. Rather than subjecting himself to the agony of six-day races, Zimmerman quickly established his name in the United States as a top short-distance and medium-distance track racer. In the early 1890s, Zimmerman headed over to Europe, where the competition was tougher. In England, he was so good he was banned from racing in that country. In France, Zimmerman became a great celebrity, dubbed "Le Yankee Volant" (the Flying Yankee) for his record-breaking string of victories.

Soon after Zimmerman, Georgia's Bobby Walthour—"the Babe Ruth of bicycling"—followed. He too became a champion and a celebrity in the United States and Europe (as did his son, Bobby, Jr., and nephew, Jimmy, Jr., in later years). Then came Charles

"Mile-a-Minute" Murphy, who earned his name when he rode his bike faster than sixty miles-per-hour while trailing a train. The two most significant cycling heroes of the day, though, would emerge in the last years of the nineteenth century. They were Marshall "Major" Taylor and Frank Kramer.

At a time when segregation was the rule in the United States and black men were barred from most professional sports, the fact that Major Taylor, who was black, was able to overcome racism and rise to the top is extraordinary. More extraordinary, though, was his talent. In the face of constant hostility, Taylor broke the sprinting world records of the time and became world champion in 1899. Though he became more famous as a cycling champion in Europe than in the United States, Major Taylor stands as both a sports hero and a civil rights hero, almost fifty years before Jackie Robinson broke baseball's color line.

Frank Kramer was cycling's biggest celebrity in the first decades of the twentieth century—his stretch of sixteen consecutive U.S. cycling championship titles is unmatched. Kramer's perfect cycling form is still imitated by racers today.

## The Tour de France

As six-day races were becoming all the rage in the United States, long-distance road racing became the main form of bicycle racing in Europe, particularly in France. By the turn of the century, races that stretched between Paris and other French cities such as Brest, Bordeaux, Lyon, and Camembert—all well over a hundred miles away—were quite common. Competing bicycle manufacturers and sports newspapers continually tried to outdo each other by coming up with increasingly long and difficult road races to sponsor and promote.

In 1902, a paper called L'Auto was looking to increase circulation and came up with the long-distance road race to beat them all. The race would circle the entirety of France—from Paris to Lyon to Marseille to Bordeaux to Nantes and back to Paris—over 1500 miles in all! The paper dubbed the race "Le Tour de France." The first Tour in 1903, won by top French rider Maurice Garin, immediately established the race as a French institution that continues to this day.

## Between the Wars

During World War I, European racing was put on hold, but after the war, the sport returned to prominence despite the death in battle of many top cyclists. New champions such as Constante Girardengo of Italy and the Pélissier brothers of France emerged, and road racing continued as a hugely popular sport.

In the United States, racing promoter John Chapman (who succeeded H. E. Drucker and John MacFarland as the "Barnum-esque" colorful showman of cycling) and racers such as Reggie McNamara and Alf Goullet kept the six-day race alive. During the 1920s, the competition evolved into even more of a show, featuring a variety of racing events. By the end of the 1930s, though, Chapman had retired and bike tracks were shutting down all over the place. The Great Depression took its toll on the sport. Just as cycling had died out as a popular form of transportation when cars emerged decades earlier, now the sport of cycling was dying out as well. By the time the United States entered World War II, bike racing in this country had all but vanished.

## Postwar Cycling

Cycling, both as an activity and a sport, remained popular in Europe—in fact, it got bigger after the war. Champions like Fausto Coppi, and races like the Tour de France and the Giro d'Italia (Italy's version of the Tour) became more popular than ever. What few American cyclists remained were forced to venture overseas to make a living. The only cycling competition in the United States for decades following World War II was at the amateur level and it kept a fairly low profile.

It wasn't until the resurgence of cycling in the late 1960s that Americans again began to make a significant contribution to the sport on a professional level. Amateur and professional cyclists such as Jack Simes III (who was the son and grandson of pro racers), David Chauner, Audrey McElmury, Sheila Young, Mike Neel, and Jonathan Boyer became known on the international scene through the 1960s and 1970s. By the end of the 1970s, with the help of the popular 1979 film *Breaking Away*, cycling again became a high-profile sport. As never before, though, road racing became the most popular biking event in America.

During this period, while Americans made their first tentative steps back into professional cycling, the European cycling scene was dominated by champions such as Frenchmen Raymond Poulidor and Jacques Anquetil, and Belgian Eddy Merckx. From 1964 through 1978 Merckx won more major road races than anyone in history and earned his place among the greatest cyclists of all time. In the 1980s, France's Bernard Hinault became the largest European cycling star. By that time, though, American cycling had grown so big the Europeans were looking to the United States as the new home for the sport.

## Greg LeMond

Ask Americans to name a professional cyclist and they often answer Greg LeMond. Though he retired a few years ago and is at least a decade older than most current cycling champions, LeMond remains American cycling's greatest figure. Though he's arguably the best American cyclist in the last sixty years (if not of all time), LeMond's significance to cycling is even greater for what he represents. Turning pro in 1980, LeMond (along with *Breaking Away*) entered American popular culture as a symbol of the United States' re-emergence in the world of competitive cycling.

Born in California in 1961, LeMond first caught the attention of the professional cycling world when, at nineteen he joined the French Renault racing team led by racing great Bernard Hinault. By 1983, LeMond had captured his first world championship. His celebrity was not fully established, though, until three years later when he became the first American to win the Tour de France in the race's eighty-four-year history. LeMond quickly became America's first cycling superstar. Before retiring, he went on to win two more Tours de France and another world championship. Today he continues to be cycling's most recognizable figure.

## Mountain Bike Racing

By most accounts, the future of bike racing seems to lie in mountain biking. When the mountain bike emerged in the last decade as the most widely used bike in the United States, it was inevitable that a new type of racing would bloom as well. Though the first mountain bike races were held in California in the late-1970s, it wasn't until the mid-1980s that the sport became organized under the direction of the National Off-Road Bicycle Association (NORBA) and, soon after, by other off-road cycling groups around the world.

The first official mountain bike world championships took place in Colorado in 1990, the same year the sport received formal recognition by the Union Cycliste Internationale, world cycling's governing body. Mountain biking reached a new level of acceptance in 1996, when it became an official Olympic sport at the centennial games in Atlanta. The first generation of mountain bike champions has included riders such as Ned Overend, Joe Murray, Jacquie Phelan, Juli Furtado, John Tomac, and Tinker Juarez.

# Road Racing

Perhaps the most common and familiar type of bicycle racing, road races have produced most of the world's best-known cycling champions. There are several types of road racing events sanctioned and governed in the United States by the U.S. Cycling Federation (USCF). In all races, the winner is the cyclist who rides the course fastest. However, there's a huge variety in the distance of races, ranging from one-minute sprints to epic stage races that take weeks to complete. Also, some races pit cyclists directly against each other, while others require cyclists to ride against the clock. Road races can stretch from one starting point to a different finish line (called point-to-point races), or they can take place on a circuit course that loops around to the starting point. Depending on the length of the course and the distance of the race, a circuit race can require cyclists to ride a single lap or many laps.

## Individual Road Races

The most common type of road racing is the mass-start race where the first rider to cross the finish line wins. In mass-start races, either the racers all begin at the same starting line or else, as in handicap races, cyclists begin at different points depending on their past performance.

Most individual road races take place on circuits at least five kilometers in length. The exception is point-to-point races, which take place on the roads from one town to another and are more difficult to organize because they require more road space and often involve closing roads to vehicular traffic. Point-to-point races are more common in Europe, where bike racing is more popular.

Unlike circuit races that are held on flat city streets, point-to-point races are highly individual because each race's course is unique. Riders who are familiar with a point-to-point's course (if they've done the race before) have a huge advantage over new racers. Much of the strategy in point-to-point races involves anticipating the road conditions and planning accordingly.

## Criteriums

Circuit races of less than 5 kilometers (but of at least 800 meters) are known as *criteriums*. These are typically set on short courses that make use of a few city blocks on which a number of laps are often required. Criteriums are similar to track races, except that they're held on roads. Because criteriums are short and usually (though not always) held on flat courses, they emphasize speed over other riding skills. And because they are action-packed and self-contained, criteriums are popular spectator events—the most common type of road races held in the United States.

To increase the competition and excitement of longer criteriums, certain individual laps may be designated as *primes* (pronounced preems)—sprints that act as smaller races within the longer race. The prime laps may be predetermined before the race or chosen spontaneously by the referee. Winners of primes are chosen separately from winners of the full race.

## Time Trials

In time trials, racers do not compete against each other directly. Instead they ride individually against the clock, and the rider with the best time wins. While this may sound like a trivial distinction—because either way the fastest rider wins—in fact, time trials require a completely different strategy than mass-start races. Where much of the strategy in mass-start races revolves around drafting, it is not possible to draft in time trials. They are, therefore, a more accurate measure of a racer's speed.

Time trials vary greatly in length, from a few miles to over a hundred miles. Races sometimes take place on a circuit but are more often *out-and-back*, which means riders race out to a point then turn around and race back to the start. Individual racers start separately, normally at one-minute intervals, but if one racer manages to catch up to another, neither may draft.

Time trials may involve individual racers or teams. Team time trials usually feature teams of four riders, who can increase their times by taking turns drafting. Team times are measured by the third rider's time.

## Stage Races

A stage race is an individual or team race made from a series of point-to-point races. The best known stage race is the Tour de France. Riders race from one town to another, stopping to rest for a specified time (usually overnight) then continuing to the next town. After the entire series of stages has been completed, the rider with the fastest overall time or the most points (awarded according to placing at each stage) is the overall winner. Other awards, such as best climber or best sprinter, may be given for specific parts of the race. The longest stage races can take up to three weeks to finish, with only a few rest days allotted.

Because stage races are so long and physically demanding, the winner is not necessarily the fastest cyclist but rather the rider with the best overall cycling skills. While most stage races are European, a few shorter ones take place in the United States as well.

# Track Racing

While track racing was the major form of competitive cycling in the early days of the sport, today it is less popular than road and off-road racing. Part of the reason for its decline is, simply, the scarcity of bike tracks. Where velodromes (cycling arenas) were once a common sight all over the United States, only a few dozen remain in use. Nevertheless, track racing still thrives as an Olympic sport.

Though all track racing takes place on sloped bike tracks, there is some variety in the material and size of these tracks. Frequently they are made of wood, though cement surfaces last longer in open-air arenas. Most outdoor tracks range in length from 150 to 500 meters (333 meters is a common size), while indoor tracks tend to be smaller and therefore more inwardly sloped.

Depending on the number of laps required in a race, a track event can last anywhere from several seconds to several days. Some are mass-start or handicap races while others are individual time trials. Because track bikes have a stiff frame, a fixed gear, and no brakes, they can be quite difficult to handle. For that reason, only the most experienced road riders should venture onto the track.

## Sprints

Sprints are the shortest track races, with the 1,000-meter match sprint the most common. While competitors ride the entire length of the match sprint, actual sprinting often doesn't start until the final 200 meters, which is timed and takes about ten seconds. These end sprints are full-speed-ahead tests of cycling power. Before that, though, the race is more of a tactical battle than a speed contest. Riders may vary speeds—even come to a standstill (called a *surplace*)—as they jockey for the rear (drafting) position or try to fake each other out.

Most sprints pit two or three individual riders against each other; some sprints have a small number of two-person tandem teams (these are typically longer races). Preliminary sprints or time trials may determine which riders in a larger field of competitors will sprint against each other. Winners are determined through elimination, and the final match is a best-of-three contest.

## Time Trials

The most common time trial for men is the kilometer, or 1,000-meter (for women it is a 500-meter time trial). As with road time trials, kilometers (or kilos for short) are raced against the clock rather than against other competitors. However, most track time trials involve two riders who begin at opposite sides of the track. The fastest time wins. Often racers are allowed to ride one or two laps before timing begins (called a flying start). Kilos are short enough to qualify as difficult all-out sprints; they typically take a little over a minute for professionals to complete.

## Pursuit Races

Pursuit races are run as elimination tournaments in which riders are ranked according to time and paired off into two-person heats. In each heat, two riders begin at opposite sides of the track, exactly half the track's distance apart. The race ends either when one rider catches the other or when the designated distance has been covered. When riders are equally matched neither catches the other; therefore the pursuit is often a simple timed race. The chase tends to make the riding faster, though.

Pursuit races are typically 3,000 or 4,000 meters in length, whether individual or team pursuits. Team pursuits are essentially the same as individual races, except they are run with two teams of up to four members each. One team catches the other when

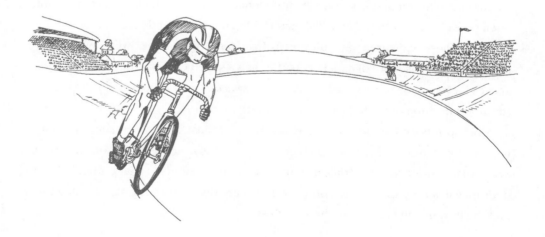

the third rider of the faster team pulls even with the third rider of the slower team. Teams ride in a perfectly choreographed formation, with the members alternating position as pace setter. While a pursuit race is too long to be sprinted, it is short enough for riders to maintain a brisk pace throughout.

### Points Races

Points races are mass-start competitions in which riders pedal around the track one hundred times or more. Certain laps, usually every fifth lap, are predesignated as sprints. The riders race these laps, and the top four winners are awarded points (five points for first place, three for second, two for third, and one for fourth). The race ends when the leading rider completes the required number of laps. At that point, the rider with the most points (not necessarily the leader) wins.

### Miss-and-Out Races

Also known as "devil take the hindmost," the miss-and-out is an elimination race similar to a points race in which after certain sprint laps the last person to cross the line is disqualified from the race. The race ends in a sprint when only a few riders remain.

### Keirin Races

A popular sport for gambling in Japan, keirin racing is similar to match sprinting, except it involves up to nine riders. The race is about 1,500 meters in length (about ten laps on a larger track) and because it is usually paced by a motorized bike or tandem, speeds of up to fifty miles-per-hour are normal. For the final lap, the pacer is removed and the riders sprint unaided for the finish.

### Madison Races

Madison races are relay races of two-person teams. Named for Madison Square Garden, the place where the six-day race became a two-man relay, modern Madisons are often 50-kilometer races in which teammates take turns racing. Other Madisons are run for a specified distance or over some period of time, and points races can be held during designated laps as well.

## Omnium Races

With omniums, racers compete in a variety of track events and earn points for placing in each race. The rider with the most total points is the winner. For the National Championship omnium, points for each race are awarded as 7, 5, 3, 2, 1, respectively, for riders placing first through fifth. Because omniums provide the whole spectrum of track events for maximum entertainment, they can be seen as the heir to the six-day racing spectacles of yesteryear.

# Off-Road Racing

The huge increase in mountain bike popularity over the past decade has predictably led to the rise of mountain bike racing. From its roots in cyclocross and BMX racing, mountain biking has blossomed to become a major form of racing. Just recently, it reached new international acceptance by becoming an official event in the 1996 Olympics.

The National Off-Road Bicycle Association (NORBA), which is affiliated with the USCF, is the governing body of professional and amateur mountain bike racing in the United States. Like other types of bike racing, riders can compete in a number of different events.

## Cyclocross

Because cyclocross race courses can be partially (though no more than half) paved, and also because cyclocross developed as a wintertime diversion of road racers, the USCF categorizes it as a road race. However, cyclocross racing is generally done off-road and is therefore the predecessor to the newer sport of mountain bike racing. Cyclocross courses even include terrain too rough to navigate on bike at all, requiring riders to carry their bikes.

Cyclocross is a mass-start race usually held on a large circuit with natural obstacles. Cyclocross bikes are neither as heavy nor as rugged as mountain bikes, and their tires are thinner as well. While the growth of mountain bike racing has made cyclocross somewhat redundant in the United States, it remains popular in European off-road competition. Cyclocross races tend to run 20 kilometers long for amateurs and 35 kilometers long for professionals.

## TRACK RACING WORLD RECORDS OF
## THE UNION CYCLISTS INTERNATIONAL

### Women's Records

| Event | Record holder and home country | Date and place | Time or distance |
|---|---|---|---|
| 200 meter lancé (flying start) | Olga Slioussareva, Russia | 4/25/93 Moscow, Russia | 10.831 sec. |
| 500 meter lancé (flying start) | Erika Saloumiaee, Russia | 8/6/87 Moscow, Russia | 29.655 sec. |
| 500 meter arrêté (standing start) | Felicia Ballanger, France | 9/29/95 Bogotá, Colombia | 34.017 sec. |
| 3 km. arrêté (standing start) | Rebecca Twigg, United States | 9/30/95 Bogotá, Colombia | 3:36.081 min. |
| 1 hour | Yvonne McGregor, Great Britain | 6/17/95 Manchester, England | 47.411 km |

### Men's Records

| Event | Record holder and home country | Date and place | Time or distance |
|---|---|---|---|
| 200 meter lancé (flying start) | Curt Harnett, Canada | 9/28/95 Bogotá, Colombia | 9.865 sec. |
| 500 meter lancé (flying start) | Alexandre Kiritchenko, Russia | 10/29/88 Moscow, Russia | 26.649 sec. |
| 1 km. arrêté (standing start) | Shane Kelly, Australia | 9/26/95 Bogotá, Colombia | 1:00.613 min. |
| 4 km. arrêté (standing start) | Graeme Obree, Great Britain | 8/19/93 Hamar, Norway | 4:20.894 min. |
| 4 km. team | Australia | 8/20/93 Hamar, Norway | 4:03.840 min. |
| 1 hour | Tony Rominger, Switzerland | 11/5/94 Bordeaux, France | 55.291 km |

## Bicycle Motocross (BMX)

BMX bikes were first popularized in the 1960s as a nonmotorized kids' version of motocross motorcycles. Since then, the BMX bike has been a hugely popular kids' bike. Whether or not kids actually race, quite often some sort of BMX-style bike is the first bike they get.

BMX racing boomed in the 1970s and continues to be very popular today for kids between five and seventeen (with professionals continuing into adulthood). Over one hundred BMX race tracks across the country host races year-round. BMX racing heats, called *motos*, take place on dirt tracks and run anywhere from 400 to 1000 meters long. Racers start the race on a short downhill ramp to build up speed, and may encounter gravel, water obstacles, and jumps throughout the race.

## Cross-Country Races

Cross-country races are essentially the same as cyclocross, except that for cross-country racing the traditional racing-style cyclocross bike is replaced by a mountain bike, and courses are shorter. Like cyclocross, cross-country racing is done on a circuit track with a variety of terrains, including trails, fields, or gravel roads. It may also be point-to-point if the course is suitably rough. Because a part of the track may be paved, cross-country somewhat overlaps the worlds of off-road and road racing.

## Downhill and Uphill Races

Somewhat similar to skiing, downhill mountain biking is an individual time trial that takes place on steep, high-speed descents (often at ski resorts). Like other time trials, riders typically begin at regular intervals and race against the clock. Uphill races, though much less popular than downhill races (for obvious reasons), can be timed or mass-start.

## Dual Slalom Races

Also based on a skiing event, dual slalom races pit two riders against each other on a downhill race through a slalom course. Racers must zig-zag around a series of gates, with time penalties for missed gates. In competition, dual slalom heats are part of an elimination tournament, where the winners advance to the next round until an overall winner is determined.

### Observed Trials

This is not so much a race as a performance. Riders follow an obstacle course, 25 to 100 feet long and often divided into separate sections, that contains natural hazards such as rocks, logs, mounds, streams, and mud. Using bike handling skills, the riders attempt to complete the course in a prescribed period of time without setting foot (or hand) on the ground. Each time the rider's body touches the ground—called a dab— the rider gets one or more points, depending on the severity and the number of previous dabs. The rider with the least amount of points at the end is the winner.

### Stage Races

Like road racing, mountain biking also has stage races. These may include a number of different events or they may be one long race broken up into sections. Either way, mountain stage racing tests all the skills of mountain biking, including downhill riding, hill climbing, and cross-country handling. The competition takes place over the course of one or more days, with the winner determined either by the lowest total time or the most overall points.

### Ultra Endurance Races

This is the general name for any mountain biking race, usually cross-country or stage, that is more than 75 miles long. They include the Race Across America (RAAM) and the Iditabike, a race across Alaska.

# A Spectator's Guide to Bike Racing

Unless you live near one of the few velodrome or bike tracks, most likely any bike race you attend will take place on-road. The good thing about road races is that they're usually free to watch, and you can move along the sidelines to find a good vantage point. But unlike track races, it's not usually possible to see an entire road race at once. A long stage race, for instance, can cover over a thousand miles, and unless you chase after the riders with your car you'd be lucky to see more than a mile of the race. For long races like the Tour de France or the Tour Du Pont, the only way for bike racing fans to really follow the event is to read about it in the paper or watch it on television.

Even on the shortest criterium courses, spectators are generally limited to seeing cyclists only as they pass on each lap. It is at criteriums, though, that spectators have the best opportunity to experience a road race. To get the best view, make sure you arrive early. Because many onlookers want to situate themselves at the finish line, it may get crowded there. But the finish line may not be the best place to watch the race from, anyway—at least not until the end of the race (or unless the race features primes).

Most of the time, a good viewing technique is to walk along the sidelines in the opposite direction of the cyclists during the race. That way, you always face the racers and you can see the race from different vantage points. Also, you get a better feel for the entire course—the turns, the hills, the straightaways. If you find a good position that allows you to see a large portion of the race course, such as on a hill, you may decide to stay there. Otherwise, continue to walk as you watch the racers.

As the race progresses, keep track of who the leaders are. It helps to know something about the history and riding style of the race's top riders (their strengths and weaknesses). Watch how they enter turns, how they brake, and when they decide to breakaway from the pack. These maneuvers reveal interesting aspects of the rider's technique and strategy. Also, pay close attention to who is drafting the leaders. Because riders who follow closely behind other riders encounter significantly less wind resistance than leaders, it is a tactical advantage *not* to be in first place for most of the ride. However, riders must take the lead at some point if they are to win the race. Drafting, as you'll see, plays a major role in bike racing strategy.

Some races allow the use of faster vehicles, such as motorcycles and tandem bikes, to pace the riders. Because cyclists draft behind these vehicles, paced races tend to move much quicker. Team races, in which a group of riders work together by taking turns leading while the others draft, also increase the average speed of a racer. In many team races, support riders (known as *domestiques*) are used to support the team leader by pacing, blocking other riders from passing, or using other strategic maneuvers.

## TOUR DE FRANCE JERSEYS

The Tour de France is not only a marathon stage race in which the rider with the fastest time wins; a lot of smaller competitions also go on. A colorful system has developed over the years to identify the leaders in various categories. While the ultimate prize is the *maillot jaune*, or the yellow jersey, other jerseys are awarded to winners in other areas of the race.

| | |
|---|---|
| *yellow jersey:* | Overall leader with lowest total time. |
| *green jersey:* | Rider with the most overall points (awarded after each stage). |
| *red jersey:* | Rider with most points at a particular point in the race. |
| *polka dot jersey:* | Rider with the most points for hill climbing, known as the "king of the mountain." |

Source: Chauner, David, and Michael Halstead. *Tour de France Complete Book of Cycling.* New York: Villard Books, 1990.

A nonriding team manager, known as a *director sportif*, may determine team strategy from the sidelines.

In mountain bike racing, some bike handling and downhill techniques will be different from road racing, though many of the same racing principles still apply. Knowing as much as you can about bikes and biking (the kind of information you gain from this book!) will help you appreciate what goes into bicycle racing. And the more racing you watch, the more you will understand the subtleties of the sport.

# How to Get into Racing

Bike racing isn't just for professionals. Amateur competitive cycling is open to just about anyone—including you. While you may not have the slightest ambition to be the next Greg LeMond, you might be surprised at how much fun and exercise you can get through bike racing. It will improve your riding form and technique immensely. And because there are many different skill levels in racing, it's easy to find a competition class that is both mentally and physically challenging while still appropriate to your experience and abilities.

## Decide on a Type of Racing

If you think you'd like to give bike racing a try, the first step is to decide what type of racing is best for you, a decision that will depend on the kind of riding you have done previously. Naturally, mountain bike riders are most likely to get into mountain bike racing. Whichever type of racing you pursue—whether road, track, or off-road—be sure that you have the right bike and other necessary equipment and that you are familiar with the basic riding techniques involved.

## Get a Racing License

All bike racers, whether professional or amateur, are required to have a racing license in order to compete. Three related organizations give out racing licenses; they are collectively known as USA Cycling. In order to receive a yearly license from any of the three, you must first join USA Cycling for a reasonable $20 a year (membership is free for riders fourteen-years-old or younger). While one-day licenses can be bought for the day of a race, they can be expensive compared to yearly licenses. If you plan to compete more than once or twice a year, it's in your best interest to join the organization. Besides, USA Cycling membership provides many other benefits for racers and nonracers, including training programs, racer's insurance, and events listings.

To race on roads or tracks, you must apply for a license from the U.S. Cycling Federation (USCF). For mountain bike racing, licenses are given by the National Off-Road Bicycle Association (NORBA). The cost is an additional $10 per year (in addition to USA Cycling membership), plus another $5 for an international license. If you plan to race as part of your college team you will need to join the National Collegiate Cycling Association (NCCA). NCCA licenses cost $10 a year as well. Pro Cycling, a fourth organization grouped under USA Cycling, governs professional racing. Special fees and qualifications apply to become pro (for now, though, let's just take one step at a time!).

To receive an application for membership and a racing license, call USA Cycling at 719-578-4949.

## Join a Club

Once you send in your membership application, pay the necessary fees, and receive your racing license, you are free to start competing. The organization you join will provide you with information on USA Cycling-affiliated clubs and racing events being held in your area.

It's a good idea to join a club if you plan to compete regularly. Many racing events, particularly road racing, are designed as team competitions. Even if you don't plan to race in team events, though, a club is a good way to keep yourself involved in competitive cycling and to meet other people with similar interests. Club members provide mutual support in racing and training, not to mention friendship.

## Race!

When you begin racing the officials will put you in the appropriate category for your experience level, probably the new licensees or beginner class. As you continue racing you'll advance to more competitive levels, including novice, intermediate (sport), advanced (expert), and national-caliber amateurs (or pros). Riders over age thirty are placed into a Masters category.

Based on your personal interests or on your cycling strengths and weaknesses, decide what event you'd like to compete in. Do you like short sprints or long endurance rides? Would you like to race with other riders, or against the clock? Don't feel pressured to decide right away, though. You may want to try out a few different events to determine what best suits you.

Though your first race can be very intimidating, rest assured it's something all racers experience. In the beginning, just try to get a feel for the competition—don't feel pressured to win or even perform well. At first, aim to simply remain with the pack throughout the race while you watch other riders and learn as much as you can from them. Ask riders and officials any questions you may have. As you become more comfortable with racing, your performance will improve.

In order to remain competitive in cycling, you must be prepared to expend effort and time in training. If you are not prepared to be dedicated to cycling, racing is probably not for you. However, a little effort can yield great results. And the more you succeed in racing, the more likely you are to train harder. As your dedication increases, so will your racing skill and fitness level.

## References

*Bicycling Magazine.* Jan. 1995–July 1996.

Ford, Norman D. *Keep On Pedaling: The Complete Guide to Adult Bicycling.* Woodstock, Vt.: The Countryman Press, 1990.

LeMond, Greg, and Kent Gordis. *Greg LeMond's Complete Book of Bicycling.* New York: G. P. Putnam's Sons, 1990.

Lieb, Thom. *Everybody's Book of Bicycle Riding.* Emmaus, Penn.: Rodale Press, 1981.

Matheny, Fred. Bicycling Magazine's *Complete Guide to Riding and Racing Techniques.* Emmaus, Penn.: Rodale Press, 1989.

*Mountain Bike.* October 1996.

*1996 Competition Guide.* Colorado Springs: National Off-Road Bicycling Association, 1996.

*1996 Rules of Bicycle Racing.* Colorado Springs: United States Cycling Federation, 1996.

Nye, Peter. *The Cyclist's Sourcebook.* New York: Perigee Books, 1991.

Perry, David B. *Bike Cult.* New York: Four Walls Eight Windows, 1995.

# CHAPTER 12

# BICYCLE TOURING

As you start to enjoy riding around your neighborhood or through the park, you may want to take cycling to the next level. Many cyclists plan entire vacations, or at least day excursions, as bike trips. Bicycle touring is a great way to combine all the health benefits of exercise cycling and the physical challenge of sports riding, with the fun and discovery of travel and sightseeing. On a bike, you're able to cover more distance than you would on foot, and you can enjoy the scenery more than you would in a car or bus. Whether you are taking in the gorgeous views in the world's most exciting cities or in the country's national parks, bikes can be the perfect vehicle for adventure.

While there's something to be said for the spontaneity of touring without a plan or destination, some degree of planning is usually necessary to make your trip as enjoyable as possible. For instance, without proper planning you could get lost or you could wind up riding through rough terrain—or worse, uninteresting areas. You don't want to push yourself to do more riding than you can handle, nor do you want to ride during unpleasantly cold or hot seasons. At the very least, planning ensures that you'll have enough supplies—particularly water and food—to get you through long days of riding. You'll need to consume a lot more food and water than usual on days that you spend more time riding. To help you plan your bike trip, a huge amount of information on touring is available through bike clubs and organizations, which we'll discuss throughout this chapter.

You have a number of options when planning a bike tour. Some bike tourists choose to sign up with tour operators, who often take care of all the arrangements, from food and lodging to support vehicles and routes. Others prefer the flexibility of going it alone. Some independent tourists carefully map out each day's routes and accommodations beforehand, and some just wing it. How you go about bike touring depends on your ability to plan effectively and your tolerance for surprises.

Once you're out touring, remember all the riding techniques and safety guidelines you learned in other chapters of this book. But if you're on vacation, don't worry about improving fitness or bike skills. Relax and have fun; everything else will come along naturally in time. Just keep in mind how far you'll be riding. Serious bike touring often involves up to 50 miles a day of riding. Make sure you're prepared for that and pace yourself throughout the ride. Ride in low gears that will allow you to spin and join pacelines whenever possible. Protect your body—particularly your rear, knees, back, and hands—from the strain that intensive riding can cause. Also, be aware that for extended tours you may need to carry a minimum amount of clothes and supplies in bike saddle bags, which will weigh you down and make riding more difficult (and braking less effective).

# Bike Clubs

For cyclists who race, bike clubs are extremely helpful and sometimes required. For recreational cyclists, though, touring clubs can be a great way to make the most of cycling. While it's certainly easy and acceptable to tour on your own, joining a club puts you in contact with other people who have similar interests. Club members grow as cyclists through mutual support and learning, plus they develop friendships in using their cycling hobby as a social outlet.

While racing clubs consist of serious teams with bike coaches and sometimes even corporate sponsorship, touring clubs just bring members together for group rides and to support bicycle interests. A good club has regularly scheduled rides of various lengths, designed for a variety of riding skill levels to encourage everyone to stay involved. Club members know the best roads or trails to ride and also organize events such as picnics and parties, to encourage family participation. Plus, clubs may have meetings for educational purposes (on maintenance or riding techniques, for example), or to organize a drive to improve bike access. Membership may provide other advantages as well, such as discounts at local bike shops or gyms.

Most large cities have a number of bike clubs to choose from, while smaller towns may not have any. Above all the other advantages of clubs, look for a club that has members you feel comfortable with and can learn from. Before joining, go out on a ride or attend a meeting to find out about the people in the club. The whole idea of bike clubs is to be social when riding, so make sure you find other cyclists who you like.

## SPINNING THE TUNES

 The best known song ever written about a bicycle is probably "Daisy, Daisy," better known as "On a Bicycle Built for Two." Legend has it Harry Dacre wrote the song back in the 1890s to commemorate the elopement-by-bicycle of champion racer Bobby Walthour and his sweetheart. Since then the song has been performed by dozens of musicians, from Chet Atkins to Nat King Cole to Hal 9000 (the computer in *2001: A Space Odyssey*) to the Chipmunks. But that's not the only bicycle song that was ever recorded. The following list contains some other bike favorites.

"Busted Bicycle," by Leo Kottke, from *The Best* (Capitol/EMI, 1977).

"My White Bicycle," by Nazareth, from *Greatest Hits* (A&M Records, 1996).

"Bicycle Spaniard," by Cracker, from *The Golden Age* (Virgin, 1996).

"Bicycle Race," by Queen, from *Greatest Hits I & II* (Hollywood, 1995).

"On a Bicycle Built for Joy," by Burt Bacharach, from *Butch Cassidy and the Sundance Kid* (A&M Records, 1969).

"Bicycle Song," by Linda Ronstadt and the Stone Poneys, from *The Stone Poneys* (Capitol/EMI, 1967).

"The Bicycle Trip," by Bruce Cockburn, from *Bruce Cockburn* (Columbia Records, 1970).

"Broken Bicycles," by Tom Waits, from *One from the Heart—Motion Picture Soundtrack* (Columbia Records, 1982).

"Bicycle Girls," by God Is My Co-Pilot, from *Tight Like Fist* (Knitting Factory Works, 1993).

"The Bicycle Slides," by Peadar O Riada, from *Wind's Gentle Whisper* (Bar/None, 1996).

"Pervertimento for Bagpipes, Bicycle and Balloons, S66," by P. D. Q. Bach, from *An Hysteric Return—P.D.Q. Bach at Carnegie Hall* (Vanguard, 1993).

# Day Rides

Day rides are just that: rides you can do in a day, usually over the weekend. That said, though, there's a huge variety in the length (10 miles to 200 miles) and difficulty of day rides. These rides are the most common feature of bike clubs across the country. Day rides can involve sightseeing in a town, or they may combine trail-riding with a cook-out or other activities.

Sightseeing on a bike can be particularly rewarding. It's a great way to see an entire town or area in a day, something that's often difficult to do on foot. However, be very careful whenever you leave your bike, for example, to visit a museum or church. Make sure you lock your bike securely and take along any bags or equipment that could be stolen, particularly in cities.

Thanks to the availability of bike rentals in many bike-friendly towns, it's possible to have a day ride even if you're not on a bike-oriented vacation. Ask the hotel receptionist or call local bike shops to find a place where you can rent a bike for a day or even a few hours. Rates are usually quite affordable.

Take only what you absolutely need on your day ride: plenty to drink, enough to eat, money (or better yet, a credit card), identification, a repair kit, suntan lotion, first

aid supplies, a bike lock, and appropriate clothing for any weather conditions you might encounter. You'll probably also want to carry a list of phone numbers of people to contact in case of emergency. Remember, though, the more you bring, the more you'll be weighed down. Get a fanny pack or small removable bike bag to hold everything.

# Extended Day Touring

Bike tours that last more than one day require a bit more planning but can also be a lot more fun. First, you will need to pack luggage, or panniers, so you'll have clothes and supplies to last the entire trip. Next, you'll need to find places to stay overnight. Campsites are popular choices but you will need to carry camping supplies in addition to clothes and the equipment can be quite heavy. Another possibility is to stay at small country inns, youth hostels, or even larger motels and hotels. To stay at these places, you only need one thing: a credit card (or a check-book). You may have to make reservations far in advance, though, which will make your touring less spontaneous.

Sightseeing on multi-day tours is a little more difficult as well. If you travel with fully-stocked panniers, leaving the bike behind safely may be unwise because panniers are usually easy for a thief to open or remove. On large group rides, the riders can take turns watching the bikes. Otherwise you may have to drag your bags along with you, or else keep riding.

A good solution is star touring in which you set up a home base—a hotel or a campground—to keep your bags and supplies. Each day you head out in a different direction, visiting new towns or sights. At the end of each day you return to your home base. You don't have to drag all your luggage with you everywhere you go, and it's safer to lock up your bike for a while.

Another way to lighten your load is to use a sag wagon. Frequently used on commercial tours or large club rides, sag wagons are usually cars or vans that ride along with the cyclists and carry their bags, food, or any other supplies. It can make riding a lot more comfortable and convenient, and easy to lock up and leave your bike behind when you want.

# Bike Camping

If riding all day on beautiful mountain roads or trails is not enough of an outdoors experience for you, consider bike camping. There's something truly liberating about riding on an extended trip, powered completely by your own body and carrying everything you need to live. Bike camping is the ultimate in roughing it and one of the most intense experiences in nature.

Bike campers may choose to stay at commercial campsites or they may set up camp deep in the woods, wherever they see fit. While staying at campsites is a great way to meet other travelers (and get a shower), finding your own place to set up a tent will give you the most privacy and intimacy with nature. Often, where you camp depends on what is available. Other times, the choice is yours.

Either way, you'll need to have the right camping equipment. At the very least, you want to have a good, breathable tent and a warm sleeping bag. Both should be waterproof. Make sure the tent is large enough to sleep all the campers comfortably (or get more than one). Since you'll be carrying all your camping supplies with you on your bike, the weight and collapsed size of the tent should be major considerations.

It's also smart to have a small lantern and a strong flashlight (a removable battery-powered bike headlight will do the trick). If you plan to cook while camping, you'll need a small grill or stove, a small pot and pan, a dish or two, and a few utensils. Keep everything as lightweight as possible. If you bring food, make sure it's nonperishable. Pasta, rice, or beans are good choices.

Bike camping is certainly not for everybody. After a long day of riding, the last thing you may want to do is set up a campground, start a fire, and cook your own dinner. Also, many bikes (even touring bikes) are not designed to efficiently carry the extra load of camping gear. Bike camping is definitely not easy. Make sure you know what you're getting into before you attempt it. Unless you already have a good deal of experience camping, don't try it alone.

# Maps and Guide Books

In order to find your way around safely on roads and trails, you'll need maps and guide books—particularly when riding in unfamiliar areas. Fortunately, there are endless resources available to touring cyclists. With a little research, it's not difficult to find bike tour recommendations, directions, and very specific road maps to just about anywhere, all geared specifically for cyclists.

The first place to go for bike maps and touring information is the Adventure Cycling Association (ACA). Formerly known as Bikecentennial, the ACA is the country's largest organization for recreational cyclists, with all sorts of programs and services for its 40,000 members. Their National Bicycle Route Network makes bike maps for the entire country, maps that can be bought through the mail or by phone. Membership in the group will get you discounts on maps as well as on hotels and other travel costs.

For off-road riders, the International Mountain Bicycling Association (IMBA), along with the editors of *Mountain Bike* magazine, published a *Mountain Bike Destinations Guide* listing trails (with phone numbers to call for more information) and a variety of other information. The book, published by Rodale Press, is available to members of IMBA.

Beyond that, bike tourists can search out good road maps for a particular state by calling any of these state government offices: Division of Tourism, Department of Transportation, Department of Parks and Recreation, State Highway Administration.

In addition, the following books, companies, and clubs are excellent sources of bike touring maps and information.

## Maps

National Bicycle Route Network maps
  Adventure Cycling Association:
  P.O. Box 8308, Missoula, MT 59807
  (800-721-8719)
Michelin guides and maps (international)
  Michelin, P.O. Pox 19008,
  Greenville, SC 29602 (800-423-0485)

Maps by Mail (international)
  P.O. Box 52, San Leandro,
  CA 94577 (510-483-8911)
Cyclists' Touring Club (international)
  Cotterel House, 69 Meadrow,
  Godalming, Surrey GU7 3HS,
  United Kingdom
  (011-44-483-426994)

## Guide Books

*The Mountain Biker's Guide To . . .*
(series of books) Menasha Ridge
Press, 3169 Cahaba Heights Road,
Birmingham, AL 35243 (800-247-9437)

*Cycling U.S. Parks: Scenic Bicycle Tours
in The National Parks* Bicycle
Books, Mill Valley, CA

*25 Bicycle Tours In . . .* (series of books)
Backcountry Publications,
Woodstock, VT (800-245-2151)

*Europe by Bike* and *Latin America
by Bike*
The Mountaineers, 1011 SW
Klickitat Way, Seattle, WA 98134
(800-721-8719)

*Mountain Bike Adventures In . . .*
(series of books)
The Mountaineers, 1011 SW
Klickitat Way, Seattle, WA 98134
(800-721-8719)

*Touring Cyclist Catalogue*
Touring Exchange, P.O. Box 265,
Port Townsend, WA 98368

## Accommodations

*Bed, Breakfast & Bike*
White Meadow Press, P.O. Box 56,
Boonton, NJ 07005 (201-584-1725)

*Bed & Breakfast In . . .*

*The Best Bike Rides In . . .*
The Globe Pequot Press,
P.O. Box 833, Old Saybrook, CT
06475 (800-243-0495,
CT 800-962-0973)

*Woodall's Campground Directory*
Woodall Publications Corp., 13975
W. Polo Trail Drive, Lake Forest,
IL 60045 (708-362-6700)

*The Hostel Handbook*
722 Saint Nichols Avenue,
New York, NY 10031 (212-926-7030)

# Packing Hows and Whats

Every traveler has a different style of packing, though most take more than they really need. With bike touring, you'll probably need to carry at all times everything you pack on your bike. And because bike weight plays a large role in pedaling efficiency and handling, it's very important to keep your packing light and compact. While it's natural to want to be prepared for any occurrence, in the end you'll be sorry if you bring more than what's absolutely necessary. That said, don't get so obsessed over packing light

that you leave important items behind—especially if they don't add much weight to
your load. As you become a more experienced bike tourist, you'll learn what you really
need and what you don't. If possible, try to keep all your luggage and supplies under
twenty pounds.

## Panniers and Bags

Supplies and equipment are carried by panniers, which are specially designed bike
bags that attach to brazed-on mounts near the front and rear wheels. While rear
panniers are more common, it's a good idea to distribute the weight on your bike
by using front panniers as well. Whether front or rear, panniers should be mounted
reasonably low—with the heaviest supplies packed lowest—to keep your weight
stable. Get panniers that are bright in color and just large enough for your needs.
They should also be easy to carry separately if you need to leave your bike behind.

A small handlebar bag is a good place to put your sunglasses, maps, suntan lotion,
identification, and a credit card. Put your repair kit in a small saddle bag just below
your seat. All bags should be waterproof, in case of rain. To be safe, though, pack

items in plastic bags to ensure they stay dry in a heavy rain storm. Carry any extra supplies, such as larger camping equipment, on the rear rack.

## What to Pack

Pack as little clothing as possible. Most tourists can get by with two or three pairs of shorts and two or three shirts, no matter how long they travel. This requires you to wash your clothes often, almost every night. Good bicycle clothing, though, is easy to wash and quick to dry. Packing light is worth it for the space you save. Make sure you pack at least one (not counting what you're currently wearing) of each of the following items.

| | |
|---|---|
| Cycling shorts | Underwear (a few pairs) |
| Tights | Cycling shoes |
| Leg warmers (in cooler climates) | Gloves |
| Jersey | Socks |
| Sweater or sweatshirt (in cooler climates) | Street clothes, including long pants, a long-sleeve shirt, |
| Waterproof windbreaker or jacket | T-shirts, and hat |

For more information on bicycle clothing, see Chapter 8. In addition to clothes, bring the following supplies.

| | |
|---|---|
| Maps | Sewing kit |
| Water bottles | Repair and tool kit |
| Flashlight | Air pump |
| Toiletries | Bike lock |
| Towels | Compass |
| Sunscreen | Optional: camera, book, notebook, pen |
| Insect repellent | |
| First aid kit | |

If you plan to camp, make sure you bring the following supplies as well.

Tent

Sleeping bag

Sleeping pad

Lantern

Pocket knife

Stove and fuel

Pot and pan

Bowl and spoon

Scrubbing sponge (for cleaning)

Nonperishable food and spices

Can opener

## ALTERNATIVE CYCLING SPORTS

A number of alternative sports were developed as the sport of cycling progressed. The following paragraphs describe the main ones, so far.

*Freestyle.* Freestyle riding developed out of the BMX subculture and is related to skateboarding. Freestylers perform various jumps and maneuvers as they ride at high speeds inside a bike half-pipe or rink. Tricks include the half-decade, the windshield wiper, the X-up, and the helicopter.

*Acrobatic and artistic cycling.* These are gymnastics with a bicycle. Participants perform routines and are graded by judges.

*Cycleball and bicycle polo.* Cycleball is like indoor soccer, except the ball is hit with cyclists' wheels. Two-person teams (one goalie and one in the field) compete, with most teams coming from Europe. Bicycle polo is played outdoors and is very similar to traditional polo, except it is played on bikes.

# Tour Operators

There are literally hundreds of companies based in the United States that offer bike tours anywhere you'd want to go in the world. Most smaller tour operators specialize in tours to one region or country, though some offer a wide variety of trips. Call many companies and ask for brochures to find the one that best suits your needs. Make reservations as early as possible because many of the best tours get booked quickly. Certainly, there is a bike tour to suit just about everyone.

The two best sources for finding tour operators are the publications put out by the Adventure Cycling Association (ACA) and the League of American Bicyclists (LAB). Both the ACA's *The Cyclists' Yellow Pages* and the LAB's *Bicycle USA Tourfinder* contain extensive listings of tour operators, and both sources are available to members of the organizations. To get these publications, call or write to the groups at the following locations.

Adventure Cycling Association
P.O. Box 8308
Missoula, MT 59807
406-721-1776l; www.adv.cycling.org

League of American Bicyclists
190 W. Ostend Street, Suite 120
Baltimore, MD 21230
800-288-BIKE; www.bikeleague.org

## How to Pick a Tour

Depending on where you want to go, there will likely be many tour companies to choose from. How you find the best one for you is a matter of doing a little research and asking the right questions. The following paragraphs describe what to look for.

*Location.* There are bike tours to just about anywhere in the world. Pick where you want to go, considering the seasonal weather and the difficulty of the terrain in addition to the sights you'll see. Be open, as well, to the suggestions of others. A trip to a place you never considered going may turn out to be an incredible experience. Before signing up, get as much specific information about what you'll see, the amount of time you'll stay, and the routes you'll take.

*A reputable company.* The tour operator should have a good reputation and a strong track record for successful trips. Get a recommendation from a friend or another bike enthusiast.

*Tour leaders and support.* Any organized trip you take should be led by experienced adult cyclists who know the area thoroughly. There should also be someone (possibly the leader) who knows how to fix any mechanical problems and is familiar with first aid techniques. Sag wagons often accompany tours, as well.

*Difficulty.* Tours can range in level from very easy to very difficult. Don't sign up for a tour you aren't sure you can handle (or one that's too easy). If you get stuck on an inappropriate trip, you won't have fun and you could injure yourself.

*Accommodations and meals.* Some tourists prefer to rough-it as much as possible, while others want luxury hotels. Either choice, and everything in between, is available—just make sure you know exactly what you're getting. The same advice applies to food. Find a tour that will provide what you want in a bike trip.

*Others on the tour.* Find out how many people will be on the tour with you. You may prefer the intimacy of a small tour, or the social possibilities of a large one. Also, some tours are designed to attract specific groups, such as singles, women, or church members.

*Cost.* Prices vary considerably, even among tours in the same area. Pay only for accommodations you want. Beyond that, as long as you get what you're paying for, price shouldn't be the main consideration. If you want to save some money, expect less from a tour operator or go it alone.

# Popular Rides and Festivals

The following lists contain just some of the major rides and festivals held annually across the country. Most of the rides are quite long, so be sure to prepare in advance. For more complete information on rides, a great source is the *Bicycle USA Almanac*, put out by the League of American Bicyclists (800-288-BIKE). For information on off-road rides, trails, and festivals, a good place to look is the *Mountain Bike Destinations Guide*, put out by the IMBA (303-545-9011) and *Mountain Bike* magazine.

## Rides

Bicycle Ride Across Georgia (BRAG);
    P.O. Box 576, Stone Mountain,
    GA 30086; 770-921-6166; June
Bicycle Ride Across the Magnificent
    Miles of Illinois (BAMMI);
    1440 W. Washington, Chicago,
    IL 60607; 312-243-2000; August
Bicycle Ride Across Tennessee;
    Tennessee State Parks,
    401 Church St., Nashville,
    TN 37243; 615-532-0016; October
Bike Florida; P.O. Box 115706,
    431 Arch, Gainesville, FL 32611;
    904-392-8192; June
Bike Ride Across Nebraska (BRAN);
    10730 Pacific St., Ste. 218,
    Omaha, NE 68114; June
Bike Virginia; P.O. Box 203,
    Williamsburg, VA 23187;
    804-229-0507; June
Boston-Montreal-Boston;
    42 Greenwood Dr., Bluffton, SC
    29910; 803-757-4191; August
Cycle Montana; Adventure Cycling
    Assoc., P.O. Box 8308, Missoula,
    MT 59807; August

Detroit Free Press Michigander;
    Rails-to-Trails Conservancy,
    913 Holmes Rd., Ste. 145, Lansing,
    MI 48910; 517-393-6022; July
Escape from New York Century;
    21-70 24th St., Astoria, NY 11105;
    212-288-6324; September
Great Annual Bicycle Adventure along
    the Wisconsin River (GRABAAWR);
    P.O. Box 310, 4182 Percussion
    Rock Rd., Spring Green, WI 53588;
    608-935-RIDE; June
Grand Canyon to Mexico Bicycle Tour;
    P.O. Box 40814, Tucson, AZ 85733;
    602-751-9938; all year
Kansas Dirt Tour; 8916 Millstone
    Circle, Lenexa, KS 66220;
    913-492-4015; September
Moose Tour; Maine Wheels, 225 Paris
    Hill Road, South Paris, ME 04281;
    207-743-2577; July
Ozark Mountains Bicycle Challenge;
    P.O. Box 579, Flippin, AR 72634;
    June
Pedal for Power–Across America; LAB,
    190 Ostend St., Ste. 120, Baltimore,
    MD 21230; 800-288-BIKE; May/June

Pedal for Power–Ride the Coast; LAB, 190 Ostend St., Ste. 120, Baltimore, MD 21230; 800-288-BIKE; September/October

Register's Annual Great Bicycle Ride Across Iowa (RAGBRAI); P.O. Box 622, Des Moines, IA 50303; 515-284-8282; July

Ride Across Indiana (RAIN); Bloomington Bicycle Club, 2818 Limestone Dr., Bloomington, IN 47403; 812-332-2409

Ride Across Minnesota; MS Society, 2344 Nicollet Ave., Ste. 280, Minneapolis, MN 55404; 612-870-1500; July

Ride the Rockies; Denver Post, 1560 Broadway, Denver, CO 80202; 303-820-1338; June

Santa Fe Trail Bicycle Trek; 885 Camino Del Este, Santa Fe, NM 87501; 505-982-1282; September/October

Seaport Metric Century; Pequot Cyclists, P.O. Box 505, Gales Ferry, CT 06335; 203-464-0174; June

Seattle to Portland; P.O. Box 31299, Seattle, WA 98103; 206-522-2453; June

See the Sea Spring Century; P.O. Box 81592, Mobile, AL 36689; 334-649-7177; May

Tour de Short/Atlantic City Rescue Mission Bike-athon; P.O. Box 492, Northfield, NJ 08225; 609-965-4823; June

Tour du Port; LAB, 190 Ostend St., Ste. 120, Baltimore, MD 21230; 410-539-3399; October

Tour of the Mississippi River Valley (TOMRV); Quad Cities Bike Club, 2023 E. 45th St., Davenport, IA 52807; 319-355-5530; June

Tour of Scenic Rural Vermont (TOSRV-East); Eastern Mass. Council/AYH, 36 Glendale St., Maynard, MA 01754; 508-897-5906; June

Tour of the Scioto River Valley (TOSRV); P.O. Box 14384, Columbus, OH 43214; 614-447-1006; May

Trans Texas; P.O. Box 1832, Austin, TX 78767; September

## Festivals

Bike Butler Mountain Bike Festival; 4770 Squiresville Road, Owenton, KY 40359; 502-484-2998

Camp Winnawombat; P.O. Box 757, Fairfax, CA 94978; 415-459-0980

Canyonlands Fat Tire Festival; 94 West 100 North, Moab, UT 84532; 801-259-5333

Chequamegon Fat Tire Festival;
P.O. Box 267, Telemark Lodge,
Cable, WI 54821; 715-798-3811

Craftsbury Mountain Bike Weekend;
P.O. Box 31, Craftsbury Common,
VT 05827; 800-729-7751

Crested Butte Fat Tire Bike Week;
P.O. Box 782, Crested Butte, CO
81224; 303-349-6817

Giants Ridge & Laurentian Mountain
Bike Festival; P.O. Box 190,
Biwabik, MN 55708; 800-688-7669

Hat City Cyclefest; P.O. Box 1034,
Bethel, CT 06801; 203-790-9352;
June

Jim Thorpe Weekend; 634 S. Spruce
St., Lititz, PA 17543; 717-626-1742

Julian Fat Tire Festival; P.O. Box 2036,
Julian, CA 92036; 619-765-2200

Methow Valley Mountain Bike Festival;

P.O. Box 147, Winthrop, WA 98862;
509-996-3287

Pedalfest; P.O. Box 1630, Park City, UT
84060; 801-649-6100

Shenandoah Valley Bicycle Festival;
P.O. Box 1, Harrisonburg, VA
22801; 703-434-3862; June

Team Big Bear's Mountain Bike
Festival; P.O. Box 2932, Big Bear
Lake, CA 92315; 909-866-4565

Thin Air Fat Tire Festival; P.O. Box #7,
Teasdale, UT 84773; 800-858-7951

Winter Park "King of the Rockies"
Mountain Bike Festival; P.O. Box
3236, Winter Park, CO 80482;
800-722-4118

West Virginia Fat Tire Festival;
Elk River Touring Center,
U.S. Hwy 219, Slatyfork, WV 26291;
304-572-3771

# Traveling with Your Bicycle

Taking your bike with you on vacation is an extra hassle that many bike tourists find
to be worth the trouble. While it's usually possible to rent bikes wherever you might
go—and tour operators often provide bikes—there's nothing like having your own
bike with you on long-distance bike touring. Your bike is already perfectly adjusted to
fit; it's comfortable and broken-in; and you know its gearing, its brakes, and all of its
quirks. An unfamiliar bike, meanwhile, can throw off your balance and cause muscle
aches for the entire trip.

## Taking Your Bicycle on a Plane

If you decide to take your bike on an airplane, be sure to call the airline in advance (preferably before you buy the ticket) to find out if there are any special rules or extra charges. Many airlines require a bike to be boxed and at least partially disassembled, though some will take the bike as is. They may have more specific rules concerning how the bike should be packed, the maximum weight of the boxed bike, and the size of the box. Checking a bike may be the equivalent of checking your luggage, or you may need to pay an additional fee according to size or weight. Some airlines are more bike-friendly than others, so check with a number of companies before booking a flight. Once you have made all the arrangements, be sure to allow extra time for checking in in case you have problems.

## Taking Your Bicycle on a Train

Most Amtrak lines allow bikes only if they are boxed or foldable. There is a $5 charge each way. On some Amtrak lines in California, Vermont, and the Pacific Northwest, unboxed bikes can be taken on the train, depending on space availability. To be safe, make a reservation for your bike as well as for yourself. Check local commuter trains individually because their bike access rules vary considerably.

Foreign trains, particularly in Europe, tend to be much more accommodating to bikes. Boxes are not usually necessary, and often you are able to carry your bike along with you. Just be sure to keep a close eye on it when you travel. Because some thieves prey on tourists, it's best to keep bikes locked up, even when they're right by your side.

# The Best Places for Bike Touring and Trail Riding

All over the world, there are so many beautiful and exciting places to bike ride, it's nearly impossible to come up with a list of great bike trip destinations without unfairly ignoring dozens of others. The destination lists below are by no means complete; they include a variety of areas, some remote and some easily accessible. Use them as a starting point when you begin to look for a bike tour.

To find tour operators that go to these areas, the best sources of information are the ACA's *The Cyclists' Yellow Pages* and the LAB's *Bicycle USA Tourfinder* (see the addresses on p. 284).

## In the United States

*Anchorage, Alaska.* Great cycling from Anchorage north up to Fairbanks, along the Denali Highway, including Denali National Park and Mt. McKinley. The combination of scenery and moderate summer weather makes for perfect bike touring.

*Kaibab National Forest, Arizona.* While the Grand Canyon National Park doesn't allow bikes on its trail, the surrounding Kaibab National Forest offers both road and off-road riding. The Arizona Trail will take you close to the Grand Canyon and the Painted Desert, through the forest, and all the way down the state to Phoenix and Tucson.

*Monterey, California.* While there's great cycling all over California, the stretch of Highway 1 between the northern Los Padres National Forest near Big Sur and the Monterey Peninsula is particularly gorgeous. Trees, rolling hills, and the Pacific Ocean are all in view, plus there's the nearby wine country.

*Durango, Colorado.* Best for serious mountain bikers, but with some great Rocky Mountain roads as well, Durango is in the heartland of off-road riding. Great skiing, too, with Telluride and Purgatory nearby.

*Cape Cod, Massachusetts.* A bike trail weaves around Route 6, taking riders from Dennis on the Nantucket Sound, all the way up Wellfleet by the Cape Cod National Seashore. Reached by ferry, Nantucket and Martha's Vineyard offer more scenic bike trails, if you don't mind the crowds.

*Missoula, Montana.* Being the home of the Adventure Cycling Association, you know it can't be bad. Full of forests and mountain ranges, stretching south to Butte and Bozeman, this area of western Montana has some of the most beautiful, wide open land in the country.

*Erie Canal, New York.* From Albany west to Niagara Falls, along Route 31, is a bike path that follows the Erie Canal. Particularly beautiful is the western stretch that passes near the Finger Lakes and on to the falls.

*Asheville, North Carolina.* With Pisgah National Forest to the north, Great Smoky Mountains National Park to the west, and Nantahala National Forest to the south, Asheville is the premier bike touring center in the South.

*Moab, Utah.* Like Durango, another mountain biker's mecca. A wide variety of trails cover all skill levels, with spectacular scenery all along the way.

*Jackson Hole, Wyoming.* Close to Yellowstone and Grand Teton National Park, and surrounded by national forests, northwestern Wyoming offers endless bike trails and sites, plus a moderate climate.

## All Over the World

*Canada.* There's no end to the possibilities for great cycling in Canada, from Vancouver Island in the west, to the Canadian Rockies, to the Toronto and Montreal areas, to Nova Scotia and Prince Edward Island in the east.

*Egypt.* Ever consider visiting the great pyramids on bike? Why not? There's plenty of flat desert land, thrilling views of the Nile River, and all those amazing historical sites.

*France.* In the land that created bicycling, you can't go wrong. There are plenty of tours to choose from and easy bike access if you want to go it alone. Try the south coast near Bordeaux, the wine country and Alps in the east, the northern hills of Normandy, or the sparkling coast of the southern Riviera.

*Mexico.* Whether you choose the Baja peninsula, with its breathtaking Pacific vistas, or the Yucatán peninsula, with its Mayan ruins and Gulf coast, there are miles and miles of adventurous cycling south of the border.

*Ireland.* Endless miles of rolling green hills and views of the sea make any Irish coastline, from Galway to Cork to Dublin, perfect for bike tours.

*Israel.* Pass Biblical towns and archeological sites at every turn as you easily make your way from fertile Galilee in the north, down along the Mediterranean coast, inland to Jerusalem, and south into the Negev Desert.

*Nepal.* The hills around Kathmandu make for some of the most thrilling and exotic mountain biking you'll ever do. If you can make it through the Himalayas to the foot of Mount Everest, you're ready for the mountain bike hall of fame.

*New Zealand*. Take a winter getaway down under—it'll be summer there. A great mixture of road and dirt biking, with mountains and towns along the coast of the Tasman Sea. There's plenty of camping too, if you don't mind a little rain.

*Peru*. Ride along the coastline desert, between the blue Pacific coast and the Andes Mountains, to visit ancient Inca ruins and modern cities. Or head up into the mountains toward the picturesque Inca city of Machu Picchu.

*Zimbabwe*. From Victoria Falls on the Zambezi River, through the highlands to spacious Wankie National Park, your bike tour becomes a true African safari. Just don't feed the lions.

# Century Rides

The grand event for recreational cyclists around the country is very often a 100-mile one-day group ride, usually sponsored by a cycling club and held in late summer or fall (September is National Century Month). These marathon rides are called *centuries*, and cyclists have been doing them for well over a century. For nonracers who want to direct their workouts toward a goal, the century ride is a perfect way to culminate a full spring and summer of cycling. In many ways, a century is the ultimate in recreational sports. It's definitely a challenge that requires preparation and conditioning, but it's well within the capabilities of most enthusiastic and determined cyclists. It's a full day of athletic activity, but the physical strain is not so great that you can't spend much of your time socializing with other riders and enjoying the outdoors.

You can find out about century rides in your area through local cycling clubs or by contacting bike organizations such as the League of American Bicyclists. For your first century, look for a course that doesn't have too many difficult hills and that is well marked. Also find a century that provides technical support for bikes and first aid for riders. Make sure your bike is in perfect condition before the ride, and carry along a well-stocked repair kit just in case. If you've recently made repairs or replaced components, be certain you're bike is broken in.

While there's a good chance you're going to struggle through your first (and maybe every) century, keep the ride in perspective. In other words, no matter what happens on your century ride, be sure you have fun.

## Preparation

Unlike racing, century riding doesn't require participants to learn any special techniques to do well. All that's needed is endurance, which is built up simply through riding a lot. Cyclists can prepare for a century by riding at a moderate pace over increasingly long distances. Start with 10 or 20 miles, easily accomplished over a few hours on the weekend. As you build up endurance and your body indicates it can handle more, ride for longer stretches at the same moderate pace. Go for 30 miles, then 40, then 50. Once you're able to ride 60 or 70 miles in one ride, while maintaining your speed over seven or eight hours, you're probably ready to take on the century.

If you're not used to riding for that long, it could take you some time to build up to the point where you're ready to do a century. Don't rush it. Even if you're in good shape, training will likely take a few months. If it takes you a few years before you're ready, it will simply make your accomplishment all that much sweeter.

## Getting Through It

Centuries require that you ride almost continuously for six to twelve hours in one day. Do yourself a favor and conserve energy. Get a good night's rest and have a high-carbohydrate breakfast a few hours before the ride. When it's time to begin, start out slowly. If you're lucky the wind will be on your side and the hills won't be too brutal (if you're concerned, check the course beforehand). Work together with other riders to form pacelines that will help you save strength for the long ride. Ride with others of similar, or slightly higher, ability. The sense of teamwork will also make the ride more enjoyable and satisfying.

In order to keep your body hydrated and to restore the energy lost while pedaling, you will need to drink and eat during the ride. Many organized centuries have rest areas at a few spots along the way for eating and taking short breaks. It will be necessary to drink, and possibly to eat, more often than a few times, though, so some of it will have to take place on the bicycle. Make sure you have plenty to drink—your body could easily need six to eight quarts of water or a sports drink by the time you've covered 100 miles. Don't wait until you're hungry to eat—you'll run out of steam if you do. Instead, eat something small but nutritious (a banana or sports bar is best) every ten miles or so.

Once you're finished, take some time to rest and replenish your body with ample amounts of food and drink. The finish lines of centuries are typically meeting areas where cyclists can compare notes on the ride and share stories. Enjoy yourself there—you've earned it. After you head home, give yourself plenty of time to recover before you start riding again. Then, when you're ready, start preparing for your next century!

## References

*Adventure Cyclist.* July 1996.

*Bicycle USA.* Baltimore: League of American Bicyclists, September/October 1995.

*Bicycle USA Almanac.* Baltimore: League of American Bicyclists, March/April 1996.

*Bicycle USA Tourfinder.* Baltimore: League of American Bicyclists, November/December 1995.

*Bicycling Magazine.* Jan. 1995–July 1996.

Chauner, David, and Michael Halstead. *Tour de France Complete Book of Cycling.* New York: Villard Books, 1990.

*The Cyclist's Yellow Pages.* 17th ed. Adventure Cycling Association.

Ford, Norman D. *Keep On Pedaling: The Complete Guide to Adult Bicycling.* Woodstock, Vt.: The Countryman Press, 1990.

International Mountain Bicycling Association and the eds. of *Mountain Bike* magazine. *Mountain Bike Destinations Guide.* Emmaus, Penn.: Rodale Press, 1995.

LeMond, Greg, and Kent Gordis. *Greg LeMond's Complete Book of Bicycling.* New York: G. P. Putnam's Sons, 1990.

Matheny, Fred. Bicycling Magazine's *Complete Guide to Riding and Racing Techniques.* Emmaus, Penn.: Rodale Press, 1989.

Nye, Peter. *The Cyclist's Sourcebook.* New York: Perigee Books, 1991.

Perry, David B. *Bike Cult.* New York: Four Walls Eight Windows, 1995.

# APPENDIX

## Glossary of Bicycling Terms

*aerodynamics* The study of the motion of air and its influence on moving objects. Aerodynamic refers to the ability of an object to move through the air with the least wind resistance.

*ATB* All-terrain bike, or mountain bike.

*ball bearings* Small steel spheres in the joints of machines (including bicycles) to allow rotation of the parts.

*BMX* Bicycle moto-cross.

*bottom bracket* Point at which the seat tube and down tube connect; incorporates the axle for the crankset.

*brake pads* Rubber pieces on the brakes that come in contact with the rim of the wheel to stop the bike.

*braze-ons* Frame attachments, which have been secured through a heated metal brazing process, that hold objects such as air pumps, water bottles, and panniers.

*butted frame* Bike frame on which tubes are thicker at the ends—where they connect with other tubes and bear the most stress—and thinner in the middle.

*cadence* Number of revolutions per minute of a pedal.

*caliper brakes* Common brake design using connected arms that squeeze around the outside rims of the wheel to stop the bike.

*cantilever brakes* Brake design using individual brake pads on both sides of the rim, pulled by a lever to stop the bike.

*century* 100-mile bike ride or race (sometimes 100 kilometers, called a metric century).

*chainwheel (chainring)* Sprockets held around the bottom bracket and turned by the cranks.

*clincher tire* Common tire design in which the tire has beads that hook into the rim and is held in place by the pressure of the inflated innertube.

*clipless pedals* Apparatus similar to a ski binding that connects a rider's shoes to the pedals without the use of toe clips.

*coast* To ride without pedaling.

*cog* Sprocket located around the rear wheel hub, connected to the chainwheel sprockets by the chain.

*crankarms* Arms that hold the pedals and revolve around the bottom bracket to turn the crankset.

*crankset* Mechanism consisting of the pedals, crankarms, chainwheels, and axle, located at the bottom bracket.

*criterium* Multi-lap circuit race, typically held on a few city blocks.

*derailleur* Mechanism operated by the shift levers that moves the chain between chainwheels in front or cogs in rear to change gears.

*development* Distance a bike in a certain gear travels in one complete turn of the pedals.

*diamond frame* Standard bike frame design in which the four main tubes form a diamond shape.

*draft* To ride behind another vehicle (often another bicycle) to reduce wind resistance.

*drivetrain* Propulsion mechanism of a bicycle, made up of the entire crankset, plus the chain, cogs, derailleurs, and shift levers.

*dropouts* Slots located at the ends of the front fork and rear stays where the wheel axles attach.

*drop handlebars* Handlebars with extensions that curve downward to enable a lower riding position.

*echelon* Staggered group riding formation used to block wind resistance.

*fender* Bike part, usually made of metal, sometimes found directly above the upper rim of the wheels; used to keep water and mud sprayed by the wheels off the rider.

**fork** Component that extends down from the head tube, then splits into two blades that connect to both sides of the front wheel; consists of a steering tube, or fork shaft, fork blades, and dropouts.

**freewheel** Mechanism on the rear wheel hub that allows the wheel to continue turning forward while the drivetrain remains stationary or moves in reverse.

**folding bike** Bicycle with a frame that folds for more compact storage and ease in carrying.

**gear** Combination of one cog and one chainwheel turned together by the chain.

**gear ratio** Ratio between the size of the chainwheel and the size of the cog in a particular gear; determines the development and pedaling difficulty.

**headset** Head tube mechanism that uses ball bearings to enable steering; an upper and lower headset are located at the top and bottom of the head tube.

**head-tube angle** Angle formed by the top tube and the upper extension of the head-tube.

**high gear** Gear with a larger development and more difficulty pedaling; used for level ground and downhills.

**honking** Riding out of the saddle; standing up while pedaling, for better acceleration.

**hub** The center piece of a wheel that rotates around the axle and through which the spokes are threaded.

**indexed gearing** Gear shifting system in which shift levers click and derailleurs move the chain precisely into preset positions.

**low gear** Gear with a smaller development and greater ease in pedaling; used for climbing hills.

**lugs** Reinforced metal joints that strengthen the connections of tubes on the bike frame.

**mountain bike** Bicycle with fat tires and low gears, designed for use on a wide variety of terrains, including off-road and nonpaved surfaces.

**ordinary bike** A high-wheeled bicycle common in the 1870s, also called a penny farthing.

**paceline** A riding formation in which riders draft in line behind a leader.

**pannier** Touring bag mounted on the sides of the rear and front wheels.

**point-to-point race** Noncircuit race with separate start and finish lines.

**quick-release** Lever located on wheels, brakes, and seats that allows fast and easy adjustments without tools.

**racing bike** Bicycle with thin tires and drop handlebars, designed for racing.

**rake** The amount of forward slope in the fork.

**recumbent bike** Bicycle operated from a reclined position.

**rim** Outer frame of a wheel that the tire is attached to.

**road bike** Bicycle—such as a racing bike, touring bike, or sports bike—designed for use on paved surfaces.

**road rash** Skin abrasion caused by a fall off a bicycle.

**saddle** Bike seat.

**safety bike** Modern chain-drive bike, introduced in the 1880s.

**sag wagon** Motorized support vehicle accompanying a bike tour or race, often carrying supplies, equipment, and food.

**seat post** Bar holding the saddle that slides into the seat tube.

**seat-tube angle** Angle formed by the seat tube and the top tube.

**spin** To pedal at a fast cadence.

**spindle** Axle that attaches to the crankarms, located in the bottom bracket.

**spokes** Network of thin metal rods that connect the rim to the hub on a bike wheel and support the wheel through tension.

**stage race** Multi-day bike race consisting of a string of point-to-point races.

**stays** Thin tubes connected to the main tubes of the frame that connect the frame to the rear wheel.

*stem* Bicycle component that connects the steering tube to the handlebars.

*stoker* Rear cyclist on a tandem.

*suspension* Ability to absorb bumps and shock from the road.

*tandem* Bicycle made for two riders.

*time trial* Timed race.

*toe clips* Frames or stirrups attached to the pedals that hold the rider's feet in place when pedaling.

*touring bike* Bicycle with wide-ranging gears, designed to carry panniers on long-distance touring.

*trail* Measure of steering geometry determined by the distance between a vertical line extended down from the wheel axle and a line extended from the steering tube to the ground.

*true* Term describing a wheel that is perfectly flat and round, with spoke tension balanced throughout.

*tubular tire* Tire that is sewn around an innertube and glued onto the rim, used primarily for racing; also called a sew-up tire.

*wheelbase* Distance between front and rear wheel axles.

## Bike Books

### General

Ballantine, Richard, and *Richard Grant. Richard's Ultimate Bicycle Book.* New York: Dorling Kindersley, 1992.

*Bicycling Magazine*, eds. T*he Most Frequently Asked Questions about Bicycling.* Emmaus, Penn.: Bicycling Books, 1980.

Bicycling Magazine's *New Bike Owner's Guide.* Emmaus, Pa.: Rodale Press, 1990.

Bicycling Magazine's *700 Tips for Better Bicycling.* Emmaus, Pa.: Rodale Press, 1991.

Chauner, David, and Michael Halstead. *Tour de France Complete Book of Cycling.* New York: Villard Books, 1990.

Cuthbertson, Tom. *Anybody's Bike Book.* Berkeley, Cal.: Ten Speed Press, 1991.

Ford, Norman D. *Keep On Pedaling: The Complete Guide to Adult Bicycling.* Woodstock, Vt.: The Countryman Press, 1990.

Forester, John. *Effective Cycling.* 6th ed. Cambridge: MIT Press, 1993.

Honig, Daniel. *How to Bike Better.* New York: Ballantine Books, 1985.

Langley, Jim. *The New Bike Book.* Mill Valley, Cal.: Bicycle Books, 1990.

LeMond, Greg, and Kent Gordis. *Greg LeMond's Complete Book of Bicycling.* New York: G. P. Putnam's Sons, 1990.

Lieb, Thom. *Everybody's Book of Bicycle Riding.* Emmaus, Pa.: Rodale Press, 1981.

Nye, Peter. The Cyclist's Sourcebook. New York: Perigee Books, 1991.

Perry, David B. *Bike Cult.* New York: Four Walls Eight Windows, 1995.

Sloane, Eugene A. T*he Complete Book of Bicycling.* 4th ed. New York: Simon & Schuster, 1988.

Van der Plas, Rob. *The Bicycle Commuting Book.* San Francisco: Bicycle Books, 1989.

Weaver, Susan. *A Woman's Guide to Cycling.* Berkeley, Cal.: Ten Speed Press, 1991.

### Mountain Biking

Bicycling Magazine's *Mountain Biking Skills.* Emmaus, Pa.: Rodale Press, 1990.

Coello, Dennis. *The Complete Mountain Biker.* New York: Lyons & Burford, 1989.

Kennedy, Martha J., et al. *Fat Tire Rider: Everyone's Guide to Mountain Biking.* Brattleboro, Vt.: Vitesse Press, 1993.

Nealy, William. *Mountain Bike! A Manual of Beginning to Advanced Technique.* Boulder, Col.: VeloNews Books, 1992.

Olsen, John. *Adventure Sports: Mountain Biking.* Harrisburg, Pa.: Stackpole Books, 1989.

Van der Plas, Rob. *The Mountain Bike Book.*
3rd ed. Mill Valley, Cal.: Bicycle Books,
1994.

Woodward, Bob. *Mountain Biking: The
Complete Guide.* New York: Sports
Illustrated WC Book, 1991.

Zarka, Jim. *All-Terrain Biking: Skills &
Techniques for Mountain Bikers.* Mill
Valley, Cal.: Bicycle Books, 1991.

### *Maintenance, Repair, and Mechanics*

Bicycling Magazine's *Basic Maintenance and
Repair.* Rev. ed. Emmaus, Pa.: Rodale
Press, 1990.

Coello, Dennis. *The Mountain Bike Repair
Handbook.* New York: Lyons & Burford,
1992.

Cuthbertson, Tom. *Cuthbertson's Little
Mountain Bike Book.* Berkeley, Cal.: Ten
Speed Press, 1992.

Garvy, Helen. *How to Fix Your Bicycle.* 7th ed.
Los Gatos, Cal.: Shire Press, 1993.

LeMond, Greg. *Greg LeMond's Pocket Guide to
Bicycle Maintenance and Repair.* New
York: Perigee Books, 1990.

Seidl, Herman. *Mountain Bikes: Maintaining,
Repairing, & Upgrading.* New York:
Sterling Publishing, 1992.

Snowling, Steve, and Ken Evans. *Bicycle
Mechanics, In Workshop and Competition.*
2nd ed. Champaign, Il.: Human Kinetics,
1990.

Stevenson, John, and Brant Richards.
*Mountain Bikes: Maintenance and Repair.*
Mill Valley, Cal.: Bicycle Books, 1994.

Sutherland, Howard. *Sutherland's Handbook
for Bicycle Mechanics.* 5th ed. Berkeley,
Cal.: Sutherland Publications, 1990.

Van der Plas, Rob. *Bicycle Repair: Step by Step.*
Mill Valley, Cal.: Bicycle Books, 1994.

Van der Plas, Rob. *The Bicycle Repair Book.*
2nd ed. Mill Valley, Cal.: Bicycle Books,
1993.

Van der Plas, Rob. *Bicycle Technology.* Mill
Valley, Cal.: Bicycle Books, 1991.

Van der Plas, Rob. *Mountain Bike
Maintenance.* Mill Valley, Cal.: Bicycle
Books, 1989.

Van der Plas, Rob. *Roadside Bicycle Repairs.*
Mill Valley, Cal.: Bicycle Books, 1990.

### *Riding and Racing Techniques*

Coello, Dennis, and Ed Chauner. *Mountain
Bike Techniques.* New York: Lyons &
Burford, 1991.

Gould, Tim, and Simon Burney. *Mountain Bike
Racing.* Mill Valley, Cal.: Bicycle Books,
1992.

Hinault, Bernard, and Claude Genzling. *Road
Racing: Technique & Training.*
Brattleboro, Vt.: Vitesse Press, 1988.

Lehrer, John. *The Complete Guide to Choosing
a Performance Bicycle.* Philadelphia:
Running Press, 1988.

Matheny, Fred. Bicycling Magazine's *Complete
Guide to Riding and Racing Techniques.*
Emmaus, Pa.: Rodale Press, 1989.

*Mountain Bike Skills.* Emmaus, Pa.: Rodale
Press, 1990.

### *Fitness and Nutrition*

Bicycling Magazine's *Nutrition for Cyclists.*
Emmaus, Pa.: Rodale Press, 1991.

Bicycling Magazine's *Training for Fitness and
Endurance.* Emmaus, Pa.: Rodale Press,
1991.

Burke, Edmund R. *Cycling Health and
Physiology: Using Sports Science to
Improve Your Riding and Racing.*
Brattleboro, Vt.: Vitesse Press, 1992.

Carmichael, Chris, and Edmund R. Burke.
*Fitness Cycling.* Champaign, Il.: Human
Kinetics, 1994.

Rafoth, Richard. *Bicycling Fuel.* 3rd ed. Mill
Valley, Cal.: Bicycle Books, 1993.

Roy, Karen E., and Thurlow Rogers. *Fit and
Fast: How to Be a Better Cyclist.*
Brattleboro, Vt.: Vitesse Press, 1989.

Schubert, John. *Richard's Cycling for Fitness.*
New York: Ballantine Books, 1987.

Van der Plas, Rob. *The Bicycle Fitness Book.*
Mill Valley, Cal.: Bicycle Books, 1990.

### History and Biography

Abt, Samuel. *Champion: Bicycle Racing in the
Age of Indurain.* Mill Valley, Cal.: Bicycle
Books, 1993.

Abt, Samuel. *LeMond: The Incredible
Comeback of an American Hero.* New
York: Random House, 1990.

Boga, Steven. *Cyclists: How the World's Most
Daring Riders Train & Compete.*
Harrisburg, Pa.: Stackpole Books, 1992.

Hinault, Bernard. *Memories of the Peloton.*
Brattleboro, Vt.: Vitesse Press, 1989.

Magowan, Robin, and Graham Watson. *Kings
of the Road: A Portrait of Racers and
Racing.* Champaign, Il: Human Kinetics,
1988.

McGum, James. *On Your Bicycle: An Illustrated
History of Cycling.* London: John Murray
Publishers, 1987.

Nye, Peter. *Hearts of Lions.* New York:
W. W. Norton, 1988.

Ritchie, Andrew. *Major Taylor.* Mill Valley,
Cal.: Bicycle Books, 1988.

Watson, Graham. *The Tour de France and Its
Heroes: A Celebration of the Greatest Race
in the World.* North Pomfret, Vt.: Trafalgar
Square, 1990.

### Bike Touring (See also Chapter 12)

Butterman, Steve. *Bicycle Touring: How to
Prepare for Long Rides.* Berkeley:
Wilderness Press, 1994.

Lovett, Richard A. *The Essential Touring
Cyclist: A Complete Course for the Bicycle
Traveler.* Camden, Me.: Ragged Mountain
Press, 1994.

Nasr, Kameel. *Bicycle Touring International:
The Complete Book on Adventure Cycling.*
Mill Valley, Cal.: Bicycle Books, 1992.

Nicoson, Michael. *The Basic Essentials of
Bicycle Touring.* Phoenix: Wide World of
Maps, 1993.

Plevin, Arlene. *Cycling: A Celebration of the
Sport and the World's Best Places to Enjoy
It.* New York: Fodor's Travel Publications,
1992.

Van der Plas, Rob. *The Bicycle Touring
Manual.* Mill Valley, Cal.: Bicycle Books,
1993.

## Bike Magazines & Newsletters

### Consumer

*Adventure Cyclist*, P.O. Box 8308, Missoula, MT
59807, 406-721-1776.

*Bicycle Guide*, 6420 Wilshire Blvd., Los
Angeles, CA 90048, 213-782-2201.

*Bicycle USA*, 190 W. Ostend St., Ste. 120,
Baltimore, MD 21230, 410-539-3399.

*Bicycling Magazine*, 135 N. Sixth St., Emmaus,
PA 18098, 610-967-8093.

*BIKE*, P.O. Box 1028, Dana Point, CA 92629,
714-496-5922.

*BMX Plus!*, 25233 Anza Drive, Valencia, CA
91355, 805-295-1910.

*BMX Today*, National Bicycle League, 3958
Brown Park Drive, Ste. D, Hilliard, OH
43026, 614-777-1625.

*Cycling Athlete*, 1417 Robinson Rd. SE, Grand
Rapids, MI 49506, 800-225-7568.

*Cycling USA*, USCF, One Olympic Plaza,
Colorado Springs, CO 80909, 719-578-4581.

*Dirt Rag*, 5742 Third St., Verona, PA 15147,
412-795-7495.

*Doubletalk*, Tandem Club of America, 35 E.
Centennial Drive, Medford, NJ 08055.

*Go: The Rider's Manual*, Wizard Publications,
3882 Del Amo Blvd., Ste. 603, Torrance,
CA 90503, 213-371-1454.

*Low Rider Bicycle*, Park Avenue Publishing,
P.O. Box 648, Walnut, CA 91788, 909-598-
2300.

*Mountain Bike*, 33 E. Minor St., Emmaus, PA
18098, 610-967-5171.

*Mountain Bike Action*, Hi-Torque Publications, 10600 Sepulveda Blvd., Mission Hills, CA 91345, 818-365-6831.

*Mountain Biker*, 6420 Wilshire Blvd., Los Angeles, CA 90048, 213-782-2372.

*Mountain Biking*, P.O. Box 16149, North Hollywood, CA 91615, 818-760-8983.

*NORBA News*. NORBA, One Olympic Plaza, Colorado Springs, CO 80909, 717-578-4717.

*Pro Bike News*, Bicycle Federation of America, 1818 R St. NW, Washington, DC 20009, 202-332-6986.

*The Recumbent Cyclist Magazine*, P.O. Box 58755, Renton, WA 98058, 206-630-7200.

*SNAP BMX Magazine*, Ride Publishing, 3021 N. San Fernando Blvd., Ste. A, Burbank, CA 91504, 818-846-5475.

*Velo News*, 1850 N. 55th St., Boulder, CO 80301, 303-440-0601.

*Winning Magazine*, 744 Roble Rd., Ste. 190, Allentown, PA 18103, 215-266-6893.

### Industry

*Bicycle Dealer Showcase*, 9560 SW Nimbus Ave., Beaverton, OR 97008, 503-520-1955.

*Bicycle Retailer and Industry News*, 1547 S. St. Francis Drive, Santa Fe, NM 87505, 505-988-5099

*Marketing and Merchandising Newsletter*, 33 E. Minor St., Emmaus, PA 18098, 215-967-5171.

*Outspokin'*, National Bicycle Dealers Association, 2240 University Dr., #130, Newport Beach, CA 92660, 714-722-6909.

## Cycling Organizations

Adventure Cycling Association
P.O. Box 8308
150 E. Pine St.
Missoula, MT 59807
406-721-1776

American Bicycle Association (ABA)
P.O. Box 718
Chandler, AZ 85244
800-878-7453

Bicycle Federation of America
1506 21st St. NW, Ste. 200
Washington, DC 20036
202-463-4622

Bicycle Manufacturers of America
3050 K St. NW, Ste. 400
Washington, DC 20007
202-944-9297

Bicycle Network
P.O. Box 8194
Philadelphia, PA 19101
215-222-1253

Bicycle Transportation Action
308 E. 79th St.
New York, NY 10021
212-288-3103

Bikes Not Bombs
59 Amory St. #103A
Roxbury, MA 02119
617-422-0004

Canadian Cycling Association
1600 James Naismith Drive
Gloucester, Ontario
K1B 5N4 CANADA
613-748-5629

International Bicycle Fund
4887 Columbia Drive South
Seattle, WA 98108
206-628-9314

International Human Powered Vehicle
    Association (IHPVA)
P.O. Box 51255
Indianapolis, IN 46251
317-876-9478

International Mountain Bicycling Association
    (IMBA)
P.O. Box 412043
Los Angeles, CA 90041
818-792-8830

International Randonneurs
Old Engine House No. 2
727 N. Salina St.
Syracuse, NY 13208
315-471-2101

League of American Bicyclists (LAB)
190 W. Ostend St., Ste. 120
Baltimore, MD 21230
800-288-BIKE

National Bicycle Center
P.O. Box 3401
Redmond, WA 98073
206-869-5804

National Bicycle Dealers Association
2240 University Dr. #130
Newport Beach, CA 92660
714-722-6909

National Bicycle History Archive of America
P.O. Box 28242
Santa Ana, CA 92799
714-647-1949

National Bicycle League (NBL)
3958 Brown Park Dr., Ste. D
Hilliard, OH 43026
614-777-1625

National Off-Road Bicycle Association
    (NORBA)
One Olympic Plaza
Colorado Springs, CO 80909
719-578-4717

Rails-to-Trails Conservancy
1400 16th St. NW
Washington, DC 20036
202-797-5400

Tandem Club of America
2220 Vanessa Drive
Birmingham, AL 35242
205-991-7766

Ultra-Marathon Cycling Association
4790 Irvine Blvd. #105-111
Irvine, CA 92720
714-544-1701

Unicycling Society of America
P.O. Box 40535
Redford, MI 48240
810-661-0334

United States Bicycling Hall of Fame
34 E. Main St.
Somerville, NJ 08876
800-BICYCLE

United States Cycling Federation (USCF)
One Olympic Plaza
Colorado Springs, CO 80909
719-578-4581

United States Professional Cycling Federation
    (USPro)
RD 1, Box 1650
New Tripoli, PA 18066
215-298-3262

USA Cycling
One Olympic Plaza
Colorado Springs, CO 80909
719-578-4581

Wheelmen
55 Bucknell Avenue
Trenton, NJ 08619
609-587-6487

Women's Cycling Coalition
P.O. Box 281
Louisville, CO 80027
303-666-0500

## Cycling Online

### Websites
About Biking: www.aboutbiking.com
Adventure Sports Online Cycling Directory:
    www.adventuresports.com
Bicycle Helmet Safety Institute:
    www.helmets.org
Bike Cafe: www.bikecafe.net
Bike Culture Magazine:
    www.BikeCulture.com/home
International Human Powered Vehicle
    Association: www.ihpva.org
League of American Bicyclists:
    www.bikeleague.org
Mountain Bike Resources Online:
    www.mbronline.com
Mountain Bike Review: www.mtbr.com
National Bicycle Dealer Association:
    www.ndba.com

National Bicycle League (BMX): www.nbl.org
One Less Car: www.onelesscar.org
Ride BMX: www.bmxonline.com
Tandem magazine: www.tandemmag.com
USA Cycling: www.usacycling.org
VeloNews: www.VeloNews.com
Women's Mountain Bike and Tea Society
    (WOMBATS): www.wombats.org
Yahoo! Cycling Directory:
    http://dir.yahoo.com/Recreation/
    Sports/Cycling

## References

Bicycle USA Almanac. March/April 1996.
    Baltimore: League of American Bicyclists,
    1996.
Bicycling Magazine. Jan. 1995–July 1996.
Chauner, David, and Michael Halstead. Tour
    de France Complete Book of Cycling.
    New York: Villard Books, 1990.
CompuServe Magazine. Columbus, Oh.:
    CompuServe Inc.
The Cyclists' Yellow Pages. 17th ed. Missoula,
    Mont.: Adventure Cycling Association,
    March 1996.
Ford, Norman D. Keep On Pedaling: The
    Complete Guide to Adult Bicycling.
    Woodstock, Vt.: The Countryman Press,
    1990.
Nye, Peter. The Cyclist's Sourcebook.
    New York: Perigee Books, 1991.
Perry, David B. Bike Cult. New York:
    Four Walls Eight Windows, 1995.
Van der Plas, Rob. Bicycle Technology.
    San Francisco: Bicycle Books, 1991.

# Index